STUDIA INSTITUTI ANTHROPOS

JOHN W. BURTON

# God's Ants
## A Study of Atuot Religion

STUDIA INSTITUTI ANTHROPOS

37

JOHN W. BURTON

# God's Ants
# A Study of Atuot Religion

ANTHROPOS INSTITUTE
St. Augustin
West Germany

1981

For Alak

# Preface

Field research for this study was made possible with grants provided by the Social Science Research Council and the Wenner-Gren Foundation for Anthropological Research. I am grateful in acknowledging their assistance. Of the many Sudanese who helped make the research possible, especial thanks belong to Francis Deng and Dorothy Ludwig Deng. Administrative officials who also aided my research include Abel Alier, then President of the Southern Sudan, James Ajith, then Commissioner of Lakes Province, Isiah Kulang Mabor Deng, then Commissioner of Bhar-el-Ghazal Province, and Hamid Yeni, then Executive Officer of the Yirol Rural Council. In the town of Yirol, Gai Tut, Marghani Bilal and his wife Nyanawil, Gum Deng and Barnada Madeo Bol all helped to make idle periods enjoyable and productive. Dr. Alfred Anyuat, an Atuot by birth, probably saved my life when I was struggling with a particularly nasty bout of dysentery. I am also most grateful for having met and later befriended Mr. Telar Deng, my most patient and demanding tutor in the Atuot language. The Atuot whom we knew willingly allowed us to share in their lives and settle among them as adopted kinsmen. *loicde ce duoth te cieng Reel.*

At the State University of New York, Stony Brook, Professor W. Arens proved to be a constant source of intellectual inspiration while I was a graduate student there and later provided the requisite moral support throughout the duration of fieldwork in Atuotland. My debt to him as a teacher is great; the value of my friendship with him is inassessible. Professors David Hicks and Louis C. Faron offered critical comments on an earlier draft of this monograph, and I am grateful for their efforts in this thankless task. I also wish to thank Professor E. H. Winter who sat as the outside member of my doctoral committee at the defense of my dissertation.

In Oxford, Dr. Godfrey Lienhardt offered us gracious hospitality and offered advice on certain matters pertaining to the Southern Sudan. He kindly consented to read and comment on a draft of this study. Though I was never a student of Lienhardt's in an institutional sense I have gained a great deal from his comprehensive knowledge of Nilotic peoples. Indeed, the present volume could at best be considered a supplement to his masterly study of Dinka social thought. If our Atuot friends could have read his book, I am certain the majority of them would have agreed, *thiec deng era nuer ce ngac cieng me car me gau e mal.*

A number of ethnological and comparative issues which are briefly noted in the course of this study have been addressed in greater detail elsewhere, and interested readers are advised to consult them (see Burton 1977*b*, 1978*b*, 1978*c*, 1980*a*, 1980*b*, 1980*c*, 1980*d*, 1980*e*, 1980*f*, 1980*g*, n.d. *a*, n.d. *b*).

More than anyone else my wife L'Ana H. Burton made this research possible and for this, temporarily left her own work behind to travel with me to the Southern Sudan. Atuot had seen a number of white males prior to our arrival in their country, but the sight of a white woman – who could actually speak the Atuot language – never ceased to be a source of conversation and reflection among our Atuot friends. In retrospect, I have the firm impression that a major reason why Atuot were so kind to us was because of the unrestrained hospitality L'Ana offered them. Having lived through many of the experiences described or referred to in what follows, she is obviously a better critic than many could be of its values and shortcomings. I dedicate this monograph to her as a modest appreciation of the contribution she made toward its completion.

# Contents

# Introduction

This book is a partial study of the religion of the Atuot, a group of Nilotic speaking pastoralists of the Southern Sudan. Their language shares its closest affinities with Nuer. The reader familiar with previous studies of Nilotic religions will appreciate this expression of Atuot social thought to be most like that of the neighboring Nuer and Dinka. The thesis of the study is to reveal the way in which their notions of God are reflected in the daily experience, and to demonstrate the manner in which personal identity is in part the result of an individual's understanding of the ways of God. Though an important part of their affective experience, Atuot, like most people, are not prone to reflect on the ideas discussed here. This, rather, is the task I have undertaken.

In the field of African studies there has been a lingering controversy about the characteristics of the "high God" in Africa. Unhappily, the issue has more often offered a context for the voicing of polemics than unfolded any valid conclusions. Lienhardt (1961) and Evans-Pritchard (1956) suggest that these religions are unlike other Nilotic expressions and African cosmologies in general. The central idea of God, and the human response to his powers, make Atuot, Nuer, and Dinka religions in some ways peculiar in the wider African context, though importantly similar among themselves. Evans-Pritchard draws frequent reference to similarities between Nuer ideas and theological notions expressed in the Old Testament, though I have not found the same recourse especially helpful or necessary in the present study.

The fieldwork on which this study is based was carried out in the Southern Sudan between October 1976 and November 1977. My concern for the Nilotic world and the problems these societies raise for social anthropology pre-dated the field research by about four years. A particular interest in Nilotic religions led to focus on this phenomenon in the course of a more general ethnographic study of Atuot society. In a series of notes and essays (Burton 1974, 1975 [together with Arens], 1976, 1977, 1978) I addressed some of the issues raised in the interpretation of themes in Nilotic symbolism, which invited either re-analysis or seemed to require further first hand research.

While a research student at the University of Cambridge and member of Churchill College, I examined archival materials in Great Britain relating to the period of British administration in the Southern Sudan. Scant mention is made of the Atuot in these files. In Oxford, Godfrey Lienhardt made it possible to canvass unpublished field notes of the late Jean Buxton, who had lived among the Mandari, neighbors of the Atuot beyond the southern perimeter of their country. Apart from these sources, only passing reference is made to the Atuot in other ethnographic accounts of neighboring peoples. In England I was also befriended by many Southern Sudanese students, one of whom was Atuot by birth. He offered my first lessons in the language. Hence, while there is neither a dictionary or grammar, I went to the field with a knowledge of some basic and helpful phrases.

As initially proposed, the research had three general aims: First, to learn of the historical affinities between Atuot, Nuer, and Dinka, primarily through the collection of oral traditions. Though there is a sizeable literature with reference to Nilotic ethnology (see e. g., Evans-Pritchard 1940, 1950, 1960a; Lienhardt 1961, 1975; Buxton 1963, 1973, 1975; Crazzolara 1933, 1950–1954; Riad 1959; Seligman 1932; Deng 1973a) there had been no social anthropological study of the Atuot, and hence no way to elucidate these and related problems. Second, I considered it important to make an analysis of the social significance and usage of the ethnic label "Atuot" in reference to historical and contemporary social relationships among Sudanese Nilotes (cf. Southall 1976; Glickman 1972; Gough 1971; McLaughlin 1967; Newcomer 1972; Sahlins 1961). Though not discussed in this dissertation, this phase of the research involved a diachronically oriented survey of inter- and intra-ethnic marriage. The central focus on Atuot religion brings to light what I characterize in this study as a passive sentiment and resignation to the "words and deeds of God" *(ruac Nhial)* which typifies Atuot religious experience. The body of data collected fills in certain gaps in the Nilotic ethnography, and is relevant for the type of comparative analysis recommended by Evans-Pritchard, who wrote (1960b: 14-15): "What is required is an intensive study of a limited and clearly defined cultural region where the facts can be examined in their full contexts of ideas and practices." To the extent that my own research was successful, this becomes a realizable goal for the Nilotic world, and more specifically to three societies which are similar in economy and ideology, the Atuot, Nuer, and Dinka.

Leaving the hot and dusty confines of Khartoum behind us in the north, we arrived by plane in the Southern Sudanese capital of Juba, and then made our way north and west to Rumbek, once a staging post for the slave trade, and presently the headquarters of Sudan government for Lakes Province. Once there, we were advised to stock up on a number of essential food commodities for there was no way to be certain if the same goods would be available in the few small shops in Atuotland. We were then driven the final seventy-five mile leg of the journey to Yirol, a sub-district headquarters of Lakes Province with a population of about three thousand. This town is often associated with the Atuot as well as the Aliab and Ceic Dinka, while in other areas of the contemporary Sudan, one may be known as a Nuer from Bentiu, a Dinka from Gogrial, and so on.

In the dry season the motor trip from Rumbek to Yirol normally requires four or five hours while at the height of the rains, if the road is open at all, the same journey takes the better part of a day. The physical remains of British "developmental" efforts in this region include a number of government buildings and an "all weather" road from Wau in Bhar el Ghazal Province to the Nile port of Shambe. Since it is now traversed by the twenty ton lorries of itinerant Arab merchants rather than horses or the light automobiles of the 1930s, the road has fallen into disrepair. Historically, their isolation was a factor in Atuot resistance against Turkish and Arab led slaving parties, and the region was not appreciably administered until the late 1920s. Poor communications and transport to areas outside eastern Lakes Province today means Atuotland is viewed by Southern Sudanese as more "backward" than areas of Nuer, Dinka, or Azande country. Though we encountered a number of imposing inconveniences because of this same isolation, Atuotland proved a most fertile location for the research.

In Yirol we were accommodated for a short while in the government rest house, and in the meanwhile arranged to have a mud and thatch hut repaired as a home base.

Located near the southern shore of Lake Yirol, this had been the home of a former chief of the Luac section of Atuot. As a result, our initial introduction into Atuot society was realized through members of this family. Predictably, the first practical problems we faced were our near inability to speak or understand Atuot, where we were to acquire foodstuffs, and how to secure potable water. Our problem with language actually proved to be a productive one, for even while we were often frustrated, learning to speak Atuot was the ideal means of entering their world. Though the context is radically dissimilar, Hicks (1976: 15) describes an experience remarkably like our own. "They were flattered by our efforts to master their language and keen to make certain we noted down words lest we forget... If there is any one path to understanding a foreign community, language is it."

We must have appeared both strange and anomalous in the eyes of our first Atuot friends. Their initial impressions were that we represented a corps of British administrators returning to rule once again. This was not an uncomfortable notion to live with, for they often complain about Arabs who now dominate Sudanese government and run the small shops, but appreciated the British for their medicines and for not interfering too much with their own affairs. However, the handful of foreigners who had lived in Yirol in this capacity spoke either Arabic or rudimentary Dinka, and at this point we were incompetent in both languages. Instead, we wanted to learn *their* language. Nothing really could have been more satisfactory, for this indicated to them that even while we were foreigners, we possessed some degree of intelligence in wanting to learn to live and speak their way. In their minds, none is better.

Together with the notes made in England it was possible to gain a sense of confidence with the language in the course of daily life. A young Atuot fellow named Malek helped with assorted tasks around the hut, and since he spoke only Atuot, he also served as a perpetual and most patient teacher. After three or four months we had mastered simple conversation. Occasionally this seemed a stunning realization for them. I once sat talking with a group of older men in a hut, when another man walked in and was seated. After a short while he turned quickly and said to a friend, "I never knew there were white Atuot!" As the research progressed I found I had tape recorded more than three hundred and fifty Atuot songs. Their ox and bull songs are especially rich in poetic metaphor, so that without a much longer experience of speaking and thinking in their language, it would have been impossible to translate them personally. Yet this was mandatory for not only are they of great ethnographic value; the social and ideational importance of song in Atuot society would be difficult to overemphasize. As undesirable as some purists (I think the word "romantics" applies better) may view my recourse, I hired an Atuot school teacher who was competent and accomplished in English, to help in the task. Those who have attempted a similar exercise will appreciate this as a long and tedious process. As often as possible, the composer of each song was present during translation, either to re-sing lines which were unclear or to elucidate phrases which seemed to have no inherent meaning. Only a small number of these songs appear in this study.

I never employed a "field assistant" nor anyone who would normally be called an "informant." This was unnecessary, and also inconsistent with precepts of Atuot social values. When one man has "spoken his word" another takes this as a signal to speak up in refutation or confirmation of the preceding conversation. Further, since we were well accepted by them, and there are few in the traditional context privy to information unavailable to others, participant observation rather than directed interviews was the general methodology employed throughout. Atuot are engaging conversationalists. The most frequent activity in the cattle camps after the cows have been released for grazing in the morning is to sit among friends and relatives and converse. Thus, there was a great deal of time to record data on marriage, relations of kinship, politics, and other social institutions, though this material is discussed here only when necessary to understand social features of Atuot religion. This information draws into relief sociological differences between Atuot, Nuer, and Dinka societies.

Our personal relationships with Atuot really made our stay in their land possible and enjoyable. Their only persistent demands were for gifts of tobacco, which in their view is simply a gesture which recognizes another person as a "human being," and for medicines such as penicillin and malarial remedies, which we gave freely. Asking for a gift is both a mark of respect and underscores a basic notion in their sense of the need for reciprocity in social relations. Often in return for these small favors, we were given gourds of milk, which represent for Atuot the most sincerely intended and precious gift. In retrospect, we were more often an imposition on their lives.

This book is intended primarily as a contribution to Nilotic studies; as those with specialization in other ethnographic areas will appreciate, there are also in this sub-field path finding, subtle and illuminating analyses which precede one's own. In the absence of Evans-Pritchard's (1956) writing on Nuer religion, and Lienhardt's (1961) sensitive and often brilliant study of Dinka mythology and religion, my task both in the field and in the course of interpretation would have been immeasurably more difficult.

As a study in social anthropology this book does not conclude with "new" theoretical insights based on the ethnographic data presented. Because its substance is concerned with belief, expectation and intention, however, the material does have an immediate relevance to the understanding of social life from a humanistic perspective. Apart from the variety of "isms" at our disposal for the interpretation of religious systems – a functional one as in the case of Middleton's (1960) monograph on the Lugbara, a structural type such as Barnes' (1974) for Kedang – there is no "theory" in social anthropology which has been accepted and consistently employed by the practitioners of the discipline with regard to the religious side of collective representations (cf. Evans-Pritchard 1965; Needham 1972). This disparity does not reflect an inability to account for religion anthropologically, but merely indicates that approaches to this sort of material have been inspired by peculiar interests and perspectives. A number of related problems are discussed in the final chapter. Functional analyses have become less frequent in social anthropology as its disciples have come to realize they are not dealing with "savages," but with human beings, whose complex psychic attitudes make the entire task of explanation elusive (see Needham 1972: 246).

The first chapter examines the historical traditions of the Atuot, with a broad concern with more general problems of Nilotic ethnology (cf. Burton n. d. c). That "Atuot" lived at some time to the north of their present country, in what is now western Nuerland, is evidenced by a number of sources. My concern then, is to understand how a Nilotic sub-division came to be known to themselves and others as the Atuot.

The second chapter describes the physical and ecological features of Atuotland, and concludes with a discussion of how these realities are reflected in Atuot conceptions of time, space and causation. Topographic features of the country force the herding groups to be widely dispersed. Gross estimates of each population set the ratio of human being to cattle as 1:2. A comparative figure for Nuerland is 1:1.4 (see Howell 1954a, 1954b). No similar ratio is available for the Dinka, though cattle and human populations reach their highest densities in the Rek area of Dinkaland (see Harrison 1955:24), and in the same region, the priestly-political master of the fishing-spear enjoys his greatest authority. They would be likely to offer the information in the absence of first hand knowledge, but the Dinka are probably the wealthiest pastoralists in the Southern Sudan. This study draws only brief reference to traditional forms of political organization. The combined effects of pastoral transhumance and a savannah environment upon political institutions is discussed masterly by Evans-Pritchard (1940), and I have written elsewhere about the related themes of population density and political centralization in the Nilotic world (see Burton 1977, n. d. c).

The third chapter introduces the Atuot concept of God, and the way in which "creation" and cosmological order is viewed in relation to the supreme being. God the Creator (*Decau*; cf. verb *cak* "to create"; noun *cak* "milk") is that being who alone is thought to have the puissance of creation. "God the father" *(Decau guar)* represents to human beings the paternalistic interest God is imagined to have in the people he has created. To highlight his magnitude and omnipotence, Atuot call themselves "God's ants" *(acuek Decau)*. Though sometimes said to be distant from the world of human beings, an attempt is made to demonstrate how an individual's relation to (i.e., understanding of) God is reflected in his own sense of individuality and personal identity. While God is central and all embracing, they know of his presence more often through lesser powers which partake of the Deity.

In the course of daily life, one often hears mention of the term *jok* (pl. *jao*), and the fourth chapter is devoted to an understanding of the variety of meanings this word has for the Atuot. Any single translation of the term is problematical, but its most frequent referent approaches what we mean by "power," "divinity," or "spiritual agent." For reasons made apparent in the course of analysis, the phrase "power (of God)" is employed to convey its implications for the Atuot. *Jok* is an idiomatic notion in Atuot symbolic thought, to the same degree that a bovine idiom communicates information about social relationships. A further division of the powers involves the distinction between "heavenly powers"*(gaat Decau,* literally, "children [sons] of the Creator") and "earthly powers" *(jao piny)*. Respectively these are classified as "passive agents" and "active agents" in accord with texts offered by Atuot about their varied qualities.

The fifth chapter leads away from formal description to a consideration of the praxis of religious and symbolic thought, as evidenced in the situation of sacrifice. Here it is argued that what is basic to Atuot religious sentiment is the *intent* of their sacrifices since by itself, the act has little meaning. Sacrifice is a petition to God in the expectation that he will look upon the people he has created with benevolence. Sacrifice dedicated to a power is different both in intent and praxis from direct petitions to God. These differences form the subject of the second half of the chapter (see also Burton n.d. *a*).

Other spiritual agents are viewed by Atuot as entering their lives in association with the recently deceased through ghostly visitation *(cien)*. In chapter six, the discussion shifts from the interpretation of symbolic metaphor to a consideration of moral values and their relation to social organization. While the physical remains of the dead are buried, the memory or "image" of the deceased lingers with living kinsmen. Failure to recognize the continued presence of the dead through the medium of ghosthood is often cited as the cause of illness or death. Hence, physical death merely represents the cessation of one type of relationship and the initiation of a new one. Collectively, these ideas seem more a part of Atuot ethics and morality, but they are discussed here, however, because ghosts are viewed idiomatically as having a "power" like a *jok*.

The concluding chapter elucidates the difference between moral and religious sentiments among the Atuot. An attempt is also made to convey a feeling for what are individual and collective religious experiences. In the interpretation of the ways of God an individual confronts powers beyond his control. Moral values on the other hand are a means of constraining the responsibilities of one person to his fellows. Atuot religion defines the relationship of man to God. Spiritual vengeance is an active agent employed by human beings in the social world, where self-assertiveness, rather than passivity, is the norm.

Atuot do not reflect imaginatively on a world awaiting them after death where they will find all their desires fulfilled. As Evans-Pritchard suggests for the Nuer, their's is a "this-worldly" religion. Atuot religion seeks to answer questions which evoke in individuals a feeling of resignation. Yet it is also a religion of hope and expectation, for through sacrifice, their central religious act, Atuot imagine that God will accept what is offered and absolve them of the problem at hand.

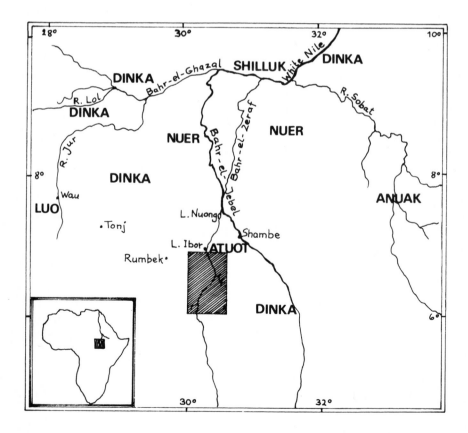

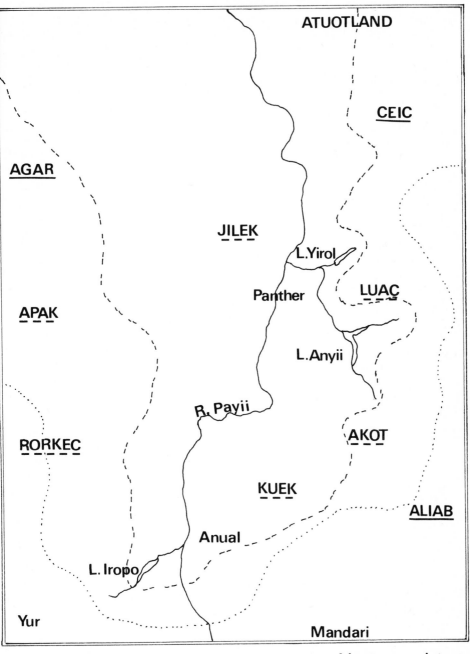

ATUOTLAND

CEIC

AGAR

JILEK

L.Yirol

Panther                    LUAC

APAK

L.Anyii

R. Payii

AKOT

RORKEC

KUEK

ALIAB

Anual

L. Iropo

Yur                              Mandari

- - - - ATUOT          ········ approx. limit of ironstone plateau
_____ DINKA          -- -- --      "         "    "  toic

CHAPTER I

# Historical Traditions

## 1. The Peoples Called Atuot

In the anthropological literature on Sudanese Nilotic societies (see Burton n. d. *c*) occasional reference has been made to the Atuot. They are estimated to number 35000. Until I had begun my own research, no Europeans, apart from a handful of British officials, had lived in Atuotland. During the colonial period no missionary work was carried out among them, and my wife and I are the first foreigners to have learned their language. The only written information concerned with the Atuot appears in the meagre and unpublished records of their former British administrators, collected in archives at Durham, London, and Khartoum.

In a review of Nilotic studies Sir E. E. Evans-Pritchard wrote (1950: 6), "The Atuot seem to be a section of the Nuer who are today separated from them by Dinka tribes. Almost nothing is known of them and they would certainly repay a separate study." Later, commenting on the breadth of our knowledge about Sudanese societies he noted (1960: 337), "I would suggest a study of the Atuot, for apart from the intrinsic value of such a study, it would shed a revealing light on the complex ethnological problem of the relationship of the Nuer and the Dinka."

Under different circumstances the study which the mentor suggested in 1950 might not have been delayed for twenty-six years. However, soon after the Sudan gained independence the country was divided by a seventeen year civil war, in which Southern Sudanese sought to gain an equivalent footing with the primarily Arab population of the north, which had been favored economically, educationally, and politically by the former overlords. With the signing of a peace agreement in 1972, the Southern Sudan was opened again to the world at large, including the occasional social anthropologist, after having been politically a "closed district" for nearly two decades.

According to Crazzolara's (1950–1954) reconstruction of the Nilotic migrations within the Southern Sudan and eastern Africa, the present area of Atuot settlement is co-terminous with what he has called the "cradleland" of the Nilotes. In his attempt to account for common clan names among the Dinka, Nuer and Shilluk, Crazzolara (1950) posited that such connections could be traced back to the time when they lived side by side in Atuot country. Linguistically, Atuot has been classified as having its strongest affinities with Nuer (Tucker 1935: 878; Bryan and Tucker 1948: 12), and, in fact, I found I could converse with Nuer while they spoke their language and I spoke Atuot, since both are distinct from Dinka. When I had first begun to learn Atuot I was querried a number of times by Dinka, asking if Atuot was spoken in my homeland, for they had lived in close proximity to them all their lives, but were unable or unwilling insultingly to understand it[1].

---

[1] In their classification of Nilotic languages, Bryan and Tucker (1948: 11) make the following distinctions: Language group Nuer consists of Nuer dialect cluster and Atuot dialect cluster. A standard orthography has been adopted for a number of the Nilotic languages, and I recorded the Atuot language in conformity with these symbols; hence, *c* as in English "church" *(col wic); ny* as in French "Boulogne" *(kuoiny); ng* as in English "singing" *(cieng).*

The criteria of language and its use have normally been noted as a delimiting feature of tribal groups in anthropological writings, and to some extent, native peoples employ a similar classification. For this reason the Nuer have become known by a term which they do not normally use for self-reference, while they *are* called Nuer by both Atuot and Dinka. Correspondingly, both the Dinka and the Nuer use the word Atuot to refer to the people who are known among themselves as *nei cieng* Reel, the people of the land (alternatively, "home," "tribe," "world") of Reel. Atuot and Nuer call the Dinka *jaang,* a word that in both languages connotes a degree of insult, as one of its meanings is "foreigners." Sociologically this presents a paradox, for the Dinka are estimated to number at least one million; thus they are the largest ethnic group in the Sudan, while the Nuer are only one quarter as numerous and the Atuot only the size of a smaller Nuer or Dinka tribal group.

The origin of nomenclature is problematical. In the Nuer language the word *gatuot* can mean "aristocrat, the most noble of the tribe" (Kiggen 1948: 100) as well as sons of chiefs or bulls (*gatatuot;* Crazzolara 1933: 49). In western Dinkaland *atuot* refers to a type of cow with majestic wide-spreading horns, said to originate from Atuotland (Deng 1973: 106). In all three languages the noun *tuot* refers to the spur-winged goose *(Plectropterus gambensis).* A number of people from *cieng* Reel wo cared to speculate on such matters told me that *atuot* really means the people who have separated. In the wider ethnological context, all Nilotes are "people who separated," while in the more telescoped historical world, this would appear to be an accurate interpretation.

The word *reel* in Dinka and Atuot can also connote "cleverness" as well as something that is difficult or unpredictable. The ox color called *rial* refers to a predominantly dark animal with a splash of white standing out starkly against the otherwise muted brown or black hide. In the Nilotic cattle idiom, this might well be instructive. We can see the similarity between an isolated patch of color against the dominant black background and a people who think of themselves as those who have separated, or in the Nuer meaning, aristocrats, those people who stand out among others. Surrounded by the more populous Dinka, the Atuot are indeed "separate," though Dinka culture in some form or another pervades throughout the Nilotic world in the Sudan. According to Evans-Pritchard and other authorities, so much of Nuer culture has to be explained in reference to the Dinka. Seligman (1911) and Westermann (1912*a*) and Hofmayr (1925) suggest that Shilluk forms of totemism are Dinka in origin, and I am certain the same can be said for the Atuot. In the "initial situation" there were Dinka, and then there were all the others. Jackson's observations offer another perspective (1923: 74):

> When first we hear of the Nuer they seem to have domiciled in what is commonly referred to as "the Island," the country west of Shambe . . . With them were the Atwot and to the north and west the Shilluk . . . Up to this period [mid-fifteenth century] it is perhaps not unreasonable to imagine that the Nuer, Dinka, Atwot, and Shilluk were all more or less congregated in the area round Shambe but were forced gradually to emigrate.

The presence of the people who later became Shilluk in the same area is likely, and since they were somewhere *west* of the Nuer, this is the probable reason why Nuer began to migrate in an easterly direction. Southall (1976) fails to recognize this point and therefore much of his thinking on the subject is misdirected. Dinka were already living in the area Nuer have now come to inhabit, and they are fully aware of having "incorporated" Dinka into their society. Likewise Atuot traditions state that the Aliab,

Ceic, and Agar Dinka were already surrounding the land where they now live, yet they have not incorporated nor been incorporated by their Dinka neighbors[2].

Approaching the question of ethnic differentiation from a materialist perspective, it would be apparent that the praxis of the evolved forms of pastoralism among Sudanese Nilotes is essentially similar, while slight (though significant) ecological differences among the three pastoral societies mentioned are apparent. Where some Nuer are said to practice only horticulture, population densities in areas of western Dinkaland are significant and their cultivations expansive. Even though they no longer keep signifi-cant numbers of cattle, Shilluk and Anuak culture evidence the well known bovine idiom. Concurrently, for the pastoralists one can argue that their economic interests encourage a degree of competition for selected resources, grazing and fishing sites being the most important. However, as there are variations in micro-environments, the secondary differences in culture and language may just as well be seen as developments which occurred over a long period of time (see Burton 1980*f*).

The Dinka world view incorporates other people. This is evidenced by a joke they tell in which the Dinka have become so many, they say there are now the Dinka Nuer, the Dinka Shilluk, and so on. The simple fact that a people consider themselves to be "different" from others is reason enough for a social anthropologist to recognize this view. In addition, data from a marriage survey shows that about eighty-four percent of Atuot marriages are ethnically endogamous[3]. The people of *cieng* Reel consider themselves to be the "real" people in a manner typical of Nilotic ethnocentricism. An older woman told me why she thought there were differences between the Nuer, Dinka, and Atuot:

---

[2] That the Dinka were not inhabiting the area now called Atuotland gains additional support from another source. Santandrea (1968: 111–112) writes, "The original country of the Luo |Jur| was south of Yirol in what is now Atuotland . . . At the time the Atuot started invading the land and hard fighting ensued, under Dimo's grandson Ajak|Dimo is often cited in the literature as one of the founders of the Shilluk dynasty| the Jo Luo left the land of their birth for good . . . No details are given about the splitting of the various Luo tribes, except that it was caused by the inroads of the advancing enemies, the Atuot" (cf. Kronenberg 1960).

[3] In the past, Atuot did not make reverse payments of cattle after the settlement of a marriage. Over the last fifty years, however, there has been a great deal more intermarriage between Atuot and Dinka due to the cessation (or at least the threat of legal punishment) of cattle raiding and warfare. Atuot explain that marriages used to be settled in the cattle camp, amid the same cows which would be taken by members of the bride's family directly after agreeing on the number appropriate. Through intermarriage with the Dinka, Atuot have now learned of *thio*, "reverse payment" (in Dinka, *arueth*) which refers to a proportion of the marriage cattle to be returned to the wife's people once the marriage has been seen to be successful. These cattle are selected from the herds of the groom's family, not from those given in the initial exchange. Today, the cattle of marriage are more often distributed in the village context, where pieces of straw represent the color and sex of animals to be exchanged. Now, a man can promise to give a "cow with no color," implying that he has no cattle free at the moment but will at some point in the future make good his intention. According to Atuot, this innovation is used by the Dinka in the attempt to steal cattle rightfully belonging to Atuot. "Now since we have a boundary with the Dinka (i. e., cannot openly fight them) we have *thio*. But before Atuot never married Dinka because they are evil-eyed people." Since this has now become a necessary part of all legal marital unions, it is possible to surmise that Atuot now have larger herds to manipulate. Concurrently, the Dinka seem always to have been in possession of greater bovine wealth.

Why are you asking this difficult question? You are the person who knows this, you have the things that walk in the air. That one there was created *jaang,* with *thong jaang* (Dinka language). Mandari have their way of speaking and we people of Reel have *thok cieng* Reel. This was God who did this. We should ask you why you have different skin. You know all the things. Now, how is it that you don't know where death comes from?

Others often answered the same querry by pointing out their marriage preferences and relating how the Dinka give their cows differently when they make their marriages, and such statements point toward a conscious feeling of separate identity.

## 2. Historical Traditions

Because documented history for the Southern Sudan does not really begin until the middle of the last century, written sources with particular reference to the Atuot are almost non-existent. This necessitates examination of oral traditions. The elucidation of a central Dinka myth by Lienhardt (1961), and the integration of structual with historical methods by Feierman (1974) suggests that this is both feasible and illuminating. I have collected a great deal of information concerning the Atuot during the period of British administration in the Sudan, but its inclusion would make this chapter exceedingly long. This material will be discussed in a separate publication since it has no direct bearing on this problem. As a preface to the interpretation of their tales of origin and separation, brief mention can be made to the earliest foreign contacts with the Atuot.

Those familiar with the writings of Deng (1971, 1972) and Lienhardt (1961) for the Dinka are aware that Arab influence in western Dinkaland has been a constant and occasionally disastrous reality of their historical experience. Many of the songs Deng (1973) has translated recall the times when their land was "spoiled" by the "circumcized people with teeth." The charismatic Mahdi at one time figured in their cosmology as a divinity. Nuer whom I met always addressed me as Turuk, a name they have often used to describe foreigners, since the first Turkish incursions into their country. With a better understanding of their history it became apparent that Atuot had experienced nothing of the same. Therefore I was called *Dingelese* (an Englishman) and this revealed that only the British had entered their lives in any significant way. In the contemporary world, many Ngok Dinka have become Islamicized, yet I know of no Atuot who has been so "converted," and Arabic influence in this area of the Sudan is minimal. Atuot are not only repulsed by qualities they see in the "inhuman" Arab character, but also insultingly refer to them as circumcized *(athoiny),* a practice they despise.

A few men were able to recall a single incident learned from their grandfathers, recounting how a Turkish garrison was surrounded by Atuot near the border with the Ceic Dinka wherein the foreigners were speared, shot with arrows, and then burned. Schweinfurth, who travelled through the southwestern area of Atuotland in the 1860s, noted that they would be a difficult tribe to subjugate for they were skilled with the use of bow and arrow. Among the Sudanese Nilotes, Atuot are unique in their possession of the bow and arrow, which they use with the more common fishing spear in warfare and hunting. Atuot say that when the Turks first landed at Shambe in Ceic Dinkaland, they forced the Dinka to act as porters, but when they entered Atuotland, Ceic refused to go further on for they recognized that the Atuot were superior to them in warfare.

Thus the Turks made their way inland from the river skirting around the northern areas of Atuotland, entering Agar Dinka country, which served as a staging point for the trade in slaves and ivory. The same route was employed by early British administrators in the Southern Sudan, and Atuotland remained effectively unadministered until 1923, when a sub-district headquarters was established at what has become the town of Yirol. Atuot also claim to have been untouched by the slavers of the last century, while they recognize that many of the people who live west of them – the Gok and Agar Dinka, the Bongo and the Jur – suffered from them. Gessi Pasha (1892: 213) wrote, "a tribe called Atuot which is till now independent and its presence renders travelling dangerous. The government has not yet succeeded in subjugating it." To effect a change in the situation he "sent three hundred men armed with guns to make a simple demonstration but my people were obliged to retreat on finding that they were facing thousands of Atuot" (*ibid.*: 337; see also Petherick 1869: 216; Gray 1961: 131). The British administrators were able to play off traditionally hostile people against each other, and eventually the government became known by the word still used today by the Atuot, *aceke*. Literally this means a revelation of the Creator, from the verb *cak,* to create. The things by which the government became known – guns and airplanes, for example – were compared to the powers of the Creator, for like their experience of God, the things of the government were beyond their control.

When Atuot recall the times of the past, their world is portrayed as a place where it was dangerous to move beyond well known areas since cattle theft was a constant threat. Even to a greater degree than is evident today, marriages were necessarily intra-ethnic. A situation of perpetual hostility (*ater* "feud") characterized their relations with the *jaang,* or Dinka foreigners. The Agar Dinka are also called *arol,* a term which gives the impression of a man who would club one on the head at the slightest provocation. In Atuot the word *aliab* means "disorder, lies and chaos," and characterizes their feelings about the Aliab Dinka. The presence of central administration has necessarily changed these situations over the last fifty years as there is much greater freedom of movement. The Akot Atuot, for example, the least numerous section, intermarry frequently with Aliab, sections of Luac and Jilek Atuot with Ceic Dinka, and the Apak with Agar Dinka. Their relations with the Nuer seem less openly hostile and accusations of cattle theft between them are rare, a point of ethnological interest addressed in the next chapter.

When a man from Atuot is asked by a foreigner, "who are the people called Atuot?" he will typically list the six sections *(dor)* of people who speak *thok cieng* Reel, the Atuot language: the Apak, Luac, Kuek, Akot, Rorkec, and Jilek. Of the Dinka he may say, "these are *jaang* over there, and they are different" *(jaang te cor wene, nei murro)* and of the Nuer, "we and Nuer are closest relatives" *(kok e nuere era kok thiako e nei).* Sociologically, the Apak are a problematical group for the fiction of their unity as a section of Atuot is revealed by linguistic and historical evidence. They speak of themselves as Apak, rather than *nei cieng* Reel, and consider all the other Atuot to be an inferior section of Apak. Their language is more a dialect of Dinka that has incorporated some Atuot vocabulary. When I had some competence in Atuot, it was still difficult to understand the Apak dialect. The text that follows indicates the Apak are in fact an ethnically diversified people, as evidenced in their name, *ca pak* (from the *Dinka puk* "to have been divided"). They are also the largest Atuot section.

Events of the past within memory occurred *wal,* long ago, while Creation and their separation with Nuer happened *ne mei,* too long ago to be certain of any details. The telescoping of historical time is evident in the texts: beyond the twelve generations most people can recount in their own genealogies, the sense of historicity merges with the things of *ne mei.* The traditions recorded here can be called *alet ne mei,* "words (deeds) of long ago." Understandably, they are not a part of daily conversation, and I was sometimes directed to "go speak to that fellow, he knows those things." On the other hand, all Atuot have access to impressions of tradition through the songs of their dances. When a man composes an ox song *(tuar theo)* or bull song *(tuar tuot)* the names of his forefathers and the events of their lives are often central themes. One could not say that they have a great interest in the past *per se,* yet whenever a group of invited men collected to speak the words and deeds of the past, invariably a large number gathered. Occasionally they interrupted to amend or disagree with what they had heard.

### 3. The Stories of Migration

In what we can call a typically Nilotic fashion (see Lienhardt 1975) the tales relate how they parted, necessarily on hostile terms, with the Nuer. There is rarely any mention of the Shilluk, perhaps because they had begun their northern migration before Atuot and Nuer separated, but as I have suggested, it is likely that they were in the same area (see Riad 1959; Oyler 1918). Creation (and conceptually, at the same time separation) is said to have occurred in a cattle camp called Akorthaar, sometimes called Korlil. Literally translated, the first name means "under the tree *akor.*" The second can be glossed in English two ways, either "at the tree *akor* in the type of pasture of the *toic* called *lil*" or "the place of the fight in *lil.*" Nuer traditions also recall Creation occurring under a tree in western Nuerland (Evans-Pritchard 1940).

This camp is shown on some maps on the west bank of the Bahr-el-Jebel river, about fifty miles north of where the White Nile branches into the two streams of Bahr-el-Jebel and Bahr-el-Zeraf. The Nile is called *kier* in Nuer and Dinka, and *cier* in Atuot. *Cier* is also the Atuot name for the first star that appears in the early morning sky during the summer months. In Nuer, Akorthaar is called Tharjath ("under the tree"). I had occasion to speak with a number of chiefs from the western Nuer area and their stories are quite similar thematically to those I recorded in Atuot.

It is likely that when they began to migrate south, Atuot moved with their herds along the inland *toic* of the river Payii and upon entering their present country, found it inhabited by hunters and trappers *(adep),* fishermen *(atuoc),* and ironworkers *(ajuong).* The Dinka who now live around Atuotland are said to have already been there. In the interest of comparison, it is significant that the Atuot do not think of themselves as having "incorporated" Dinka into their society, a starkly converse situation than that recorded in the Nuer ethnography. When compared with other Nilotic separation myths (see Lienhardt 1975) the Atuot and Nuer legends seem rather uncomplicated. In a general way these reflect the political themes of separation and segmentation, while the affirmation of collective interests typifies Dinka political and religious experience.

The first text was recorded with an elder chief of the Kuek Atuot.

> There is always a certain amount of envy and enmity between brothers. The words we heard from the old people when we were children say we were part of Nuer. They were brothers, Reel and Nuer, and had a quarrel about the bead called *tik yang*. Reel couldn't find the bead once, and he accused Nuer that his cow had swallowed it. Reel said the cow would have to be killed and they looked at the insides, but found that the cow had not eaten it. So they fought and settled by an oath. They said if we stay together then we will always go on killing each other. So Reel left [by demanding such extreme action in the first place this would summarize a long period of disagreement. Reel is portrayed here in a strict sense as the one who separated]. Reel left a bull crying in the camp and then rounded up the families to move by night to make it safe so Nuer wouldn't attack them on the way. When Nuer returned to the camp and heard the bull crying, he stayed for one day but then he realized that Reel had left. He was too far away to follow him. Reel went until the people came to this place. We praise ourselves by being called Reel because we despise these *jaang* around us.

The text offers a number of interesting points, perhaps most importantly the conclusion that if one cannot live with another, the only possible recourse is separation, not compensation. Alternatively, if one does not separate there is the possibility of becoming only a part of the other group. The ideal marriage is one which produces many children, so that the father will be assured a lasting name of his own by his *very own* sons. The text gives the impression that the events occurred entirely within the course of two days, but as the man states, there is always a lingering potential for hostility between brothers. I have witnessed the severance of relations in this dramatic fashion in a cattle camp, where driven to a climax, reconciliation was thought to be impossible and a man drove out his cattle from the camp in the company of his two sons. In a like manner, Evans-Pritchard (1940: 209) noted, "Nuer say that feuds and quarrels between lineages chiefly led to their dispersal."

A shorter version of the same legend was recorded among the Luac Atuot.

> At one time the father of Nuer and Atuot became very old and he told his two sons to come early the next morning so that he could divide his cow and calf between them. They left together, but Nuer went his own way because he had arranged to meet with a woman. Atuot came very early the next morning and took the calf, while Nuer appeared much later in the day because he had been with his woman. He found only the old cow remaining. Then the father died. Atuot came by later and Nuer accused him of stealing the calf, but Atuot answered that he didn't know where it was and that unless he had evidence to make his word, he had better be quiet. They killed and ate the old cow and then departed. Because they had eaten together, they could never fight each other.

This suggests that Atuot is the younger son, without a wife, and eager to increase his own numbers, for he takes the cow calf, a symbol of the potential for a herd. Though no one is killed in this version, their separation leaves them in a situation of "negative reciprocity," with a feeling of respect, yet emphasized by distance. Their relations with the Nuer are indeed quite like this. The accusation of theft, however, is only the first blow, as they would certainly have fought with spears if the situation had been repeated. It is thought better for an Atuot man to walk off alone when one has been insulted the first time. If the first fight between two men is with heavy ebony clubs the second is with spears. The sentiment of Atuot on this point is identical with that expressed in a Dinka proverb (Lienhardt 1975: 220), "The second hit is much greater than the first." Since it was necessary for Atuot to come early in the morning and steal the calf it implies that his own people were not many and had yet to begin to increase their numbers.

Two other texts, one I collected from two Nuer chiefs and the other found in Jackson (1923) offer further insight on these ethnological problems. The Nuer chiefs spoke of their relations with Atuot long ago in this way.

> One time the father of Jagei (Nuer) had a cow and Tuot (Atuot) said this cow swallowed his *tik yang*. The cow had been left behind in the camp when the others·went for grazing because it was calving. Tuot claimed that since the cow of Jagei had swallowed the bead it would have to be cut open to recover the bead. This was done but the bead was not found. No one knew then that a kite had swooped down and flown away with the bead. Jagei became enraged because the cow that was going to calf had died. He demanded to fight Tuot, but Tuot did not want the fight and offered to compensate it with three cows of his own. Tuot then decided to leave the camp secretly to avoid the fight and he pegged a bull in the camp so they wouldn't think he had left. His father Reel and brother Thiang remained behind. Thiang later bore the section of Nuer in Panjok. He had refused to stay with Jagei when he learned of how unreasonable he had been with the brother Tuot. Thiang crossed the Bhar-el-Jebel and died in Nuerland. Tuot later became known as Atuot and went to stay where they are now. The Nuer used to be called Reel because their father was Reel.

Two points need emphasis. First, there is a hint that the people of Reel became known to Nuer as Atuot from the bull, *tuot,* left behind in the camp. The second is that the text suggests again, that if a man is unwilling to accept compensation, he must sever the relationship entirely. As this tale was collected in western Nuerland, it would be difficult to know without firsthand knowledge if the eastern Nuer, that is, those people who also fought and separated, would also say that Nuer used to be called Reel. In both the Nuer and Dinka languages, the term for person or human being is *raan*. In Atuot the corresponding word for "person" is *nuer*.

The long citation from Jackson's account is presented for it differs remarkably from the three texts above. The mention of a stool in the story recalls certain themes in Shilluk oral traditions which trace the migration of the figure who became known as the *reth,* or "divine king." In Atuot, the term in the contemporary world translated as "chief" is *reth*. Jackson writes (1923:71),

> Alyett, ancestress of the Nuer, is said to have issued forth from an aradeib tree beside the river Guoal, the river of smallpox, which runs through the country called Raiyung, not far from Shambe . . . The tree was held in greatest reverence and sacrifice of a bull, or at any rate a sheep or goat was invariably made to it at the beginning of the rains . . . After Alyett gave birth to Akol she produced a canoe from the river as well as a cow and a calf. Nuer, the descendent of the marriage between Akol and Garung had two sons, Ga'a and A'ak . . . Wherever she [the wife of Ga'a] went water sprang from the ground and formed a khor or watercourse which was given the name Lil, and is reported to exist somewhere to the west of Bhar-el-Jebel in the neighborhood of Shambe.

I should think this is likely the place recalled in Atuot tradition as Korlil. The theme of crossing a river or emerging from a river figures importantly in most all Sudanese Nilotic oral tradition. Crossing a stream recalls creation and migration, and both Nuer and Dinkaland are crisscrossed by many small streams. Most Atuot know of only two rivers, the Payii, that dissects their land, and the White Nile to the east. The absence in Atuot cosmology of this otherwise common theme of crossing or emerging from a river is instructive: it implies they have not migrated as far or as often as the Nuer and the Dinka. This in turn accords with their proximity to western Nuerland. The text continues (1923:76):

Before the general migration of the Nuer and others from their original homes, there was a man called Darkok [reminiscent of the Shilluk figure Dak] a descendent or possibly son of Ga'a, living with Lang. Najh, Bor, Wott and Ror sections of the Nuer in the Island of Shambe. He was a chief of the leopard skin and lived in a hut rather removed from the rest of his neighbors. When visitors from other sections went to see him he had a habit of detaining them on some pretext or another and killing them secretly by night. His sister's son, however, happened to discover what was going on and told the people who collected in large numbers, after they had hidden their spears in a spot near at hand. These people then pretended to take part in a game with friends of Darkok, running this way and that, until they had decoyed the murderer's friends to the place where the spears were hidden. These spears were then suddenly seized and most of Darkok's followers were done to death, with only a few succeeding to make their way back to bring the news to Darkok. He then told the remnants of his family to drive the cattle away, leaving a large shining spear fixed in the top of a dom palm. He left behind a black cow and Darkok himself, being old and infirm, decided to remain behind. The Nuers heard the cow lowing and thinking that the rest of the people were still in the cattle byre with their animals, then collected and rushed the cattle byre capturing the spear, the cow and the stool of Darkok. The old man then came forward and asked why his people had been treacherously attacked. On being informed that it was in retaliation for the people that he himself had put to death, he enquired as to who had taken the spears. Lang replied that he had, whereupon Darkok said to him, it is yours and when you wish to use it, address it as the spear of the dom palm. Who has taken the cow, queried Darkok. I, said Najh. And he was told that henceforth it would be his. And who the stool on which I used to sit? I have, replied Ding Targei. Then it is yours and you are henceforth chief of the leopard skin. Whereupon Darkok left to join the remnant of his people, and from that day to this, the Atwot as his descendents are called, have lived a separate existence and become a distinct tribe from the Nuer and the Dinka. In fact, Nuer regard them as standing in much the same relation to them as to the Dinka.

The name Darkok does not appear in the Atuot texts, though it is a common personal name. Since he was a man said to have been "separate," there is an analogical similarity between this ancestor and the referents of the Atuot words *reel* and *atuot*. In a like fashion, it parallels also the cognitive meaning of a bull that stands out among others, and the splash of color against a muted background. Though the text offers nothing conclusive in terms of historical materials, it does point toward the identity of Atuot as being different from Nuer and Dinka.

I here record six legends, one from each section of Atuot, which I have selected as representative of their traditions. I have combined texts from each section in a number of cases. A man with the power *ring* (literally, "flesh") from the Jilek section related this story.

According to the words, all people were created in the place called Korlil. Sometimes we call this place Akorthaar. Nuer and Reel were brothers then, but Anuak and Shilluk and any others were there also. Later it happened that there was a very big thunder brought by God and this caused all the people to separate and then they began to get their own way of speaking. Nuer used to speak like us but then he took the language and made it crooked. Nuer and Reel quarreled and Reel later left without Nuer knowing it.

But where each section came from is uncertain. Luac, Jilek and Akot came here. The father of Luac was Cuonga, and he was an ugly man with one eye, one arm and one buttock. When he left he came through where the Ceic are and took a very ugly woman from Ceic called Ingoth [literally the name can mean, "she was fucked"]. They joined and had many children. They went to the place between the land of Kuek and the lake Yirol, called Yomboi, and settled there. Jilek came from Napgan [from *nap*, to hold up, and *gat*, child: other stories tell how in the fight with Nuer, they had to leave in a hurry and hang children from trees in the carrying skin, leaving them behind] following the other side of

Payii and settled among some fishermen called Jekaduoi who had been chased there by Rorkec, and they had suffered badly. When Lek [the founder of *ji* Lek, the people of Lek] came here he settled and made peace with them and married their women, but they had no cows. There was a relation between Jilek and Luac of *malen* [son of the mother's sister]. They decided to leave that place where Jilek was at Payii because it was muddy and there was no food. Luac also left the place at Yomboi, and they crossed the river together and found that the Akot who were also *malen* to Luac were there. They begged from Akot to use the pasture to graze the cows and then they were accommodated. Now this is the land that Luac and Jilek claim, but they were not born there.

The Akot have been marrying with Mandari and Aliab. Most of the Apak come from Jur and others from the other *jaang*. Now they are mostly speaking Dinka. All of these Atuot were divided from the Nuer, but they all have their own explanation.

*Lek* refers also to a type of fish, and in other versions of the story, Jilek are said to be the people of the river. A woman of Jilek long ago named Ipot was said to have the power *ring* as well as the ability to call rain. She was later married by a man of Luac. One of the songs of Jilek includes the lines,

Ipot, the woman of *ring*
To whom will I give you
Luac asked me where did the floods come from
Kuek asked me where did the floods come from
Ipot, the woman of *ring*
Jilek are the people of the river

The fish *lek* is respected *(thek)* as a power or "totem" *(wet)* of Jilek, for it carried the first man out of the river. This is evident in the text, for when they first entered the land, Jilek lived with fishermen, and hence the fish gave them life, here associated symbolically as emerging from the river.

Next follows a combined version of Kuek and Luac traditions, recorded in a village in Kuek. As we will see, their traditions are quite alike, and are the most similar of any of the texts I collected. The integrating role of the "culture hero" named Cuonga will be discussed after the texts have been presented.

Kuek had come from Napgan and were in the place called Agori, close to Luac in Yomboi. It happened that the old man of Kuek called Awuio and the old man of Luac named Cuonga were playing the game *agaak* every day. Cuonga was always losing to Awuio. When Awuio won he said to Cuonga, I have defeated the lame circumcized witch. This happened all the days, and the next day when they played again Cuonga had become tired of the insulting words of Awuio, and after he lost again, he went home and told his people the bad words he was always insulted with and he asked them for advice. Cuonga said if he had the power it would be better for the man to be killed. He then called together his four sons, each one from a different wife.

The first son he spoke to was Reel, but his mother refused to let her son listen to his father's plan. She would not have her son kill anyone. The mother of the son Arel also refused as did the third, the mother of the son Kuon. The mother of Lanjok, the fourth son, said that since the others had refused, her son would help. In the evening that day Cuonga went out to meet Awuio under the tree where they played *agaak*. Lanjok followed his father with spears and he stood and watched them play. Awuio won the game and said to Cuonga, I have defeated the lame and circumcized witch. Lanjok then speared Awuio and the spear came out the other side. Awuio fell dead instantly.

Cuonga and his son then left and made it back to their cattle camp where they collected their herds, knowing there would soon be a big fight. People of Awuio heard what happened and went off to collect their bows, arrows and spears, and then went back to the tree. Luac had already gone, so they took Awuio's body and buried it. This is what started the enmity between Luac and Kuek.

The fight which followed is a common theme in a number of Kuek dance and fight *(yaai)* songs as it is for the Luac.

> In my dance in Padier,
> Luac brought on the fight
> The fight of the old days
> The fight of the man called Cuonga
> This is the fight that is still coming
> The confusion of Luac troubles me still
> This is the old way, the ancient fight of Luac
> A message comes from the camp
> It comes from Panther
> When the fight comes, the cry is heard

Panther, literally, "the ancient home," refers to an area of cattle camps, of which Yomboi is one. The camp is still inhabited and used by both Luac and Kuek. Each year when people move to this camp sacrifices are made by elder representatives of both sections.

A longer version of this story of the separation of Luac and Kuek was collected from a *gwan riang* (man of *ring*) from the Luac. The man is from the clan called Nyang, which is also represented in Rorkec and Kuek. Long ago they were primarily fishermen. Nyang became part of Luac by the marriage of one of its daughters to a great great grandson of Cuonga.

> All the people of the world were created by Decau at Korlil in Nuerland. Cuonga was a son of Reel. One time Cuonga left Korlil and went to the camp Alol (in Agar Dinka) and stayed there for thirteen years. They offered Agar milk but they refused it saying what do people do with this? This was a lie because Agar had been in the forest for three days and was hungry. Agar lapped up the milk like dogs and went away for two days, then repeated the same thing. Cuonga asked his eldest son Lanjok to make a test to see if Agar really had cattle. He was told by Cuonga to take ashes from the dung fire and rub them over Agar. If the sweat came out in drops, it would show they had cattle and if it streamed off it would show they had none. Lanjok did this and the sweat came out from the pores. Cuonga then went to see Awuio in Panther. He met Awuio in the camp Tutmaker (bull of the color *maker*). Awuio told Cuonga that his home was Yomboi. Cuonga ate food given to him by Awuio and then he left.
>
> Cuonga saw that the grazing in Panther was good and free from the raids of Agar. He went back to his camp and selected thirty-six cow calves to bring to the camp of Awuio in Panther. Cuonga stayed in his own camp for three years and then went to Awuio. He found that the cows he had left were healthy and many had calved, and he gave Awuio a gift. Cuonga said to Awuio, now I am going to come live here because the *toic* is good and the land is safe from Agar. Awuio listened to the word of Cuonga and accepted, but he insisted that they should live in separate camps in Panther. Cuonga asked why, and Awuio replied, you have your problems and live apart, for why should we increase our chances of having more problems?
>
> After eleven days there was a very heavy rain and Cuonga went to the shelter in Awuio's camp. Awuio asked him scornfully, why have you come here? And Cuonga answered because he wanted shelter. Awuio gave in to Cuonga and built him a shelter *(adhang)* and then Cuonga built others himself.
>
> Cuonga had produced a child with a Ceic woman named Inor Tiok. She was very ugly and had only one wrinkled sagging breast. He engaged her and the child was born before any cows were given. He was mocked by the people for having such an ugly wife. Cuonga had gone to fetch the child and bring him to Yomboi. But when he arrived the Ceic refused him. Cuonga went to some fishermen and explained his problem and they agreed to help him. He told them to row across the river and take the child and tell Inor they would come back for her. Cuonga said if they returned with her, he would refuse the

child. The child came across and then the boat sank. Now Cuonga and Inor stood at opposite sides and Inor yelled to him, is that not your child? Cuonga answered, yes, and I have refused you. Inor shouted back, you will always follow my child. He will be the only true one among your children.

Cuonga returned to Tutmaker and became sick with a power of Inor [the text reads literally *ce Cuonga yuic de rom jok* "Cuonga was speared in the head with a *jok*"]. Five cows were sacrificed, one given by Awuio and the others belonged to Cuonga. He became well. Inor went and had a child with the fishermen and when she was delivering she and the child died. Cuonga then gave Awuio more cows as a reward for looking after his.

Then Cuonga and Awuio had a fight over the game *agaak*. Awuio always won and insulted Cuonga by calling him a lame circumcized witch. This had gone on for four years and Cuonga finally decided that Awuio should be killed. Cuonga asked his wife Ilok to give him her son to kill Awuio but she refused as did the second wife Ingar. The third wife agreed because she said it was her son given to her by Cuonga. Cuonga instructed the son called Rialkuei to go and stay behind the tree, and in the evening when the game had ended he should spear Awuio when he began to insult him. They played the game and Awuio began the insults. Rialkuei emerged from behind the tree and speared Awuio in the side but did not kill him. The son of Inor, named Lanjok, then came and speared him through the back and Awuio fell dead. Cuonga decided they would have to leave and he told Rialkuei to go bring a white cow. The cow was left that night without being milked and a white bull was slaughtered [this is part of the normal burial for a person of *ring*, described in a later chapter]. Cuonga then left a bull tethered in the camp to make the people of Awuio think they were still in the camp. Cuonga's people deserted the camp and it rained for eight days. Cuonga remained behind and every night small children would come and bring him milk. One man from Kuek knew the bull was only a decoy, but was afraid to go and tell his people because of Cuonga. When Kuek came to revenge the death of Awuio they found Luac already gone.

When Kuek left Cuonga called for three cows to be brought. One was killed by the spot where Awuio had been stabbed and it was not eaten. The other two were killed in Cuonga's camp and his people ate them. Cuonga decided to settle permanently in Panther. People followed him for generations and then began to move elsewhere.

Cuonga and Awuio are cited as two of the first people of *ring,* and many people of *ring* respect *(thek)* heart, that is, the heart of any animal killed or sacrificed. Long ago it is said that only people of Kuek respected heart, and Luac said among themselves, why should it be that Kuek always gets the flesh *(ring)* and all we are given is the heart? The next time we are given heart we will say we respect it and cannot eat it. The story is told lightheartedly though it may have symbolic meaning. Luac also take the heart in order to get *ring* the same way that Cuonga killed Awuio and took his *ring*. The recourse to murder over a game is trivial in the same way the slaughter of a cow to recover a bead is a drastic overreaction to the loss of something so small. In this situation however, the loss of life does not lead to separation, for there is (and apparently always has been) a great deal of intermarriage between Kuek and Luac. They agree to marry one another, and to settle compensation in their fights. The dance songs of Luac and Kuek are often insults of one section against the other. United by the cattle of marriages between them, it is inevitable that they will fight. Atuot say there is always a degree of enmity between brothers. In one song of Luac the lines say, "You people of Rorkec, you take you fight to Jilek and Apak – that is were your wives are." Another song begins, "The feud of the cow / And the feud of the vagina are one."

The next text is from the Akot section.

Akot were Nuer long ago. Their grandmother was *reth*. They one time quarreled among themselves about the meat of a sacrifice. The husband gave it to the junior wife and the elder wife was insulted and she told her children to fight the children of the younger woman. One of the sons was killed and they left Napgan and crossed through Ceic country. When they came to Panther they found Luac and Kuek already there. They all put up in Panther. The grandfather had a son named Karbeu and Luac gave them a daughter to marry and they became in-laws. After a long time Luac and Akot had a fight over a girl who had been given to Luac, but the cows had not been paid. Akot took the cattle they claimed and went to the camp Lual Karbeo and shared the toic with some of Luac. We stayed there a long time and a quarrel arose between Kuek and Luac, caused by some Akot called Athac and some Kuek of Nyang. Athac and Nyang fought for a long time and many died. They were fighting over a fish speared by a man of Nyang and then a man of Athac claimed it was his. Later another section of Akot called Bil [Bil was the man of Akot who is said to have married the daughter of Luac long ago. Usually in their songs, the Akot section is referred to as Bil] joined with Athac to fight Kuek. Luac then asked them to stop and establish peace. Then, after the word of Cuonga, Akot left that *toic* and went to live where we do now around the *toic* of lake Anyii.

I always tried to ask if they thought that all of the Atuot came together into their land from the north, and was invariably told that they had all come together, but settled in different areas. The old home of Panther and the man called Cuonga are once again seen as unifying elements in their traditions.

One additional short text from Jilek is interesting in regard to Rorkec traditions. When it was told to me, the middle of the text included a short song with the line "people bribe me to raid cattle." This was explained as referring to a time when the Agar Dinka asked people of Jilek to help in a fight against another section of Agar. Jilek killed them with their bows and arrows, and later took the cattle of the defeated section.

The man named Lik came from up the river with his boat and the fish called *cuur* to the place called Callau [in the center of Atuotland close to the river Payii] and he got out of his boat. A blacksmith came out of the forest to the riverside. This man did not know his father or mother, and had come from Panther with three things: his anvil *(dei)*, axe *(jep)*, and hoe *(lindo)*. When the blacksmith came to the river he asked Lik where he had come from and Lik replied, I am a man coming from an unknown people. Lik then asked the blacksmith to be his brother, and they became three, Lik, the blacksmith, and the fish *cuur*.

One night when the river had become full from the rains the fish jumped out of the boat into the river, and the other two went on. Some of the blacksmiths went to Luac and others went to Kuek and Rorkec. [The song follows next.]

Do not listen to the lies that Awen came to Payii
   [Awen is the largest section of Jilek]
People bribe me to raid cattle
Thiang [a section of Rorkec] came and crossed the *toic*
Fishermen of Thiang go another way
I am the man who is feared by people

Lik went and settled on an open bank by the river Payii and had two daughters, Pier and Amaker. Pier was married to a man from Aliab but stayed in her father's home until she was old. Amaker was married to a man from the Jiluoth section of Kuek, and she also stayed in her father's home. Awen Delang (the ancestor of the Awen section of Jilek; his father Delang is an ancestor of Rorkec) came with his cattle from Kuek to live here and these became the sections of Jilek – Delang, Pier, Amaker, and Lik.

To return to the preceding point, one has the impression the migration of the peoples from Nuerland did not involve all people at once. The congregation in the area called Panther, however, seems implicit. Some were pastoralists, while fishermen and blacksmiths "became" Atuot and owners of cattle through intermarriage. The text from Rorkec likewise "begins" when people are already there.

Kec was the owner of the land of Rorkec. There was a man called Mabiljuot who was a lion and sometimes ate people. He had two wives. One produced children and the other had none. One rainy day early in the morning he felt very hungry and had nothing to eat, so he turned into a lion and ate the wife with no children. The son of the other wife came into the hut and saw his father eating his stepmother, and ran off in fright to tell his mother. When she heard, she was certain that she would be eaten next so she collected her things and went off with the children. The woman, called Irou took her three children, Acinpuo, Anyal and Durjong and came to a river that was very high and steep. She pleaded with a fisherman to take them across the river in his canoe. This was in the land of Atuot Abongbar [a section of Ceic, who are known of throughout Dinka, Nuer, and Atuotland as being lions]. The man agreed to help her, and when they reached the middle of the river, the father had arrived at the bank. He called to the eldest son Anyal to come back. The son refused as did the second son Durjong. The third son heard his father calling and said yes, I will come. [The name Acinpuo means "no heart."] He was a lion like his father. When the others had crossed the river Acinpuo returned with the fisherman to the other side where his father waited. The mother took off through the forest until she reached the place called Anyijong and she put up there, on the other side of the river Payii.

A man named Dekaai, the owner of the land, had his cattle camp nearby. Irou saw the camp but decided not to enter, but made a place to sleep nearby behind an anthill. Their "totem," *thiang* (antelope), stayed with them there. They slept at the foot of the anthill and the antelope slept on top. One time Dekaai was returning to the camp in the evening and he saw Irou and her two sons and asked what they were doing. Dekaai asked her to come and she made a shelter with a grass roof. It rained the next day and Dekaai returned very wet. The two sons approached him and said he should go into the hut to dry off. They said this so that Dekaai would sleep with their mother. He slept with her and she gave birth to a boy named Atiik.

Sometime later there was a fight between Dekaai and Paleu [now considered a section of Rorkec, having come originally from Jur], and the son of Dekaai killed a man and Paleu came to avenge the death by demanding a son to kill. Dekaai offered them a son, but they refused and said they wanted the son Atiik instead. Dekaai protested and said it is not my son. It is the son of this woman. Anyal and Durjong became very angry with this, and they left the camp of Dekaai to go to Luac and speak with Cuonga.

They found his camp and were welcomed into it. They were offered milk and meat but refused it. At midnight they discussed their plight. They said to Cuonga, if a bull lives over there and comes here and makes a calf with one of your cows will the calf belong to you or to the owner of the bull? Cuonga answered that the calf born of my cow would be mine, not the owner of the bull. The brothers answered, this is the same with our brother. He is wanted by other people to be killed in revenge. Cuonga told them to return to their camp and that he would follow the next day, while in the meantime he had to go to Apak. He told them he would approach the cattle camp from behind and that they should then call out, who is the lame, blind, circumcized witch with his anus showing over there? When you call out this insult, said Cuonga, I will answer, let my people see who is insulting me.

They did as told the following day and Cuonga appeared. Dekaai and Paleu were in the camp. Cuonga said to them, you Dekaai and Paleu, this man you have chosen, he is a different person. Let those people go with your son. You Paleu, take the son of Dekaai for your revenge. If you do not want this son there can be no vengeance for the man who died. Cuonga then brought out the blade for making an oath and he made a curse and blessed it with mud from the earth. Then he broke it in half giving a piece to Dekaai and one to Paleu. This ended the fighting.

Then Jrou and her children left along with Atiik. The people born from her became the Kok [like Awen for the Jilek, Kok is the dominant clan. People of Rorkec are usually referred to as *ji* Kai, the people of Kok].

Why we are called Rorkec is because the man they found there was Dekaai, but the other people came from different parts. There had been a cattle camp that way (south) of Payii. The seven that were there were Pario, Yuom, Thianglual, Angol, Tieplier, Bel, and Ngo. Pario, Yuom, and Angol were all together in Rorkec [there are five sections of Rorkec: Thiang, Yuom, Pariak, Paleu, and Nyang]. The people of Thianglual and Tieplier are all gone [the names suggest either Ceic or Aliab Dinka origins], and people of Ngo [probably an iron-working group] scattered among the Luac, Kuek and Apak, and Bel went to Kuek. At first only Dekaai had cows and the others hunted or made iron.

Other Atuot suggest that Rorkec are the most "mixed" people and at the same time suggest that their language, along with that of the Kuek and the traditional iron-working people of Lualajuong within Kuek, is the "purest" form of Atuot. Many people from the other sections are fully bilingual in Dinka and Atuot, while a great many people from Kuek are monolingual in Atuot. Their songs are almost entirely sung in Atuot, while many of the other section's songs are composed in a mixture of Dinka and Atuot. Kuek and Rorkec do not share any border with Dinka, unlike the Akot, Jilek, Luac, and Apak.

The final text, from Apak, was recorded from the chief of the area who comes from the dominant Awan clan. Awan are said to have come from Jur, and in the story, the first child born to human beings is said to be the father of all the Jur.

In the beginning there was a man called Koc Decek [the text was recorded in Dinka, the language most commonly spoken in their country. The name means literally, "people of the Creator"] and he was a son of Nhial Garang [a powerful Dinka divinity]. Garang bore a son called Raan and Raan had a wife named Tiek [Dinka respectively for man and woman, or wife). The woman was given to Raan by God. The first child was called Majok, the father of all the Jur people. Mabor was born next, the father of all the Bor Dinka, and then Nuer was born, the father of all Nuer, and then Arol Raan, the father of the Agar Dinka, and then Kotjaang was born and married the woman called Atuot. Together they bore the sons Apak, Luac, Kuek, Akot, Rorkec, and Jilek. There was also a girl named Luo who married a man from Bor Dinka, and they bore the Ceic Dinka.

All the people of Apak had collected in the village of Jongkuac, and it grew and then they began to disperse back again to where they had come from. The first Apak was Awan. He was followed by Aper, Acok, Lual, Riir, Aparer, Guer, and Bok. Atoc went back to Rek Dinka and are now known as Luac in Rek. Aparer returned to Ceic and a part of them stayed here. Acok and Aper went to Aliab. Guer and Bok never moved. Riir went to the *toic* to fish. When people again returned to Jongkuac the man called Mer brought a cow to sacrifice. Mer of Awan was a brother of Cuonga. Cuonga had died in the land of Luac but Apak were not told of this and were not invited to make sacrifices there when he was buried. They went to Luac and found that Cuonga had already been buried. When people returned Mer told them to gather around the bull Mapuor. They played the drum for eight days and then the bull was slaughtered. At the very moment the bull was sacrificed, Mer said, from now on we will all be known as Apak. Then he said that Apak were first, they are the eldest son.

There are many aspects of this story which could not possibly be true, and others that have the quality of a charter in the manner described by Malinowski (1954). Lienhardt notes for the Dinka a practice common to pastoral Nilotes (1961: 295), ". . . in Dinka tradition, the establishment of a new community – a new 'cattle-camp' or section – is achieved by sacrifice, and the names of some Dinka sub-tribes today are explained as

being derived from the color-names of the beasts sacrificed to establish them." A number of lines from one other of their dance songs can illustrate well their feelings of
superiority:

> The *jaang* left
> I am the owner of this land
> You Apak, my people
> Do not call me Awan of lies
> I am the old protector of the land
> You go and see it – you will find Awan
> If you were to surrender
> Reel (Atuot) would be dispersed
> I keep the land alone
> I care for the hunger of cows
> I am the bull of the land
> You just leave it
> And leave me to put my arrows through you

A general summary of these texts suggests a number of reasonable conclusions.
First, Atuot and Nuer recognize a common origin and to some degree this affects their
contemporary relationship. Second, there has been a slow but continual process in the
past of the integration of indigenous peoples such as iron-workers and fishermen into
their society. This has necessarily had its effects on the culture, both material and
social, of the Atuot. If we accept the authority of Evans-Pritchard (1940) that rinderpest
entered the Southern Sudan within the later nineteenth century, their herds must have
necessarily been larger than at present, though by comparison with the Nuer, they are
much more wealthy in cattle. A third and perhaps more important point relates to the
integrating role of the culture hero Cuonga in giving a common identity and common
ideal of compensation to the peoples called Atuot. A song about the initial situation is
known by most people with the power *ring:*

> You children of Ijer and Aduk
> We go and sit in Korlil
> We sit in Korlil where we were created
> Ayan is going to our camp
>   [Ayan is said to be the first cow given to man by God]
> Oh, we are going to where we were created
> If there is a man who does not recognize me
> I will burn him with my fire

The song refers to the situation of creation at Korlil, the first cow given to man by
God, and the power of people of *ring* to influence the lives of all, here characterized as a
fire. The man called Cuonga is in other contexts simply an ancestor of Luac, but we
have seen how each of the other sections recognized him in the past as *the* man with the
ability to burn people with his words. Yet reference to him as a lame, circumcized witch
with only one buttock seems something of an insult at first glance. We shall see later,
however, that the same is said of the power *ring,* for this too is thought to be lame and
slow, but determined and inevitable. The lesser powers that influence their lives come
and strike them with the speed of lightning or a spear, and their influence is equally
transitory. The power *ring,* like the person Cuonga as portrayed in their oral traditions,
is permanent. Evans-Pritchard (1940*b*: 31) notes a similar sort of relationship for the
Anuak. A man named Cuai "was the leader of the Anuak till the ancestors of the noble

clan came out of the river and usurped his position. He is therefore the proto-type, as he was the first, of village headmen. He is also sometimes represented as the first man and ancestor of the Anuak people." In the texts of Kuek and Luac there is an indication that Cuonga gained part of this power by taking the life of Awuio, and later, the Luac respect the heart. Because these two traditions have the most in common and are consistent with each other, one is inclined to reason that the original people long ago descended from Reel, were the founders of these two sections. The primary feature of the other stories that offers any sense of unity, is reference to Cuonga.

In comparison with other Nilotic traditions there is thus an important similarity with the figure of Cuonga for the Atuot and that of the Dinka culture hero Awil Longar, the person recognized by *all* the Dinka peoples who live dispersed over such a vast area in the Southern Sudan. Correspondingly, within each Dinka section, only certain families are directly associated with him in an historical sense. The integrating function of the mythology of Awil Longar is seen to be identical among the Atuot, though on an exceedingly smaller scale. Atuot traditions in this manner are more like those of the Nuer, who also recognize a single common ancestor initially, while any one tale is peculiar to a particular tribal group.

In the contemporary world Atuot think of themselves as a people united by their common language, religious ideology, marriage practices, and territory. The latter aspect is in turn related to their economic pursuits. In light of the ecological constraints and their resulting territorial dispersal, it is unlikely Atuot ever acted corporately as a tribe. In practice, compensation for physical injury was limited to people who lived together as one of the six sections, as was the responsibility to unite for common defense and warfare. A sense of their moral unity is revealed in other stories relating specifically to the death and burial of the man called Cuonga. The Apak, as we have seen, were excluded from participating. It is now common practice in the situation of the death of a *gwan riang* to act corporately in the same manner, by bringing bulls for sacrifice on the grave to evidence their spiritual and moral unity.

*a)* A man handling tassels from the horn of his ox.

*b)* A shrine for the heavenly power *kwoth*. *Kwol* are hanging from the branch.

*c)* An older woman treating the drums with *ngat yang*.

*a)* A *ric* or "marriage class" dancing in a cattle camp.

*b)* A man amidst his cattle in a camp.

CHAPTER II

# The Physical World and Cosmology

The area here called Atuotland and what they refer to as *cieng* Reel, the home of the Atuot, lies on the average some sixty miles west of the White Nile at six degrees thirty north latitude and thirty degrees thirty east longitude. Today this area falls within the administrative boundary of Lakes Province, named for the many shallow water-filled depressions which dot the country. The town of Yirol serves as the sub-district headquarters and has a number of government offices as well as some shops.

The majority of Atuot wet season villages *(cieng)* and wet season cattle camps *(wuic)* are built on the ironstone plateau which forms the southern perimeter of the swamps of the upper Nile basin, and falls between the macro-ecological zones of open grassland savannah to the north and tropical forests to the south. On the ironstone plateau average elevation is approximately 435 feet above sea level and receives about eighty inches of rainfall yearly, mainly between March and November.

Atuot divide the twelve months (or moons) into the season of rains *(deker)* and the time of dryness *(mai* "fire"). Rainfall actually occurs in two periods, the first commencing in March and becoming less frequent in May. The heavier rains which nourish their staple crops of sorghum and ground nuts then begin in July and taper off in late November. The Atuot practice a mixed form of agriculture during the rainy season, while the cattle are moved seasonally between dry season camps in *toic* land and more permanent wet season camps in the forest *(gok)*. The Nilotic root *toic* as a noun refers to low lying areas near rivers which remain with pasture throughout the year. The word also has many important symbolic associations. The soils of the *toic* are primarily of the heavy cotton type *(muon me car* "black earth"). These are ill-suited for the types of agriculture they practice. The soils of the forested country on the ironstone plateau are classified as laterite catena. As their economic pursuits change from season to season, so do their social relations vary in the cattle camp and in the village. A marked difference exists between what I shall call their "religious experiences" in each type of settlement, an understanding I attempt to reach in later chapters. Cattle[4] are

---

[4] See Joshi *et al.* 1957: 178–179. In regard to "Nilotic" cattle he writes,

"The cattle type appears to be of great antiquity and is generally supposed to have resulted from an intermixture of the original wild longhorned cattle of Africa *(Bos africanus)* with later incursions of Asiatic zebus *(Bos indicus)* . . . local differences in conformation and size as exist appear to be very largely of environmental origin . . . Nilotic cattle are of an undifferentiated type which has developed as a result of a form of natural selection under the difficult conditions imposed by an environment dominated by seasonal and prolonged flooding and the prevalence of insect pests . . . Trypanosomiasis is widespread, particularly in Bahr-el-Ghazal where the cattle graze in the wooded ironstone country during the rains, but has been successfully controlled in much of the area by the veterinary authorities."

In view of the genetic characteristics of Nilotic cattle we must assume that pastoralism has been practiced for an extended period of time in this region of Africa. Sophisticated adaptations to this environment, evidenced through the enormity of their herds, further indicate the antiquity of pastoral transhumance in the Southern Sudan.

rarely if ever brought into the village settlements. Unlike the Nuer and Dinka, Atuot do not construct cattle byres or shelters *(luak)* for their cows, but simply tether them in the camp in open air within an enclosure of thorn and scrub bush.

Passing through the center of their land is the permanent river they call Payii (known also as Lau or Yei). It is also known by different names according to activities normally carried out there, such as growing tobacco, and after long deceased ancestors who built dry season cattle camps along its banks. The river draws water in its upper reaches from the Nile-Congo Divide, and when it enters the flat plains of the Nile Basin it floods its banks seasonally, transforming the dryness into a vast area of rich pasture. Smaller feeder streams *(nyin)* of the river lead into lakes Yirol and Anyii. As the river flows north and slightly west into Nuong Nuerland, it floods the expansive *toic* at lake Ibor, and seeps through swamp to join the Nile at lake Nuong, about thirty miles north of Shambe. Long ago, I was told, Payii was called *cier,* the same word that now refers to the White Nile, for at that time, people had not yet seen the much larger river.

As the dry season advances and the waters recede the Atuot subsist primarily on the many species of fish which inhabit the lakes and rivers. At the height of the dry season almost the entire population is living in the cattle camps and some families move deep into the *toic* to live in temporary fishing camps *(bur)* without cattle. Fishing is done with spears *(biith),* nets *(abuoi),* and baskets opened at both ends *(thoi)* in which fish are trapped. One can walk around lake Yirol in April, but by early June the mouth of the lake floods at its western end, where it feeds into the river Payii. Their fishing technologies make this vocation an uneconomic pursuit when the rivers once again rise with the rains of March.

The inland *toic* is an essential resource for the modes of pastoralism that have evolved in the Southern Sudan. This is especially the case among the Atuot who are bordered by the Ceic and Aliab Dinka on the eastern side. The presence of Dinka here precludes access to the *toic,* which spreads inland along the banks of the White Nile. With the exception of small variations in types of grasses found there, the riverine and inland *toics* are identical micro-environments. Howell (ed.)1954/1: 237) has commented on the inland *toic* surrounding lake Ibor. I have added parenthetical statements for clarification.

> In years when the Bahr-el-Jebel (White Nile) *toic* remains inundated and largely inaccessible during the dry season, large numbers of Nuong Nuer move southward into the Lake Nyibor area. This area is fully utilized by the Agar Dinka and the Atuot (primarily the sections of Apak, Jilek and Luac) and also in some years by the Ceic (who more normally pasture their cattle along the banks of the White Nile in the dry season). While the Nile remains high, congestion and overgrazing along the Lau (the Dinka name for Payii) reaches a climax. Pressure between the Nuer and the Dinka increases and trouble follows.

Having visited the area myself in the dry season, it is very much of an overstatement to suggest that there is "pressure" here for grazing. The only time when problems arise between the Dinka, Nuer, and Atuot who meet here in the dry season, is when people neglect to ask permission to exploit fishing and grazing areas traditionally owned by another. There is in addition a high incidence of intermarriage between the Dinka and the Nuer who share a boundary in the area, and this necessarily tends to curb cattle theft and fighting. For the Atuot, in addition to the dry season grazing found there, lake Ibor is close to open salt licks where the cows are taken for about ten days every year. Because they must move their herds far from their homeland to reach Ibor they except some sort of difficulty. Even though there is now a centralized administration, "the things of cattle," as they would say, may always bring trouble. This is expressed most clearly in a song composed by a man from the Luac Atuot:

> I decided to move to the camp, oh Maduol [his bull]
> When people were troubled with their lives
> You, the sons of Jilek,
> Do not take the bull to the side of salt [lake Ibor]
> The trouble with Nuer fell on Lau [a section of Ceic]
> You, the sons of Nyanyong
> Do not say releasing a bull to graze is an easy thing
> The land of Nuer is the land of troubles
> The troubles with Nuer destroyed our land long ago
> You are always insisting to go to *baar* [salt lick]
> But later, when the raiding of Nuer has come
> You will remain with only the ropes [of the cows]
> Oh this trouble
> You keep it on the left [watch for it cautiously]

In passing it may be noted that meetings have been organized at lake Ibor periodically since the 1930s (I attended the most recent one in March, 1977) in an attempt to stop the alleged raiding of Dinka cattle by Nuer. The myth of the predatory Nuer has been institutionalized, for in the modern context, the temporary courts set up there enable a Dinka to accuse a Nuer of cattle theft, even if he knows it was taken by his half-brother or some affine. I know of only a few similar accusations by Atuot against Nuer. Based upon his findings in western Nuerland, Evans-Pritchard (1940*a*: 127) noted, "It seems also that Atwot were not considered such legitimate prey as the Dinka on account of their Nuer origin, and it is probable that they were seldom molested as they are remotely situated."

As the map of Atuotland indicates, Atuot share a boundary with the Ceic, Agar and Aliab Dinka. To the east, an occasionally dense forest separates them from the Nile. The Luac, Jilek, and Akot Atuot who have settled here make their permanent wet season camps in this *gok* forest, and some are able to pasture their herds along the Nile in the dry season because of intermarriage with the Dinka. This is especially true for the Akot (the smallest section of Atuot), whose land merges with that of the Aliab Dinka. The Kuek, Rorkec, and Apak Atuot make villages and wet season camps on the south and western side of the river Payii inland *toic.* Seen from the air this *toic* appears in the wet season like an immense dark green putting ground, reaching down the middle of Atuotland from its southern boundary in Kuek, northward into Nuerland, a distance of about one hundred miles. Here the *toic* is about fifteen miles broad and eventually leads into the central *toic* land in Bahr-el-Ghazal province, stretching from Gogrial in Dinkaland to the west and into Nuerland across the Nile, a distance of nearly two hundred miles. There is no evidence of overgrazing in the area, and if anything, the cattle population is still far below carrying capacity (see Howell [ed.] 1954).

Game abounds and while animals are not systematically hunted, the Atuot acquire ornaments for decoration from the rhinocerous *(cicil),* elephant *(guor),* buffalo *(muk),* and ostrich *(wuot).* Fighting shields *(kot)* are made from the hide of buffalo. Ironsmiths, who live within their country, make spears *(mut)* and a variety of bracelets. It is interesting to note that blacksmiths told me that long ago they only knew how to make the fishing spear *(biith)* and that the fighting spear *(mut)* is by comparison a new thing. As there is considerable low grade iron ore in their country, Atuot never seem to have placed special value on iron products, unlike their distant kinsmen, the Nuer. The bird life of this area of the Southern Sudan is astounding in its diversity, and from these natural species they derive many of the color patterns after which they name their cattle and smaller stock.

The types of land they exploit are named for their economic uses while the primary distinction is between the *gok* forest and the *toic*. I have recorded ten different recognized species of grass which the Atuot distinguish as having varied nutritional value for their herds. Each of these is generally found in a named area of the *toic*. Other place names refer to topographical peculiarities within the two categories. In addition to economic value, land has also a moral association. A particular cattle camp is not simply a place to tether cows, but is also the camp where one's father and grandfathers before him stayed with the herds. A number of such camps are mentioned in the historical texts discussed in the first chapter. Panther ("the old home"), for example, the camp where Luac and Kuek first settled and then separated, is such a place. Each dry season, when leading members of dominant families move to the camp, sacrifies are made in the name of the long deceased ancestors.

We have learned enough already from previous studies of Nilotic transhumance (Evans-Pritchard 1940*a;* Lienhardt 1958) to appreciate the conditioning and constraining effect physical environment has had on the formation and function of political organization. Since I am not concerned in this study with an explication of traditional political institutions among the Atuot, it will be sufficient to relate a number of facts about their traditional leaders and their functions within a similarly dispersed and transhumant population. The figures that Atuot call *gwan riang* (literally, possessor of the power of God known as *ring*) have their greatest similarity to the Nuer "chief" of the leopard skin in that his powers combine religious with political sanctions. In the past, they were men who had no more real power than a curse *(cien)* and were only involved in a conflict to make a peace ceremony (*dor* "to collect, gather, unite") once the opposed parties had already agreed to a settlement. When we lived in their country we not infrequently witnessed fights that policemen armed with rifles had difficulty in stopping. I naturally expressed a degree of cynicism when older men explained that the word of the *gwan riang* was believed in, feared and respected. To understand how this could be possible requires a more lengthy discussion of the power *ring* (literally, "flesh") which is attempted later. Ultimately, this respect shown to people of *ring* invites a philosophical inquiry into the way in which Atuot resolve the contradictions of belief and experience, intention and consequence. In the modern world *gwan riang* are still shown deference for their wisdom and counsel though their political influence has largely been usurped by bureaucratic administration. As more children are given the opportunity to attend school, the basis of this political authority, the curse *(cien),* has been questioned. Most elder men and women from any of the six sections of Atuot can recall a number of living and dead *gwan riang,* who were known throughout Atuotland in the past. More numerous, but lacking any political power at all, are persons known as *reth,* a name derived from the word *ruac,* "to speak." A man is recognized as a *reth* for his eloquence in speaking and his ability to see all sides of an argument before offering a solution. Potentially any man can be recognized as a *reth* though not every man seeks the role of politician or spokesman. One man once compared the role of the *reth* to the function of the axe *(lildo)* used for hoeing. "When it is time to cultivate, everyone wants the *lildo,* but when the work is finished, it is just left around out in the rain. This is the same with the *reth.*" In the cattle camp a *reth wuic* may be consulted for advice about where rich pastures may be found, or where the cattle should be watered that day. Since he takes on this sort of responsibility he is often the man who will be expected to pass around tobacco on demand. In a small way, we here see a sort of leveling mechanism of status at work. No man has any inherent superiority over anyone else. Constant demands for tobacco and small demands are a means of reminding him of this basic premise of Atuot ethics. Correspondingly, the *reth cieng* serves as a focal point for the concerns of people in an area of village land.

Presently in Atuotland there are six *reth,* each man representing his area of Atuotland in the local administration. Responsible to him are any number of *gol yuic,* heads of smaller descent groups within the major sections, whose duties are primarily concerned with tax collection as well as collecting cattle required for the settlement of court cases. Each section has also a court president, who decides cases for the government. I have avoided translating the word *reth* by the term "chief," for in a strict sense, Atuot never recognized any person to have the status the word implies. When the British first began to administer this area in 1923, their dictates were known to local residents through the Dinka language, and less frequently in Arabic. Because the Atuot are so few in number compared to the million or more Dinka in the region, it was understandably considered inefficient to attempt administration in anything except the Dinka language. As a result, those selected to represent the Atuot and carry out government functions, were known by the Dinka term *beny,* "master" or "chief." In the past, a *reth* was a man expected to return something for having been recognized as a person who could act as a "mouthpiece" for others. While in the past there was no status differential recognized among the pastoral population, education has become one such index among a small elite.

In comparison with other Sudanese Nilotes, the political system of the Atuot could be seen to be most like that of the Nuer, and each of these in turn contrasts sharply with the centralization of political authority among the Shilluk. In the first two cases, political, economic, and religious functions are dispersed, like the people themselves, among a variety of specialists (collectively known as *kur*). In effect, the lack of a centralized authority functions to distribute status evenly. The political, ethnic, and symbolic unity of the Shilluk, by contrast, is made possible through the institution of the *reth*ship, creating a situation that implies inequality in wealth and status. In a gross sense, the difference between these people in the mode of their political life can be "explained" by population density, while the economic adaptation of pastoralism precludes the possibility of settled and centralized village life. This was made evident to British officials early in the present century, for the Shilluk were among the first of the subject peoples to accept the presence of an external government, while the Atuot and the Nuer resisted their existence as much as they were technically and organizationally able. In addition to the openly self-assertive attitude of a typical Atuot man, the objective factor of low population density mitigates against political centralization (see Burton 1977). Population density for Atuotland can be estimated to be on the average ten persons per square mile. Because people are either living in cattle camps or spread out over large distances in village settlements, effective densities necessarily vary. At any rate, their independent ideology is certainly in line with the implausibility of a well defined political theory. In their own way of thinking, they recognize the strongest economic and therefore moral commitments between persons who build their village homesteads in proximity and among the people with whom they tether their cattle.

A description of other aspects of Atuot social and spiritual lives encounters the problems of translation, even with regard to such things as settlement pattern. In the most general sense, western observers have always assumed that the village is the primal domestic and social arrangement. It is the existence of some sort of village organization that gives permanence to social relationships. Thus in the Nilotic world, *cieng* (Nuer and Atuot) and *baai* (Dinka) have always been glossed with the English words "village" or "home." Traditionally we have called the settlements where herds are tethered "cattle camps," immediately suggesting a different quality of social relationship among its residents. In our manner of thinking a camp seems necessarily temporary when contrasted with a sense of "permanence" associated with the word "village." The word "village" also refers to some degree of population density. Thus, for a time in central Africa a village was selected for study on the premise that it could represent the entire social universe of a people.

A better understanding of Atuot social realities might instead view their two modes of settlement as cattle villages and agricultural camps. A single cattle camp often has as many as three hundred people living within the circular confines of an area with a radius of two hundres yards. A typical village is widely dispersed over miles of territory. In addition to meaning "home," "land," "tribe," and "way of doing things" the Atuot word *cieng* can refer to a geographical area, and only when it is named (e. g., *ciengde* "my home") does it refer to a particular household in that land. When a man says *wa cieng,* I am going home, he is referring to an area, rather than a cluster of homesteads that we would think is typical of a village. Conversely, the phrase ɣen e wa wuic means "I am going to such and such cattle camp."

A second problem of translation relates to the same theme. Seasonal movement of human and animal populations between two relatively well defined and separate types of environment (i. e., "transhumance") has most often been viewed as a movement *toward* villages after the cattle have been fed and watered in the dry season. Here again, we take village life as the norm, and movement from it as a disruption of normal life. The village is usually thought to be the place where social integration is recreated at yearly intervals. I began to reason differently in the course of a conversation on quite a different matter. A man was relating how at one time he had been moving with his cattle *away* from the rising waters of the flood. For the Atuot, and I should think also for other Nilotic pastoralists in the Sudan, this would indicate an emphasis on the camp as a permanent enterprise, that is seasonally interrupted by high waters. This in turn forces people to seek higher ground where they can carry out cultivation. This suggests a radically different view of Nilotic ethnology than those that have been implicitly accepted, and while I cannot in this context address the notion in the detail that it demands, a few brief points should be alluded to. When considering the economic and cultural aspects of Nilotic pastoralism, it is possible to surmise about the "initial situation," where to my reasoning, people lived a great deal closer to the riverine life and perhaps depended upon its resources to a greater degree than is apparent today. The Shilluk and the Nuer, in a variation of the same model, approximate this adaptation closest. While the differences in vocabulary between Shilluk, Nuer, Dinka, Anuak, and Atuot are occasionally extreme, there is a core segment of vocabulary that is duplicated in each of the languages. These include words which describe technologies and resources of fishing. The terms for "to fish," "fish," "hippopotamus," "fishing spear," "river," and so on, are identical in these languages, and this suggests in an evolutionary sense the primacy of this mode of economic production. By contrast, even the generic term for cow differs in Dinka and Atuot (see Burton 1980*f*).

For the people themselves, economic realities are revealed in cultural terms. As demonstrated, the greatest concentrations of Atuot occur in the dry season camps, which also serve as fishing camps. While others may think of villages as permanent entities, Atuot consider their cattle camps to be permanent, and can recall the many names that a particular camp has been known by in its long history of settlement and use. Conversely, they recognize that village lands used for cultivation eventually become exhausted and therefore are transient rather than permanent locations. *Cieng* in this sense refers only to general geographic areas within forested regions that are cleared and cultivated.

Conceptually, the year begins in January *(hor)* when the majority of people are living in the dry season cattle camps subsisting on the cow milk and fish. If I am partially correct in suggesting that this is the initial situation in evolutionary terms, it is therefore significant that their stories which account for creation, the origin of marriage, and the appearance of the powers of God *(jao)* to man are all set in the environment of the dry season camp, the world closest to the life-providing sources of the river. Lienhardt (1961: 195) records a similar theme for the Dinka. In the songs that they compose to praise their oxen and bulls, and by association themselves, a very common theme is one that recalls the camps where one has lived. It would be inconceivable for a man to sing laudingly of life in the village. Perhaps in part this is simply a further expression of their cultural idiom – the fluidity with which the identification of man is transformed to his cattle and *vice versa* – but it refers to a different experience. It is possible to argue that it is purely a matter of semantics when asking if they are moving toward the village or away from the rising waters, but this would be to miss the very essence of their experiential world. A short women's song expresses the sentiment well:

> I choose the camp
> The camp where people with beads remain
>   ⌊wearing beads here represents "traditional" life and the cattle⌋
> I choose the camp
> Oh, our girls, of what do they speak?
> They speak of the camp
> I bought the tassel for the horn of Majok ⌊an ox⌋
> Our staying in the camp
> There is no confusion
> I have chosen the camp
> The camp where people with beads remain

With this question in mind, that is, what did they think was the ideal or first world, an elder woman offered her comments:

> All the vegetables ⌊*adjuaic* "green things"⌋ people now eat were only added to what was. When they tasted food, and it did not kill them, the people continued to eat it. Cow is a bad creation *(yang era Decau jek)*. It has been the cause of people being finished. People had arguments over the cow. They had a long feud *(ater)* over the cow, and the Creator at last allowed the cow to stay with human beings. When a man is speared and he dies it is because of cows – because no one accepted to leave the cows ⌊i. e., would not give up pastoralism⌋. This is why the cow is very important. A man is killed for the sake of cows. The feud of women, like this woman sitting here with you, also kills people.

> People have these fights over women. Durra [i. e., cultivation] and cows were given by the Creator. These are two things people live on and stay for. Cows and durra stay together. People decided to cultivate it with the hoe. It used to be only one small durra, and when it was pounded, we satisfied people, and still a part remained. A newly married woman put a lot of grain in the mortar one day and pounded. Since then, we have always had to pound too much grain. This is how the cow came with cultivation. People take porridge to the camp and bring milk to the village.

Atuot gain by far the greater part of their subsistence needs through agricultural effort while their ideational and religious experience refers always to the world of cows. Their dependence on their herds was likely greater in the past before there was a central government to assist them with additional grain in times of famine. A strict materialist interpretation of human existence is inappropriate for the Atuot therefore, for what is fundamental to their livelihood is in no way mythologicized in their ideology. In a developmental sense they migrated into a country that was well suited to both agriculture and pastoralism. Occasionally, a man mocking the fate of Nuer can be heard since they occupy an environment well suited to pastoralism, but must also live in fields of mud for half the year.

What Atuot call the "hungry months" (*peth a biath;* from *buoth* "hunger") are a yearly reality, while their cows are more or less productive throughout the year. Milk production is actually greater during the months that follow the rain, for there is an abundance of green pasture and sufficient water. The drier months produce a proportionately inferior quantity of milk. Because the output of their agricultural effort is dependent upon rainfall that occurs in an inconsistent pattern, Atuot see in their cows the potential to provide them with life when all else fails. Their involvement with a monetary economy has importantly enhanced this value, for now it is possible to sell either sheep or goats or a sick cow in a market, and thereby acquire money with which one can purchase grain. Logically then, these experiences feed back to reinforce the central values associated with the life of the cattle camp. To further my argument, I believe that these points serve to support my understanding of their physical world as a movement *away* from the rising waters of the wet season, rather than *toward* a village settlement where they plant their crops.

The higher ground away from the *toic* is dominated by deciduous woodland savannah. Moving eastward toward the Nile the forest thickens and there appear small rock pools which are frequented in the course of moving with the cattle. Atuot recognize the disease carried by tse-tse fly but consider it a problem only south of their country in Mandariland, where few people pasture their cattle. South and east the forest is also thicker in Jurland, and this environment is well suited to the traditional economy of hunting, trapping and iron-smithing for which the Jur are known. Except in the north, Atuotland is thus more or less surrounded by forest that opens up in the middle of the country into *toic* land. They consider their country to be a good land, for they find in it all they need for their lives.

## 1. The Ecological Year (ruon)

In Atuot the word *ruon* implies a full passage from dry season camp to dry season camp, or a full cycle of cultivation. The reason of rains falls into four categories, each period known by the quantity of rain it brings: *kwoth iguong,* the first rains that bring the turtle; *peth deker,* the months of daily light rains; *peth ba tot,* months of "big" rains; and *peth bau,* the months when the rains cease or separate. The word *kwoth* also refers to a "breath," one of the defining characteristics of life. Man has life because God has given him breath. For the Nuer *kwoth* can refer to God and also to lesser spiritual powers, while the Nuer term for rain, *nhail,* means God in Atuot. The season of no rains *(mai)* is the time when the grasses in the *toic* and the forest are burned. This is an essential aspect of their ecological adaptation, for it has been found that many of the species of grass which they are dependent upon do not germinate unless there is sufficient heat. The fresh green tufts of grass that sprout soon after burning are an important resource for cattle at the beginning of the dry season. The most common of these *(mayar)* has symbolic associations with life and fertility. In an obvious sense their entire pastoral and agricultural life is dependent on rainfall, yet they show little interest in trying to predict the weather, and express rather a passive sentiment toward what is ultimately thought to be the work of God. This is a general feature of Atuot cosmology. If I saw heavy dark clouds in the distance and suggested that it would probably rain soon, the most common reply was, "Hold on friend, let's see." Less frequently I was curtly told, "Oh really, have you called the rain?" It is toward the end of the dry season, when rain is most needed and soon expected, that a *gwan kwoth,* a man who possesses the power of rain, will make the sacrifice of a sheep to "call" rain.

In the areas of homestead cultivations on the ironstone plateau the dry season brings only small quantities of muddy water in their wells, and women often sit by them all night collecting the slowly seeping water. I have seen a young boy lowered into a well to dig out mud, but since this is an unpleasant and dangerous task, it is seldom done. "This is work for people like Azande *(nyam),*" I was once told. Happily, we found we were not the only people who suffered from the intense heat and dryness of March, when the land is said to be on fire *(ca piny mai).* With the coming rains these hardships begin to dissipate. When people begin to return to the village sites at the end of the dry season, food that has been stored in their huts is prepared, while the first cultivation begins. The change in settlement is heightened by the change in season. The rain clouds that appear to come so close to the earth and the echoing thunder of March and April are taken as evidence of the presence of God. To the Atuot the dramatic change in season reflects the power and omnipotence of the Creator. My wife and I often shared their company in their huts during the rain and were always told, "You will have a cool and restful sleep." The darkened hut becomes quiet for they feel "humbled" and respect God's presence, evidenced in association with the rain. Lienhardt (1961: 92–93) comments on a similar sentiment among the Dinka. They are grateful not just for the water that will bring life back to the land but also for what they interpret it to be, as further evidence of the continual concern of the Creator for his people. A similar notion is evident in a short tale accounting for the origin of death. Briefly, God at one time wanted to return the dead to life again, for he saw that people were sad when a person died. He later agreed with the suggestion of Fox, however, that if people were to return forever, there would soon be not enough pasture for all the cattle. Fox tied a bell on its tail and ran through the camp, making people laugh. God then saw they had forgotten about the dead man and were no longer mournful. Man is portrayed as satisfied with the most trifling of things. God too accepts the insignificant things of man. An important part of the sacrifice to call rain is the offering of four wild cucumbers *(kuol)*, an inedible vegetable of the forest.

God is said to bring back the life of rain every year. In the cool air that follows the rain children leave their parents' huts to run and slide in the mud. The softened ground is once again surveyed and weeded as cultivation *(apur)* begins.

The ecological year is summarized according to economic activities and settlement patterns on the following table. We should not confuse our linear conception of time, evident in the straight lines I have drawn to separate events, with their own perception of the fluidity of activities. As it is difficult to represent on such a diagram, I omit the periods of transhumance, generally between December and January in the move to the dry season camp, and in the middle of April to the village. Obviously, the events and processes represented here change in accord with the intensity and duration of rainfall. In years when the river floods *(yier e abor)* it is either difficult or impossible to fire the grasses, and this necessarily affects their well-being during the coming dry season when grass will be sparse. Conversely, people may suffer hunger as a result of drought, a situation which we encountered when we lived among them. The harvest of the previous year was insufficient to tide them over during the months when they expect hunger, and consequently six people died from what was diagnosed as starvation. The names of the months refer to what occurs during that period, so that *abothnon* (September) is "period of hunger," from *abuoth,* hunger. *Biildito* means the big durra; *akiodit,* the big coldness, and so on.

The first crop of durra, *rap jaang* (literally, "Dinka durra") is sown in late April in a "halo" around the hut and beyond this circumference the longer maturing sorghum known as *kec* is planted. The terms for the types of sorghum are Dinka; however, no one ever suggested they learned its cultivation from the Dinka. This fact is of some ethnological significance. A man with a number wives is expected to help in the clearing of the garden as well as sowing the seeds for each spouse. Amidst the early maturing *rap jaang* are sown pumpkins, millet, sesame, and a variety of beans. Gourds that will later be used for making calabashes, used as milk gourds, bowls and a variety of other functions, are planted some distance from the hut. In the larger area surrounding the hut where the long maturing *kec,* sorghum, is planted, large plots of ground nuts are planted, occasionally amid the durra. A number of species of both durra and ground nuts are planted. Increasingly in the northern part of their country maize *(karath)* is planted. In Kuek Atuot, the land that borders the Mandari, sizeable plantings of bitter cassava can be found. The term for cassava, *mabundo,* is not a Nilotic word, and it is likely that they originally learned of its cultivation from the Mandari. People of Kuek also call maize by the Mandari term *mataba.*

The months of July and August are given to weeding. Depending on rainfall, the first planting of durra may be ready to harvest toward the end of August. By the middle of July early ripening ground nuts, in addition to those that are in the ground from the previous year *(abuol)* are dug from the ground. Ground nuts are often the only food eaten during the hungry months. In early September a typical meal is made by mixing the paste made from ground nuts with boiled pumpkin, eaten with a porridge of durra *(kuen)* if available. The harvesting of the main crop of durra *(dieng,* the season of

## THE ECOLOGICAL YEAR (ruon)

|  | Dry season (mai) | | | | | Season of rains (deker) | | | | | |
|---|---|---|---|---|---|---|---|---|---|---|---|
| JAN<br>*hor* | FEB<br>*kon* | MAR<br>*nyith* | APR<br>*kaol* | MAY<br>*akoidit* | JUNE<br>*akoi tot* | JULY<br>*admuong* | AUG<br>*alathbor* | SEPT<br>*abothnon* | OCT<br>*biildito* | NOV<br>*biiltoto* | DEC<br>*lal* |

dry season camp (*wuic*) (cattle camps in the *toic*)

wet season camp (*wuic*) (cattle camps in the forest)

most people in the camp

settlement in villages (*cieng*)

period of greatest social density

period of greatest dispersal

fishing

first cultivation

second cultivation

hungry months

burning grass

harvest

hot winds from the north

cool winds from the south

pastoralism

harvest and also the verb for the act of breaking the head of grain away from the stalk) in November coincides with the period in which most marriages are settled. Many important sacrifices may also be delayed until the harvest so there will be sufficient beer for the people who gather. I am not aware of any seasonal rites performed specifically "for the land," though a man of the power *ring* may bless the seeds of crops with clarified butter to ensure their fertility. This is not, however, a ritualized yearly event. There are minor variations throughout Atuotland in the actual time of cultivation and harvest which reflect differences in rainfall. In addition, micro-environmental differences favor different crops. The further south one moves toward the country of Aliab Dinka the less one finds ground nuts. The soil in Aliab country is primarily of the cotton soil variety, and is said to "hold the ground nuts in the ground." In the past if their own harvest was insufficient, Atuot would travel to Aliabland to exchange livestock for durra. Considerable honey *(gu)* is collected seasonally in Rorkec and Kuek where the forest is heavier. A delicious, highly caloric paste is made by mixing honey with ground nut paste. Chickens are always found in the village homesteads, though people say they will not eat them *(Reel a thil ke ter cam)*. The feeling of revulsion is especially strong among young and elder men, for how could such a small thing satisfy his hunger? They are used often in sacrifices in the villages and the flesh is either cooked for children or disposed of in the forest. A discussion of their etiquette concerning food is better attempted in a different context.

Between July and December the wet season cattle camps are relatively close to homesteads, and there is a continual exchange of milk and agricultural products between each type of settlement. Small children often make a twenty mile round trip visit to the town of Yirol at this time to sell milk, which is richest and most plentiful during they rainy season. In the village the preparation of food is the work of women with the help of their daughters. In the cattle camp small boys and girls generally milk the cows, while men control the handling, use and distribution of milk *(cak)*. Milk is said to be the sweetest of all foods *(cak e lim e lim)*. "Leaving milk behind" *(pel ngac)* is the central notion expressed in the initiation of a young man (see Burton 1980*d*).

In September young men who are actively engaged in seeking amourous enjoyment from young women collect in age-sets *(ric)* in the larger cattle camps, and then move off by themselves to form separate camps called *dwil*. For the next ten or fifteen days they practice what is called *tonye* ("to lie down") and drink nothing but milk, and do little more than lie down in order to become fat, strong, and attractive. Bulls are given to them to slaughter and eat. This period of their life marks the culmination of their independence and is recalled with a sense of satisfaction in later years.

When we lived with them, many Atuot were only beginning to carry on their lives as they had before the years of the Civil War. The towns of Yirol, Rumbek, Tonj, Juba, Malakal, and Wau grew dramatically during the war, for they were the only places to live in relative peace. There is now a feeling of cautious serenity in the countryside, as more and more people have begun to move back to traditional village areas. This was our experience in Atuotland; since building new huts and clearing forest are continual processes, however, what I describe here can be seen as historically typical, rather than the result of resettlement.

The village of Anuol in Kuek, where we lived in December 1976, has a single well used by those who live within a radius of five to eight miles and may effectively be called the residents of the village.

When a plot of land is cleared for the first time for a garden *(kak),* nearly all trees save the *lulu* or shea nut tree *(butyuosperum parkii;* in Atuot, *arok)* are felled. The *lulu* tree is indigenous to this area, and its leaves are sparse so that sufficient sunlight reaches the sorghum and other plants. The bush and trees collected within the plot are burned in December, when the grasses of the *toic* and forest are set afire. The *lulu* nuts *(dau arok* "calves of *lulu")* are pounded to extract oil used for cooking and bodily decoration. Once cleared, suitable timber is sought for erecting the piles on which the hut will sit, normally about ten to twelve feet above the ground. The area underneath the hut is closed off with durra stalks and used for cooking, sleeping and tethering goats and sheep. Construction of the hut goes on simultaneously with clearing the garden. The door of the hut should always face toward the *toic* and the cattle, for if it faces another direction one is suspected of being a witch *(apeth).* A larger homestead normally has an additional hut built on the ground for livestock. The *adwil,* as it is called, is an extremely solid structure and will last the twenty years a garden is expected to be fertile.

After the first rains the man in the process of making a homestead will return to the village early to plant beans, sesame and durra in order to loosen the soil for ground nuts the following year. Normally the goats and sheep graze the stalks of durra and eat the leaves of the ground nuts after the harvest, but fields are not manured with any intent. Remaining fodder is burned with the grass in the forest. Another crop of durra and millet is planted in the second year, but not much is expected as a harvest in the early years of cultivation. The same process is repeated in the third year with ground nuts and possibly cassava added to the garden. By the fourth year it is hoped that a large planting of all the crops will repay their labor.

Every year the garden pattern changes slightly and is larger or smaller depending upon how much was planted and expected after the first rain. After fifteen or twenty years cultivation has depleted the soils so that additional ash fertilizer helps little. In the intervening years a type of slash and burn is practiced. As the garden expands seasonally the bush cleared from the boundary is piled throughout the garden and burned with the remaining vegetation.

The forest between homesteads is littered with old and sunken posts of what was an *adwil,* and a nearby forked branch shrine which served as the home of the power *(jok)* owned by a family. When an area has returned to its forest-like state, it is seen as suitable for cultivation again, and a new homestead may incorporate the site of an old *adwil* within the garden. Gradually over extended periods of time their villages occupy slightly different areas within the abundant forested region. The land itself is rich, and as a result, the Atuot and Ceic Dinka practice a more diversified form of agriculture than is typical of other areas of Nuer and Dinkaland (see Howell [ed.] 1954/1: 365). The home sits in the middle of the cultivated fields and this gives the impression there are no focal points of the settlements, apart from a common well. In a recently settled area such as Anyuol, savannah type forest separates one homestead from the next. In one way or another every homestead within a "village" is connected to another by narrow winding paths leading from one hut to the next, as though they were strung together. The average area under cultivation for a single homestead is about ten to twelve acres, dependent upon the factors outlined.

A man normally builds his *adwil* in the same area as his fathers. Not infrequently a youngest son comes to live in his natal home with his wife, especially if his father died a long time before. Rights to uncultivated land are recognized for any male member of a family. The localization of descent groups from a common male ancestor within the same general area is explained by Atuot as a preference related in the past to protection in warfare. There is considerable variation in actual residence, so that effectively one's kith may or may not be kin.

Among the Nuer and the Dinka the typical homestead consists of a cattle byre and a hut for each wife of a polygamous union. Two points are worth emphasizing for comparative purposes. Among the Atuot cattle are never brought to the village except for sacrifice. Second, while each wife has her own hut built by her husband, not infrequently the huts of co-wives may be separated by as much as half a mile. In other cases they may be in entirely different regions of Atuotland. Residence ideology favors patrilocality but just as often relationships of affinity are exploited for the same ends. By their reasoning, the separation of homesteads of co-wives is preferred so that the people will have respect between them. They might instead build their huts all together and then walk off some distance to their gardens, but everyone wants a hut surrounded by their cultivation. This does reflect upon the position of women among the Atuot while no ecological reason for the practice is apparent. When married, a woman keeps her own name. If she is called Alak, her child will be known as *gat* Alak by his maternal relatives, and *gat* Mayen, should that be the father's name, among paternal relatives. Some of the greatest hostilities develop between half-siblings, especially over the use of cattle for marriage. A woman prefers the independence and status of her own garden. And understanding of the meaning of what is one's "very own" is central to Atuot values and ethics. In his study of Southern Luo ideology, Ocholla-Ayayo (1976: 42) observes a similar sentiment. "'I', 'we' is a basic philosophy: I must have it; I am better; We must have it; these are important and what is outside is not valid or proper." The Atuot homestead is an independent unit and the larger conglomerate of a village area is the result of fictional or historical rationalizations about the occupation of the area. In the daily course of events economic cooperation is limited to the members of a household, for common tasks require no reciprocity.

In the more densely inhabited cattle camp, the fundamental rule is cooperation. A large cattle camp not only has high prestige value for its members but is also less likely to suffer raids. A particular camp is normally said to be the camp of a named descent group but just as often, affines tether their cows together. We lived for a time in a camp that was said to be a camp of Luac. We slept in the *gol* of Maker. To our right was the *gol* of Igai, the brother of a wife of Maker from Jilek. The *gol* closest to us on the left belonged to Cep, the husband of Alak, the sister of Maker's wife, also from Jilek. On the far side of the camp were a number of people from Ceic Dinka. Since they camp together, they first recognize their common economic interests in their most valued possessions, the cattle. The life of the camp and the needs of their herds are permanent activities, while cultivation is a seasonal task[5] (see Burton 1980*a*).

---

[5] Literally, the word *gol* refers first to the dung fire that burns continually under the roof of the *adhang* in the camp. An average sized camp has from thirty to forty *gols* and fourteen to fifteen hundred head of cattle. *Gol* also refers to the minimal descent group of the family. Thus *ji gol*, the people of my family, implies a degree of relationship absent in the phrase *ji wuicde*, people

The shelters *(adhang)* built over *gols* in the wet season camps are more or less permanent. There is no limit to the time a camp can be occupied. Indeed, the "ancient" camp is praised in ox songs, for here the ash from the dung fires has accumulated for so many years and is therefore most enjoyable to lie in. Life in the camp is necessarily a permanent part of being a pastoralist, but the actual social composition of any single *gol* changes continually. All the young children of a marital union are brought to the camp to live and drink milk at the beginning of the wet season. As milk productivity decreases they are taken home again until only the youngest, and therefore most deserving, child remains. Younger unmarried men *(acöt)* actually have the greatest amount of work for they take the cows to drink, and remain with the herds throughout the day in the forest. The dry season camps are by comparison extremely temporary. Shelter is either non-existent or made of grass. Cattle are left to graze untended in the *toic* in the dry season because there are no predators. In contrast, tending cattle in the rainy season is often a difficult, exhausting and tedious responsibility. The cattle normally have to be driven some distance for water and the ten to twelve foot grasses of the rains may shelter lions, leopards, or hyenas. If they are caught in the rain herdsmen often return to the camp late at night in almost total darkness. One has to experience this to appreciate what a trauma it can be. Atuot will say, however, that the cattle know where they are going, and this must be partially true, for when they return late at night, in an astounding display of bovine intelligence each animal makes its way through the darkened camp to stand by its cattle peg to await tethering.

The cattle camp and the things of cattle are the things of men, while life in the village and cultivation is associated with the world of women. An ox-name for a man such as Acilobaai ("I never go to the village") illustrates this. There are few women in the wet season camps for they are in the villages weeding gardens and harvesting the ripening ground nuts. Women rarely milk the cows and in the dry season camps they carry out a great deal of the fishing, in addition to porting cooking utensils. There is no wood in the *toic* for fires, so their tasks are made even more difficult.

Finally it should be mentioned that *jao,* the "powers" or "divinities" which bring ill health and misfortune, are experienced only in the village. Atuot say, "Only God comes to us in the cattle camp." This is a fundamental distinction to be understood for a proper appreciation of Atuot religion.

### 2. Ecology and Cosmology

Traditionally the Atuot say the world is a vast flat plain. The sky *(nhial)* is seen to be in permanent juxtaposition above the land *(piny)*. On a heavily overcast day, when the sky appears to have come closer to the world of people a man may say, "God has come close to the earth today." The separation of night and day represents a variety of experiences, one of which is made evident in simple conversation. When sleeping in close company during the night a respectful greeting in the morning is *ce ker, ce nien?*

---

of my camp. A camp may be known as the camp of *cieng* Angainy, which represents a clan. The terms *ji gol* and *nei cieng* (people of my clan) have primarily a domestic reference while *ji wuic* points toward a political entity, and in the past this was necessarily the most important economic and political group since fighting and cattle raiding were organized by people who camped together.

"Have you awoken?" or "Has the night separated from the day for you?" followed by "Have you slept?" meaning do you have your health. At the same time this means the powers that guide life have returned after sleeping. The daytime has associations with God, for life begins anew each day and this is God's doing. The darkness of night offers refuge for potentially malignant powers of the land *(jao piny,* sing.: *jok)*. A man in repose is especially prone to the evil intentions of his enemies through their *jao.* If he is already in a state of ill health this time is even less propitious. A man told me his father, who had killed many people when living, slept with spears around him, as protection from their revengeful ghosts *(tiep).* When sick, Atuot say, "It means your *jok* has gone for a walk far away and left you alone." The sleep of another should never be disturbed, for he will awaken before his own *jok,* that has gone off in the night, returns to him. When a person has slept it means he has stayed with life. "Decau has given us sleeping and waking, and when we awaken, it is from Decau." To wake in the morning is thus to re-enter the world protected by God. Discussing what would be done with the corpse if a man died at night, a woman replied quickly, and with some indignation, "We do not die at night. Only witches die at night."

The sun is said to walk or travel across the sky. In the evening when it grows dark the sun wants to return to its cattle camp. The moon is much slower in its movement, so that a night without a moon *(muoth)* signifies that the moon is still walking back to the eastern sky. Each new phase *(paai tieth)* marks the beginning of a new cycle of crossing the sky. The rains are said to follow the new moon. When it appears in a sky still lit by sunlight the moon is called *amel* (sheep). This is of religious significance. Men and women agreed to the idea that the sun *(cang)* is male, that is, has qualities that make it like men, and that the moon is female. *Ring,* a power later discussed in detail, is among the oldest of powers. Like the moon, it "walks" slowly, and desires sacrifices of sheep. The moon is said to be slower than the sun because "it is like women." There is evident here an implicit analogy between *ring* and the quality of femininity, a notion that will help us understand better the intent in their sacrifices, for women and *ring* are bringers of "life."

In geographical space east *(cuic* "right") is the direction from which life emanates. Daylight is associated with the world and character of men, for it implies honesty and forthrightness. The fierceness of the heat of the sun is seen to be like the strength and hard things of men. West *(cam* "left") is the side of death *(cam era thaang lieth)* and has associations with the qualities of women. The daytime is like men because they always see things clearly. Women hide their feelings, but when they finally reveal them it is always in a bad way, as though something of a disastrous nature occurred at night. North is referred to as the left side *(thaang cam)* and south, the right side *(thaang cuic).* In his life a man is thus oriented facing with the front of his body toward the east and the light of day and with his back and what is behind him *(jokde)* toward the west. In a conceptual and moral sense the things behind him are always a part of him. Whatever a man may do tomorrow, "he always has his back," that is, the things in his past. The things he follows, or conversely, the things in back of him, reflect the morality associated with deceased ancestors. North, or the left side is also seen as the direction from which bad things have entered their lives, including rinderpest *(makeeth),* malaria *(juei),* syphilis *(pajila),* and the killing brought by the Civil War. The hot and dusty winds at the zenith of the dry season blow from the left side and Atuot recognize that many people are stricken with cerebral-spinal meningitis *(dong yieth)* soon after. The cooling winds of the rainy season come from the right, or south side (see Burton n. d. *b*).

To account for seasonal changes and what we think of as the passage of time, Atuot say *piny ce jaal,* "the land has travelled," implying that it has changed character. Atuot would agree that time is relative. A period in the past is related in time and space to the memory of when people were in a particular camp. The past, present, and future are merged in experience, a point noted by Lienhardt (1961) and Deng (1971) for the Dinka, and clearly expressed for the Nuer by what Evans-Pritchard called "structural time." Time is relative to person, place, and activity. There is no Atuot word we can properly translate as "time," though the word *cang* (sun) also delineates the twenty-four hour day.

Today, *wale* can mean the way things are in the world we know as well as the period of sunlight, including the morning *(piny bau),* midday *(dercang),* afternoon *(en gang),* and evening *(en thiang).* At night the land has "gone," *piny wer.* In a similar manner the word for the following day *(iruon)* can refer to the next sunrise or some indefinite period in the future. I bought an ox soon before we left Atuotland to be left in the *gol* of a close friend. He was understandably pleased for a number of reasons, and knowing we would be leaving in a few days he said, "Tomorrow, I will buy a bull and a cow so the herd would grow." Tomorrow can be in ten years. Likewise, yesterday, *a thin,* means in the past or the preceding day. *Wal* refers to the living days of dead ancestors whose memory is still with the living and *ne mei* fills in all the forgotten "space" between ancestors and the situation of creation.

Increasingly a form of the Arabic word for time, pronounced in Atuot *thaa,* is used, but only to denote different "times" of the day. To understand the Atuot usage we would have to translate the phrase *thaa na barou ba piny* as "when the sun is sitting in the morning sky at the place you call seven."

To ask the age of a person one says *teke yin ruon na di,* "how many years do you have," and most people have not the vaguest idea. When one considers the question, there is little reason why one Atuot would want to ask another how old he was. Physical age is immediately common knowledge in fact, for the beads one wears communicate the information. Age is also perceived in terms of economic activities, so that young children collect the dung to dry in the sun in the cattle camp and married women make their way to wells to draw water, and so on. Naturally, within this classification of status and age, roles change with seasonal differences in residence and activity. For simplicity of presentation, I record here statuses and their meanings.

| Male | Female |
|---|---|
| *gat:* baby | *gat nyal:* baby girl |
| *dhol:* small boy, before puberty | *nyal:* small girl, before puberty |
| *acot:* a male at the age of initiation. His testes have "dropped" or appeared | *nyal ce kaai:* a girl who has "ripened" or matured |
| *awuot:* a man of marriageable age | *nyal awuot:* a young woman (15–16) of marriageable age |
| *cou:* "husband" | *cek:* "wife" |
| *nuer me dong:* a person who has become old | *cek me dong:* a woman who has become old |
| *gwadong:* literally, old father; grandfather or deceased ancestor | *madong:* literally, old mother; grandmother or deceased ancestor |

Age has no value in itself, but it implies maturity and knowledge of the world. A person who has survived the hardships of existence as they know it, has proven to have a deep knowledge of the world. By association he gains a better understanding of the ways of God, who directs and controls their lives. They would certainly view a "youth culture" with some disdain. An older person is also assured a place in the memory of the living through his or her offspring, a value so strongly a part of Nilotic culture that women are married on occasion to the *name* of a man or woman who may have died forty years before but left no offspring who could carry his name (see Evans-Pritchard 1945; cf. Burton 1978).

As a foreigner who had come a great distance to live with them and learn their language, I continually had the opportunity to perceive their associations of time and space when asked to explain where my land was, and how the journey was made. When these things were explained they quite naturally expressed a degree of amazement when confronted with the fact that distances which they considered so great appeared so trifling by comparison. Like a number of other travellers through the Nilotic Sudan who went about asking anthropological questions, I too was queried if I had "gotten" or found God while travelling so high in the sky, though I had the definite impression my friends knew that neither I nor anyone else had seen God. The most frequently asked question was if food and water could be acquired on such a journey. Satisfaction of both needs are met as a matter of course among kin and family in Atuotland, and this question points again toward the moral values associated with their land, for in one's own home one is ideally assured of physical and spiritual well-being. During the many times my wife or I suffered from malaria or dysentery, their constant assurance was that God had seen our way safely to their land, and since they had nothing bad in their hearts for us, surely he would see this and make sure we returned safely with our health to rejoin our own families in our own land.

The natural world follows a pattern over which they have no control, but instead is seen as the work of God. In a discussion of ideas of polarity, such as that initially proposed by Hertz (1960), we could certainly add additional ethnographic material to confirm the worldwide prominence of such dichotomies. The nature of the world as they experience it, as opposed to any attempted structural interpretation of such phenomena, is understandably more complex. For the Atuot, the things on the right which together share the qualities of maleness, brightness and life have a further moral superiority. Yet what gives a human being existence *(tau)*, what we can call the life of a man *(yei)*, is said to be on (in) his left side. If he is speared in his left side it is thought that the chances for a man's recovery are much less than if he had been inflicted with same wound on his right side. Left-handedness has in fact a positive evaluation, for it is said to be a sign of cleverness. In a functional sense it is considered much more difficult to fight a man by club or spear if he is left-handed, for it changes his character and behavior, and makes his moves unpredictable. In some folktales a man is able to disguise himself amidst enemies by pretending that he is left-handed. Most significantly, God the Creator is said to be "left" *(Decau era cam)* or on the left side. Thus the association of women with the world of darkness, death and the left points toward a paradox in the values and cosmology of the Atuot, who, like the Nuer, trace the descent of their people through males, but recount the generations of their cattle through the dams that gave birth to them. While their secular roles are degraded by men, only through women can they acquire cows. Both women and cows provide for their well-being physically, and also symbolically as representative of creative abilities. Though she may be ignored in the affairs of the daily world, an elder woman who has lived a productive life, and by analogy a cow that has born many calves, is seen to have been favored by God. Her spiritual qualities have been manifest in the physical world.

Having offered an outline of the ecological year, it is now possible to address the central concern of this book.

# CHAPTER III

# Atuot Cosmology

The remainder of this study addresses Atuot religious ritual and belief. Though I provide an account of the manner in which belief, intention, and ritual action are conjoined in an experiential sense, this formal presentation necessarily misrepresents the disorder of social realities. To a certain degree this is inevitable, for if the data were to be described as they actually occur in time and space, the reader would find himself in a quandary similar to that which Needham (1963: vii) portrays for a blind man who first gains sight. Likewise in this context, the reader would have little chance to grasp the essence of the Atuot religious experience.

Hence, in this chapter I write in a general way about their conception of cosmological order in the world. The presentation is then divided into a formal outline of spiritual powers, and the manner in which these are appeased in a variety of religious rituals. While acknowledging the shortcomings of this method, it does offer a concise blueprint for understanding the sometimes disparate sentiments and ideas which collectively form an integrated system of thought which is Atuot religion.

Social anthropologists have increasingly realized the difficulty of the task of translating concepts with a psychic reference. Thus, I have not seen it crucial to explicate the meaning of religious "belief" for the Atuot, for according to some, this is not a universal experience. Further, as Needham (1972: 100) argues, it is to some extent arbitrary to select action as a criterion of belief. No attempt is made to reveal the inner psychic state, if indeed there is one, in the Atuot understanding of God. Yet it is possible to gleen from the data a central thesis of this study, that of the ultimate and passive acceptance of the ways of God in Atuot religion. This is made apparent in the discussion of the intent of the sacrificial act among the Atuot. The offering of the life of an animal to God in the expectation of his blessings for human beings is fundamental to their religious sentiment, though there is no single term which refers to *all* sacrificial acts. The Atuot phrase "to kill a cow" *(be nak e yang)* explicitly connotes, however, the sacrifice of its life to benefit their own (see Burton n. d. *a*).

This is a difficult undertaking, and in a real sense, the problem is unresolved until the data have been presented. Only then it is possible to appreciate the analytical problems raised in the study of Atuot religion.

The material world and all it includes is said to have been created by the Creator long ago *(muon kuonon ce cak e Decau ne mei)*. To their understanding, *Decau* is the Being or Divinity who alone has the puissance of creation. In the Atuot language, "to create" means to bring into existence something that never existed before. A man and woman give birth to a child *(ce gat dieth)* while it is the Creator who creates the human being in the womb and gives it life *(ce gat cak Decau)*. Likewise, a woman forms a pot from the clay she finds by the riverside, but God brought into existence the water and soil from which it is made. This radical distinction is more or less apparent in all their religious ideas. Depending on the context, this Being may be referred to as *Decau,* connoting the one who creates and created all things, or as *Nhial* which I translate as God. Thus, *Nhial Decau* means "God the Creator." The phrase *Decau guar* ("the Creator, my father") indicates that the English pronoun "he" may properly be employed when referring to God. Confronted with a problem for which there is no immediate or direct recourse, an Atuot may utter the phrase *Nhial guar lueke,* "God my father, give me help," inferring a sense of paternal love. When they are utterly resigned to an unexpected misfortune and say *Decau guar,* "Oh Creator, my father," Atuot sentiment is that of a people who passively accept the world as they know it and as it has been created, who can at best try to gain a sense of satisfaction in their lives. The two terms, *Nhial* and *Decau,* do not therefore refer to different beings or ideas, but to different experiences of God. The people of the world are called *acuek Decau,* the tiny black ants who walk on the earth. In this way the Atuot contrast their minuteness and insignificance with the omnipotence of God, the Creator.

While we normally conceptualize categories of social life with terms that delineate spheres of activity, such as economics, religion, and politics, Atuot generally make no such distinctions. Yet is it possible to refer to those things we call religion in their language by the phrase *ruaic Decau,* "the words or deeds of the Creator." Likewise I do not think there is a single term which can be translated as "belief," though semantically this quality of thought does exist for them. The word *tak,* to think or expect, suggests that there is a high probability of something being or existing. It is different from the word *ngac,* to know, which in turn is less definite than the verb *nhok,* to agree or to be persuaded. The phrase *a ce nhok γen me lat e yin,* I have been persuaded by the truth of what you have told me, can be taken to represent their sentiments about the reality of God in their lives. This is an *a priori* acceptance, for it is everywhere and always evident in their lives, and because it is for them a primal truth. Another phrase, *kan pere ke,* suggests that one has no definite idea of what may happen while the outcome of events is ultimately predictable. While there is no single word that can be glossed with the English word believe or belief, a number of Atuot usages can be seen to approximate this quality of thought. While an outsider travelling through their country may ask the awkward question, do you know God? *(ce ngac yin Decau),* their response is usually, we have God and he is the same as your God, for he created everything and all people. The reality of God's existence is implicit, so the Atuot notion of belief is less restricted than the strictly theological connotation one normally understands by the use of the word in western societies. To say that they do not *believe* in spiritual phenomena, would incorrectly portray their feelings of something they accept as reality.

These points are relevant for they are also related to the lack of formalized liturgy in Atuot religion. Their rituals are loosely organized rather than permanent and consistent sequences of behavior. It is also necessary to note the absence of what is called pious intent at their sacrifices. They know God will see their plight and reconcile their suffering, and this is why they give him the life of an animal. At the same time they know they will later cook the flesh *(ring)* of the victim and eat it in a festive mood. Seen in combination, these factors suggest that a separate word to describe an attitude of strictly religious sentiment would be redundant where experience itself points toward a reality for Atuot that we refer to with the qualifying term "belief." Their notion of the word transcends and incorporates the boundaries of meaning which we normally ascribe to it. Atuot religion is at one level an inward, personal ideology. If a man knows he has transgressed a moral right, he is also aware that God will see it *(a be juic Decau)*. But the problems of one man necessarily affect the well-being of a family and even a larger group of kin. Each person may offer his own invocation in the course of a sacrifice while the import of collective sentiment is deemed equally important for efficacious action. Therefore, a sinner cannot profit from the misfortune of others, for other people will notice this as will God. The inevitability of individual assertiveness and conformity to social ideals is reflected in the confrontation between man and God.

Like the Nuer and the Dinka, Atuot do not have an elaborate myth of creation. God created human beings in the initial situation, and the birth of every new child is evidence of the same act, as is the year's first rains which bring back life to the world. Plants and grasses are part of the world of creation, as they provide for human subsistence. However, the word *wal* generically refers to all the kinds of grasses and is also the singular form of *wel*, medicines which are active agents. The animals considered to have existence or intelligence like human beings are their cows and the elephant. A story relates how at one time Elephant *(guor)* was once a woman because it has breasts which produce milk. A girl had remained unmarried and then went to the forest to become Elephant. At one time older people would not allow young men to see elephants because they feared they would become excited by the vagina of the elephant, which is also said to be like that of women. A young man who had an erection after looking at an elephant would soon become impotent *(rol;* cf. *rual* "incest"). Other versions relate how the elephant was created in the shape of human beings except for two additional legs. The elephant's trunk is said to allow eating with hands like people. The association of the quality of life of people and that of cattle goes beyond this, for they say that one could not live without the other.

Human conception it is said to occur when the woman's blood ends. The sperm *(laic)* meets with the blood *(riem)*. Decau mixes it for a long time until it becomes a lump. If the child is going to be male then three lumps are formed, and if female, four. It is the word of the Creator (*lat* Decau) which brings the child out of the womb. When the time for delivery comes, God turns the child upside down so it will come out head first. If there is some deformity or irregularity in the birth, such as six fingers, a breech birth, or when a boy is born without a foreskin, the child will be called Acao, a thing of the Creator, for God has had a special mark of his presence.

Once born the child becomes a human being *(nuer)* in which God has combined flesh *(ring)* with life *(yei)* which is defined by whether or not a person has breath *(kwoth)*, an active life principle God blows *(kwoth)* into the child at delivery. Other conceptual principles of life are associated with the blood that moves through the body which itself has no definite connotation of life or death, as evidenced by the same term *nuer*, referring both a human being and corpse. The elements are combined in the situation of creation and are refracted once again at death *(lia)*. They speak of their own life, and the life of all things in their world as a gift of the Creator (*buol* Decau). What they see as having been given to them for their lives, they return to God through sacrifice. Their association of human and animal blood with "life" is better considered later.

While I have said there is no one story that offers a full explanation for Creation, Atuot see in their physical world continual evidence of the presence of the creative power of God. When a clear dark night is illuminated by thousands of stars, they liken each star to a dung fire of a huge cattle camp. The presence of so many camps means God is close and there are no lurking dangers. When the night sky is overcast by clouds this indicates lions are present roaming freely among the herds. Yet, while God created lions, he did this with the concerns of human beings in mind, for he made them give birth infrequently and to only a small number of offspring. If a man is said to have the character of a lion, a common theme of their folklore, he will not father many children. They suffer the heat of the sun throughout their lives, though God was considerate enough to have left the sun without a family, while he gave the moon very many children, and the coolness of a moon-lit evening is the evidence.

One story relates how God created the first man from the black cotton-soil found by the riverside and in the *toic,* into which he blew the breath of life. A more elaborate tale recounts the beginning of the most important elements of their life, marriage and cattle, and thus has greater similarity to what we normally would call a creation myth. I have recorded many versions of the same story and combine them here.

When people were created, there was the family of Raan (man) and they lived all together in one cattle camp by themselves. The family of Acol [the first woman; literally, "the one who was called"] lived in their camp alone with their cows. Men wore the vagina on their arms and whenever they wanted to have sex, they would untie it from their arms and have intercourse with it. You could just untie it and fuck it anywhere. You just untied it and hit it against *bum* (the pubic area) and then you would feel vagina. The cattle of Raan were buffaloes *(muk)* and he did not know anything about cattle that we have today.

One time a calf of Raan's wandered off from his camp and his people had to go and look for it. They walked through the forest and traced the path of the calf to the camp of Acol. He asked them if they had seen his lost calf, and they said no. Before this the husband of Acol was the waves of the river. When she wanted to have sex she would walk to the riverside and open her legs, and bring the waves into her vagina. This is how she had children, but they were all female. The vagina of Raan only made men.

When those of Acol saw Raan they asked what his name was and he told them, I am called Raan. Then they came closer to him and looked and said, what is that thing hanging between your legs? Raan answered, this is called penis. They said next, what do you do with this thing? Raan answered, I fuck this thing here on my arm with it. Acol asked, is it sweet? Raan did not answer but asked instead, and what is that opening there between your legs? Acol answered, this is called vagina. Raan said, well bring it here and let me see if it is sweet. Raan fucked Acol and she said it was very very sweet. Then all the other people heard this and went to Raan and started pulling at his penis, and they all fucked him. They fucked him so much that he died – he died completely.

After they had all been fucked by Raan, the women then became lax with their cows. When a woman said who is going to take the cows to pasture today, everyone said I cannot do it. I am here drying the flour I pounded from durra. After a time, those of Raan heard of his death, and they followed his path to the camp of women. The men were very angry and the women of Acol all ran away in fright when they saw them coming. The men left behind them the cows that were buffaloes, and the women did not come back to their camp for one month. When they returned the men had taken over the cows. Each woman then went to a different man, and they fucked, and then those of Raan untied the vaginas from their arms and threw them into the forest.

After this they agreed to live together in the same camp but Acol said there were two conditions. First, if they wanted to stay keeping the cows, men would have to abandon the cattle they called buffalo. The second was that if they wanted to marry a woman, they would have to give the people of the wife cattle to replace her. The men agreed to this.

When they stayed for some time together, they found that when they fucked they cried like the sound of birds, and they said, what are we to do with this noise? They found a *tiet* (a man of powers) and he said they should sacrifice a goat. They killed the animal and spread the meat all over the roofs of the shelters, and the kite came down and swooped up the meat, and when he did this he also carried away the crying sound of intercourse with the meat, and the silence of the kite remained with the people.

Now women say if Raan had not been killed, they would not have come upon the cattle of women. Now if a man does not have cattle he cannot have a woman. If women fight with men now they say, we are the people that showed you the land. The vaginas and the cows were ours (cf. James 1979).

A short song that women sing together as they lead a new wife from her home to that of her husband condenses the same story of the initial situation:

A girl is taken to her husband
The husband is proud
He has deceived people with the horns of cows
⌊his cows were once buffaloes, with buffalo horns⌋
We came upon Raan ⌊all that is maleness⌋ taking a bath in the river
Raan fucked them all
What trouble is it that you have with us
We, the age-set *(ric)* of Acol
We ⌊had⌋put Raan into the river
You, those who look for marriage
Give me *manyuat* to eat
⌊a bull; "to eat," *mieth*. It means, give me wealth to live on⌋

If we understand the story primarily as a folktale, we could perceive its immediate domestic and secular referent in the daily world. Beyond this it portrays aspects of their cosmological world as well. Women and their creative abilities are recognized as primal (along with cows) in the definition of society. Another story tells a familiar Nilotic theme of the separation of the earth from the sky, or more precisely, how the connection between the sky and the earth was severed. Here again the role of women (in the last story, sexually) and their behavior accounts for the contemporary order.

At one time the sky and the earth were very close and people walked back and forth between them by means of a rope like a ladder. This was when if a person died, Decau would raise him up and he would have life again. When the people were hungry the woman would put one grain of durra in the mortar to pound it into flour and there would be enough to feed everyone. One day a newly married woman said she would work harder and pound more. She lifted the pestle so high that it hit God, and he was angry and said, before you were always satisfied with only a little food, but from now on you will always know hunger, even if you cultivate a great deal.

The act itself is so trifling, just like the swallowing of a bead, or losing at a game. The text continues,

Then *atuc* (durra bird) flew by and cut the rope, and later a man died, and people were stricken with grief. They covered themselves with ashes.

The story continues to show how God took pity on man when he saw the suffering. In these secular affairs the suffering of people is seen as their own doing. In the religious context women and cows represent life. Perhaps it is simply a homonym, but the verb "to create" *(cak)* is the same as the noun for milk, *cak*. This is not to suggest these ideas and associations are idiomatic of Atuot religion, but only to outline what are some of the ideational parameters of their poetry, thought and expression. We see here again the theme of God's paternal interest in the affairs of people for he tries to alter the situation and bring them back to life again:

> Then Decau said, let me return the people to them. He threw a piece of gourd into the water and it dropped into the pool for a moment and then re-emerged. People will always die and come up like this, he said. The fox disagreed and said, if that happened soon there would be no more grazing area. The fox threw a piece of broken clay pot into the water and it sank immediately. Fox said, people will always be like this potsherd, and will not raise up again. Decau disagreed and said, they are suffering from misery, and it is better that I bring them up again. Fox then tied a small bell onto the tail of jackel and sent it running through the cattle camp. When the people saw this, they began to laugh and forgot about mourning. When he saw they were happy, Decau left bringing them back after death.

The hunger caused by women is often said to be the oldest power *(aboth yen a kaai jao)*, the oldest thing that kills people. In their daily lives these aspects of life are much more obvious: life is given by God to man, and it returns to God when he dies. What is said to happen to a human being at death, necessarily reveals what are the components of life.

What one finds so remarkable about these stories is the insignificance of human beings and their tendency to fall upon burdens of life as a result of trivial actions. The physical privation people sometimes suffer is immense. A person must be strong and self-assertive to a maximum degree to be a successful pastoralist. Atuot suffer attacks of lions, droughts, floods and a variety of tropical illnesses, and yet compare themselves to their notion of God as mere ants. This passive sentiment characterizes their religion. For the Atuot, God should in one way be understood as a being that is ultimate, and logically therefore, beyond their control. But depending on the degree to which they can manage their lives in their own interests, they are more or less self-assertive and individually motivated. God may be ultimately responsible for life and death, though if a man's brother dies from illness, he will want to find out what particular *jok* (power) was responsible.

An illustration will highlight this difference. On one occasion my wife lay sick inside our hut with a particularly severe attack of malaria. I sat nearby talking quietly with a *tiet* about the powers and God. Through a window I could see a vulture descend and land on the roof of the hut, directly above the area where my wife was lying. Atuot say if this type of bird comes and sits on one's roof, it is indicative of bad things to follow. Somewhat alarmed that this had happened in this situation, I ran out of the hut and hurled a stone at the bird. Later when we were talking, the *tiet* took this same event as an example of the difference between powers and God. When I threw the rock at the bird, he said, this was like when a man is sick, and people look for a *jok* in his body as the cause, but God is there all the time with life.

Their relations to God and powers are divergent. Their sacrificial rites are not direct attempts to influence God in their favor, but rather to affect the powers which are ultimately under the control of God.

The powers themselves, discussed more fully in the following two chapters, are divided into further two further categories, powers of the above or from the sky *(jao nhial)*, and powers of the below or of the earth *(jao piny)*. This dichotomy obviously invites an analysis of these notions along the lines of similar binary discriminations.

However, this would portray a false picture, for collectively they are all powers, and ultimately share more in common with each other as having the property of non-human essence than being different in association with heaven and earth. The translation of the word *jok* points toward these similarities. In one sense it means spiritual powers, in another divinity, or, in the words chosen by Evans-Pritchard (1956), refractions of the divine powers of God. The essential distinction for the Atuot is not the nature of the power, but its source and the manner in which people encounter and confront it. All powers are from God who has shown man different ways of resolving their influence. Within this general sort of distinction between powers associated with the sky and those of the ground fall a number of other manifestations of the powers of God, and these do not fall clearly within either of the other two categories. I discuss them now as a preface to a later discussion of each type of power.

The birth of twins and the situation when a man has been struck by lightning are seen by Atuot as a direct manifestation respectively of the creative and destructive powers of God in their lives. Neither phenomena can properly be called a power *(jok)* and an examination of rites and beliefs associated with each will highlight the manner in which they are temporal and transient in contrast to other powers they encounter in the world which are seen as permanent features of their lives, since they are part of the world created by God. Unlike the general sentiment of passivity, twins and lightning require also assertive action by human beings in the same way that God has actively come into their lives. A further difference between these two phenomena and the powers in general is that people cannot control their occurrence. In a structural interpretation of Atuot religious beliefs, these would necessarily be classified as categorical anomalies. Rather than impose this focus on the data, however, I simply record the ethnography and discuss their own interpretation of events.

In discussing Nuer religion, Evans-Pritchard (1956: 60) suggested that the spirit *col wic* "is a conception which appears to be, unlike many of their conceptions, not only native to the Nuer but also peculiar to them." What follows, then, refers necessarily to a wider ethnological comparison not attempted here. The Dinka also recognize lighting as a special revelation of divinity, but the differences in their thought reflect other differences between them and the Atuot of a social and religious nature.

Everything recorded about lightning is based on verbal accounts, and fortunately I have never seen anyone burned by its force. Like any other natural phenomenon, Atuot attribute lightning to God. The occurrence is most prevalent at the beginning of the rainy season and is a vivid accent to the dramatic climatic change. In one of the myths explaining the separation of Nuer and Atuot, a great lightning is said to have caused them to disperse. The poetic image is consistent with their experience, for it is said, when lightning strikes a house there is a violent explosion, scattering people, wood and clods of mud in all directions. When a man is killed by lightning *(nuer ce mer ke nak Decau)* they say, the Creator has thrown down his fire to man. The lightning itself is sometimes said to have a physical property, for one could, if one wanted, dig up the shaft of fire from the ground, to ensure that it would not fall in the same place again. If struck directly, death is immediate. People come running to the burning house and before entering it, scoop up a handful of mud and smear it across their faces, shoulders and foreheads, then try to bring out the people from inside. A small ram *(ruath amel)* or he-goat *(ruath dil)* should be thrown alive into the burning hut before they enter. They will then carry out the unconscious people *(nei ce buor)* and smear their bodies with mud in the same fashion.

If a victim falls on his face from the force of impact, he will die shortly, but if he is fortunate enough to have landed pointed toward God, he will retain his consciousness and life. In passing it can be noted that in their verbal accounts the setting of such events is always the village, rather than the cattle camp. Living in a camp during such a storm, I commented on the way the cattle appeared to try to lower their backs to the ground when hearing the crashing thunder. A man told me God would never want to take the life of a cow this way, but if he did, it meant they would have to sacrifice a cow to God soon after it happened.

If struck dead, the corpse should be buried as soon as possible, because God has taken the life immediately. I doubt that anything is done with the ash of the fire. They told me that often the deceased is found dead lying on his left side, because God throws the lightning with his left hand. In a like manner, they smear the mud across their bodies with their left hands. When the hut is still draped in flames, people from nearby homesteads bring fire from their own hearths and throw it into the hut, which is said to stop or cancel out the flames brought by God, who will see that he is being respected *(be thek ke be juic e Decau)* and extinguish the flames. I asked why it was necessary to cover the mouth, chest and shoulders with mud. The explanation offered was "When they rub the earth on their bodies, people make an oath to God and say, you God have created this land and it is your earth. We know it is you who creates all things. The people are like this mud and so they show God that they are also his things."

Atuot are here resigned to the power of God, and he shows himself forcefully as the grand master. Lightning does not fall arbitrarily but only on a household God has selected. Burial should be followed by the sacrifice of a bull over the grave and no member of the household may eat its flesh. There then follows an illness which is associated with the immediate family of the deceased called *col wic.* We can translate the phrase literally as derived from *car yuic,* "black head," with apparent reference to the burned condition of the corpse. This also draws attention to the fact that the man is perceived as having been struck in the *head* by lightning, or God's fire *(mai Decau).* The symptoms of *col wic* are essentially alike those of illness brought on by a *jok.* The symptoms are akin to tuberculosis. A person is said to look malnourished and shriveled, and becomes lifeless and coughs a great deal. For *col wic,* there is unlike the situation of a power coming into a man, no medicine *(wel)* that can be used to remedy the condition, for it is brought upon him by God. It is however seen in an idiomatic way as like a *jok,* and after recognized as *col wic* it becomes a power of that family, and requires periodic sacrifices of sheep. Unless recognized soon after the travesty, lightning may fall upon the same house again. The fact that it later becomes classified as a *jok* while at the same time there is no medicine for it, makes *col wic* a singular type of spiritual agent in Atuot religion. When a family has taken it on as a power, it cannot be used to bring misfortune to the lives of others, and sacrifices to the power or divinity only act to inhibit it from coming to them again. There are songs for *col wic* which long ago were brought to human beings by the first people to suffer from its effects, but these should not be sung on a grey and overcast day, for this is a time when God is closer to the world of people. To sing the songs and thereby invite the presence of the power would be in their eyes courting disaster. The power *col wic* presents us with a clear illustration of the manner in which they attribute strong powers to a presence in the sky *(nhial)* and to God, *Nhial.*

Atuot prefer to gather together either inside a village hut or underneath the *adhang* in the cattle camp during a violent storm. The silence and respect accorded to God at this time again highlights their feelings of impotence by comparison to him in the context of such a dramatic exposition of his power. Atuot also point out that in the course of a sacrifice to *col wic* the collection of people is normally larger and inclusive of those who may not normally be defined as kinsmen. Like their experience of the being God, all people are affected by lightning, whereas other powers are limited in a domestic sense to a proportionately fewer number of persons who are all kinsmen.

If God turns the victim's face downward from the force of the impact, his eyes have been away from life toward the world of the dead, who are buried in the ground. Conversely, when thrown to his back, the victim faces God, and is assured of the life associated with the Creator. *Col wic* is different from other natural phenomena, because it can be said to be a power, whereas rainfall, earthquakes or drought are not considered in the same manner as revelations of this aspect of the quality of God. Rain, *kwoth,* is simply God's gift. Rain is regarded positively for its beneficial effects as a natural element that helps their lives. *Col wic* does not give a man any special powers, but merely protects him *from* a power. The comparison with Lienhardt (1961) for a discussion of the Dinka conceptions relating to rain *(deng)* will demonstrate a marked divergence between the two peoples in this regard. For the Dinka, *deng* is among the most important and powerful of all divinities. The Dinka reaction to lightning can also be seen to express a different sentiment. Lienhardt *(ibid.:* 93) writes,

> Those killed by lightning are described sometimes as "whom Divinity has seen" or "whom Deng has seen," or Divinity is said to have struck them on the head. They are not mourned. The Dinka will not even try to save the contents of a building fired by lithtning, nor to put out the fire, for this would interfere with Divinity's or Deng's direct expression of will.

Atuot, by contrast, take an active role, first by adding fire to the flaming hut, and then, having shown God their recognition of his presence and power, try to extinguish the fire and remove the contents and people from inside the home.

For the Nuer (Evans-Pritchard 1949*a*: 7), a man who has "become *col wic* is revered as a sacred spirit of his lineage and is called on for aid, especially when a man pursued by his enemies seeks a refuge." Nuer rituals performed in association with *col wic* seem much more elaborate, and a family which experiences the phenomenon is regarded as having been shown a special revelation by God, or *Kwoth.* A number of the widely recognized political leaders in their history also gained part of their authority through their association with this spirit. Evans-Pritchard wrote *(ibid.:* 9), "Occasionally the spirit remains in a man after he has recovered from his sickness and he then becomes a *guk Cuol,* a prophet of *Col,* and the god of lightning speaks through him to the people." Atuot would never speak of *col wic* as a god, in this manner. While the Dinka, Nuer, and Atuot have different ideas and associations, the characterization of *col wic* as a uniquely Nuer phenomenon is misleading.

The songs said to belong to *col wic* are sung in the course of the burial of a person killed by God with lightning. I present a few here which were elicited only with considerable pleading. Friends agreed to sing them only in a whisper. Atuot rely on God to give them life, but consider any direct "contact" with him as inauspicious and to be avoided. Hence, to sing these songs for no apparent reason is to court disaster.

If a person remains in a state of unconsciousness or is only partially conscious *(ce buor)*, and thus appears to be part dead and part alive, the following may be sung.

Children of *acuok*
⌊the tiny black ants, blind to the ways of God⌋
You ⌊God⌋ will see it with your eyes
The world of a great man is refusing to break
⌊the night and day will not separate; "life" will not come⌋
Oh, God our father
A great man's world is refusing to break
*Alier* is coming with a strong wind
⌊the cooling wind of life that follows the rain⌋
*Alier* is breaking the branches of trees
You hear it –
Abuk ⌊in some stories, the first woman⌋ is coming with a great wind
A great wind is coming
⌊wind here is associated with the blowing, *kwoth,* of the breath of life into a man⌋
Children of *acuok*
You will see it with your eyes
*Nhial* is coming with a strong wind
Sons of man will see it with their eyes
The world of a great man is refusing to break ⌊separate⌋
The cattle of Majong are tethered
The wind brings life ⌊in Atuot, *kene yei nong ben*⌋
Abuk, come with life
*Alier* is coming with life
The head of a man moves
Like the branches of trees in the wind
The life has come in the wind ⌊*ke yei ca alier ben*⌋

Another song was introduced by this short story.

A long time ago the sons of Ayi would pick up shields, arrows and bows to fight God when there was lightning. They would rush to the place where the lightning was but by the time they arrived, it was gone. One day Decau became offended by this and grew angry and he struck them all down with lightning when they were in their camp. They all fell unconscious, except for the ox Mabor and a small boy who ran to the village to tell people of the catastrophe. They took the ox Mabor and sang the songs of God and *col wic* and then all the people rose up again. This is why the song ways "Mabor gathered the lives."

Mabor is accepted by God
To gather the lives of cows and men
Oh, the ox of Ayi Malual
Mabor is accepted by God
The life comes with Mabor
To gather the lives of cows and men

Another longer song is helpful in further characterizing the confrontation between God and man in association with lightning. Man necessarily knows his way of life in an economic sense. Self-assertion and individuality are basic to their ethics. Yet in these "hymns," or songs of God *(dit* Nhial) dependence on God is poignantly phrased. Like all their songs, phrases are repeated over and over until another is introduced. They flow in this manner from one to the other. Except where it is necessary to convey its poetic element, repetitions have been deleted.

God, you see it and help the land
A power came in the evening
    [literally, *jok a loiny a thin* "a power fell in the evening"]
Where has the power fallen
Help yourselves, you children of Abuk
We argue whether or not we were really created
Has creation come here?
It is said that a great man hopes for nothing
He has lost his way
Oh, I pray my father
He kills *acuok* with a strong wind
I pray until I sit like a monkey
    [on his haunches, with arms extended out, palms up]
Hear the word of Nhial
I am going to the door of the hut
[after it has started on fire]
*Acuok,* that is the people, compared with the Creator
Life is the sweet thing
That is why I pray my father
The *ring* of my mother makes the land
    [allows us to live in the world]
I pass with Ayan around the camp
    [the first cow given to man; leading it around the hut or camp is a basic act of
    all their sacrifices]
Ayan is blessed [invoked upon] by the people
The power of my Creator
People all collect together
Mayan [an ox of the color *ayan*] walks lamely
The spear has entered
Mayan, do not spoil the edge of the spear
    [that is, accept your role as being sacrificed for their lives]
I do not bring on the fight

The *toic* is our *toic*
I am bewildered with this life
My father, help my life
Where does the life come from?
Oh, am I a man hated by all the people?
We fought for this land
Abuk, my mother, look upon me
Give me a bowl of water
Give me a bowl of blood
    [the meaning of this is discussed later in the description of sacrifice to God]
Give me my life
Go and bring life into the house
Take the life of this cow to give me life
This is a cow for blood *(yang riem te thin)*
I pray to you like an orphan –
I am a man left away
I pray to you my great father *(laang e yin Nhial dit)*

Later on, when a shrine made of a forked branch is placed in the ground for *col wic,* an act called *tet e col wic,* the next two songs are sung.

You, the *jok* of Nuer
You, the *jok* of Nuer, do not fear
Macar [an ox name of the power] do not have a fear
*Col wic* [you] lead the cow
Macardit [the big ox Macar] you guide the cow

You, the *jok* of Nuer
Raise up the head and the neck
⌊let the sacrifice bring life back to the people⌋

This leads quickly into the next song.

Oh it is the *jok* that is uncontrolled
The *jok* that does not distinguish between strong and weak
⌊it strikes anyone at will; implicit here is reference to the distinction between
other powers which are *always* directed against specific individuals⌋
We have gathered, all of us
God has gathered us all together
This *jok* is two
⌊*col wic* and *arop,* the second being a power said to walk with *col wic* but never comes
alone⌋

A final song is short and repetitive.

*Col wic* is the relative of the cow
When *col wic* has fallen
*Col wic* calls for a cow

This emphasizes that the power (ultimately, and here directly God) will not be appeased with anything but the sacrifice of a cow or a sheep. Unlike the majority of earthly powers it will not accept the blood and meat of a goat.

There is no single individual who acts as a master of ceremonies in this situation, for a large collection is present, and each is given the opportunity to introduce a song while the others follow with the chorus.

Atuot say God is directly manifested in their daily lives through the birth of twins. A discussion of the songs and rituals performed on such an occasion sheds further light on the relation of God to man. Like most peoples, twin birth is regarded as an exception to the normal expectations. In Atuot society, where status and role are primarily based on age and sex differences, twin birth has additional implications. Twins are welcomed, for the Atuot are happy with the live birth of any child. Twins are also created by God, but are thought to be given to a particular woman, who therefore is seen to have been specially "touched" (something like the way he may touch them with lightning) by the Creator. Twin birth is especially an occasion for women to gather, indeed, almost the total exclusion of men, as an occasion which emphasizes the creative abilities of women. The birth of twins does not convey an entirely distinct status for a woman, though a number of those who had borne twins were pointed out to me without having solicited the information. As in the case of lightning, God has come especially close to human beings. Twins share a relationship which is qualitatively different from that of other siblings, and they act in each other's company more like age-mates than brothers or sisters. Twin brothers may go off at night to flirt and court with girls, something other brothers would never do, for it has overtones of incest *(rual)* and likewise, twin females may entertain their suitors in each other's company. The division of sexual from purely domestic activities is noticeably marked among siblings and parents within a typical family. While I was present at a number of dances held to praise the mothers of twins, what I describe here is derived mostly from verbal accounts.

Soon after twins are born an exchange involving two bulls and rams is made between the families of the father and mother. The animals are kept in the homestead until there has been sufficient time to prepare food and beer, which is then brought to the parents' homestead. When people have gathered, the woman's dance (*dainy* "women's dance"; also called sometimes *bull acueo,* the drum or dance of twins) is begun. The maternal female relatives form a line moving counterclockwise around the hut, while her female affines begin to dance in the opposite direction circling the homestead, each passing by the doorway of the hut three times. As they dance, they sing,

> The spirit has come between man and woman
> And given them these twins
> The spirit has come between this man and woman
> And brought to them these twins
> Let us go up to the *papuol* tree and cry out there,
> Eeeeeee, Eeeeeee
> Let us go to the palm tree of nyawer and cry out there
> Eeeeeee, Eeeeeee
> The spirit has brought these twins
> When he (it) came between man and woman

The sound "Eeeeeee" is said to mimic the song of a flock of birds as they leave the trees and ascend into the sky. In doing this, the women announce that birds (*diet,* that is, twins) have been brought to them from above. One such dance, which happened to coincide with a wedding dance, was organized two months after the birth of twins, and early in the morning the sacrifice of an ox and sheep had been performed. Like all other sacrifices where God is directly addressed, morning is the auspicious time of day for the rite. The dance began soon after, and continued into the late afternoon, by which time men from the wedding had also joined in. Another dance is held after the twins have been weaned, perhaps at the age of three or four, and the sacrifice is repeated. A final dance, this time including those of all ages and sex, is performed after they have gone through their initiation *(pel ngac)* or in the case of female twins, when they have become physically mature.

After the first dance around the hut, the bulls and rams are tethered in front of the doorway of the hut and are aspersed with pounded durra flour *(tiiar)* as are the people collected. I was told an older woman would normally do this, or another woman who had borne twins previously. During the course of invocations over the animals they sing,

> Oh mother of twins,
> We make a sacrifice [literally, *naka yang,* kill a cow]
> We sacrifice for the mother of twins [*nake yang man acueo*]
> Mother of twins, we are praising *(laic)* you
> The grain of last year is better than this year's
> Mother of twins, mother of twins
> Your house [the text reads literally, nest] in the trees,
> Your house is in the forest
> I have put a string on my bow
> And I shoot the arrow to kill the bird
> Let us go to the *papual* of Mayer
> And cry out there, Eeeeeee
> Let us go to the bank of the river
> And cry out there, Eeeeeee
>> [this recalls the situation when there were no husbands and women went to the riverside to become impregnated by the waves. This is a very common Nilotic symbol, and merits an in depth comparative study]

Let us go to the *agep* [Dolieb palm]
And cry out there, Eeeeeee
Mother of twins, mother of twins
We are praising you for these twins

"Going to such and such a tree" and going to the river bank here represent announcing to birds the birth of twins. Birds often collect in these places. The reference to shooting a bird with an arrow was explained as meaning they thus show the birds that twins (birds) have come into their home.

In explaining why the Nuer say twins are birds, Evans-Prichard (1936) again suggests this is something peculiar to their system of thought, while in reality the association of twins with birds is rather a common Nilotic theme. In Atuot, twins, or birds, are especially associated with the bird they call *amor,* a small species which frequents the mahogany *(papual)* tree. Here again, we could discuss an ethnological parameter of the association, for the tree where human beings were created is sometimes said to be the mahogany. There is a strong symbolic association between this tree and the life creating power of God. As in Nuer, Atuot say that twins are birds, though the metaphor is incomplete, because not all birds are equally called twins. While they are considered to be of one birth, the first twin is called Ngor, the one who leads, and the second, Cien, the one behind or the one who follows. If both are male, the first is named Diet (bird) and the second Cien. In the case of female twins, they are named respectively Ayandiet and Acien. If the first is male and the second female, they are called Diet and Acien, and in the opposite order, Ayandiet and Cien. A male child born after twins is called Bol and a daughter Ibol.

While happy with twins, Atuot women also recognize that the labor and delivery are more difficult. It is said that few people give birth to twins, and this is taken as further evidence of the will of God in the life of a particular woman. A woman who has given birth to twins more than once *is* considered to have a special association with creation and with God. No one recalled any woman delivering more than two children at the same time, but they suggested that the children would also be called twins. Twins are welcome *(acuio lang e)* though people are somewhat apprehensive of the situation, as evidenced in a short passage of another song.

We do this now
For if we do not dance
When the twins come again
The children may cease
So we celebrate for these twins

The sacrifice accompanying the dance involves cutting the animal's throat and then the carcasses are divided into two halves from head to tail. The father's people receive the right halves, and those of the mother's family the left. Elder men and women from each family eat the intestines, stomach, and liver. One kidney from each animal is put aside in a pot for later use. In the division of the carcasses and the consumption of the flesh, only those persons past the age of fertility along with pre-pubescent youth participate. In nearly all other sacrifices, it is precisely these people who are generally only secondarily participants. In the situation of sacrifice for twins, the wife, her husband and their respective age-mates are prohibited from eating or even being near the cooked flesh. I was told this was done, because twins are a gift of God, and they are *gaat Nhial,* children of God. In order to respect the revelation of God's creative power, those who still have the ability to produce children are excluded by respecting *(thek)* or avoiding the flesh. The mid-wife is said to be given the meat of the hips of the animals sacrificed. While they are excluded from eating the flesh *(ring)*, the husband and wife are each given one kidney from each of the sacrificed animals to be eaten later in their hut as a minced paste. The internal organs (collectively, *jic)* are particularly associated with the life of the sacrificial victims, rather than the flesh, which is considered to be only the physical embodiment that is given life by God. The internal organs, in our own words, carry on the "life functions" of the body. The mother of twins is also given the two vertebra closest to the pelvic bone, and the husband four bones from the central spine of the bulls sacrificed. The bone *(acao,* from *cak* "to create") is that part created *(ce cek)* by God in conception. These are selected from the point where creation has divided into two, from the center of the pelvis. The parents of twins thus partake of the "life" and "created part" of the animals, a practice one could interpret as emphasizing their own act of creation through twin birth. Following the sacrifice, their hut is aspersed with the remaining durra flour. Pounded flour is associated with women and their economic labor, and the use here may represent her life-providing functions.

With the first new moon after the birth of twins, relatives representing paternal and maternal kin return again to the hut to asperse the interior with flour. This continues each month until the twins are weaned. After an unspecified period of time the father of the husband gives him a sheep. The animal is pegged at the doorway, and while those collected stand on opposite sides of it, the throat is cut and the sheep sacrificed. The flesh of this victim is reserved for the same group of people who were prohibited flesh in the first sacrifices. Apart from the dance made after their maturity, this act is said to be the last rite performed for the parents of twins.

Traditionally, if one of the twins died before reaching physical maturity, the corpse would be placed in a small hammock-like swing and fixed up high between the boughs of a large tree. Twins do not die, but are said to fly away *(ce paar)* while the corpse is raised high above the ground for God to see. God would see that the child had died regardless of this act, and it seems to be the necessary closing analogy of the "twins are birds" metaphor. The act is sanctioned by the belief that if it were ignored, the woman would produce no further offspring. The cosmological order would remain confounded.

Socially twins have certain peculiarities, though once past infancy, I did not gain the impression that they were bound by any ritual prohibitions. Their marriages are performed in slightly different ways than those for non-twins, a point discussed later. First we can consider a brief comparative sidelight.

Evans-Pritchard gave special emphasis to the notion that twins could not eat birds, that they respected *(thek)* them. Atuot offered the same observation, but under normal circumstances no one other than small children would eat them. Birds are valued positively, for they pick off the ticks from their cattle and smaller stock while grazing, and they name the colors of their oxen and bulls after the configurations they observe on these natural species. Yet birds alone are not singled out as part of a food taboo. One could say that Atuot also respect, in the sense that they avoid eating, chickens, turtles, eggs, guinea fowl, and for men, even small portions of food. This is not immediately related to respect of totemic species (indeed, no one recognizes any of these things as a totem) but is rather a custom related to proper behavior for age categories. Further, one could not cogently argue that they respect birds because of their association with twins and creation, for they eat their cows and fish which equally partake of creation. To follow Evans-Pritchard's logic, it could be argued that an adult man respects ground nuts, for he would never be seen eating a handful of them. The respect for birds has an aesthetic quality but this seems to be a matter of age instead of a cosmological classification and avoidance. The corporateness of age categories is evidenced in the rituals associated with twin birth.

The cosmological import of twinship is carried through a man's life into the world of adulthood, symbolized most strongly by marriage. The singlar identity of each twin is maintained throughout the course of the marriage ceremony. If both are females, either one can be married first, while the rule of the eldest son being married before the others is transferred to the eldest twin, who emerged first. When a female twin is married and accompanied to her husband's home, the women's marriage songs are sung in addition to those for twins. After two days, her twin sister will come to the same hut. In the evening a sleeping hide is placed on the ground for the husband, and each twin lies down on either side of him and anoints his body with oil form the shea nut *(ngat arok)* and, when it is available, clarified butter *(ngat yang)*. The first night he sleeps with his new wife, the twin sister sleeps together with them and remains in the hut for the duration of the night. In the morning, the husband must give his wife's sister a cow calf *(dau acuio* "the calf of twins") or a gift of a string of beads called *tik yang,* the beads of cows. Unless either gift is given, it is thought that his wife will produce no children, for what one twin has, the other must have also. Hence a cow calf represents the fecundity and eventual offspring of the unmarried twin. When the unmarried sister is married, her twin will also spend the night with her new husband, and should be given the same gift.

In many of the marriages I knew of in some detail, the betrothal and exchange of marriage cattle actually occurred after the girl was pregnant or had already delivered. Atuot say that if this were to happen to a female twin, she would never bear a child. That is to say, the evaluation of this as a sinful act *(awec)*, likened to incest or adultery, is emphasized, but could not be called a fault or mistake *(dwer)*.

For an elder male twin, his younger twin brother is also required to spend the wedding night in the same hut. In this case, the new bride sleeps on a mat between the two, and together, they anoint her body with oil. Atuot say, the wife has become a twin *(cek ce cuok)* for now, as with her husband, she is considered to have a special relationship to birds. The following morning, the husband will procure a string of *tik yang* ("bead of cows") and cut it in half, each part to be worn by his twin and by his wife. This offers evidence of their continual relationship. Under normal circumstances a brother may refer to his brother's wife as *cek cang,* "my wife of the daytime," while in the case of twins the cosmological bond is more intimate.

By the time each twin has entered into his or her own marriage there is little to distinguish them from others, and they are not buried differently from others.

The relation of man to God can be examined in another way by reference to Atuot ideas pertaining to what is usually called totemism. This is included in the discussion to reveal its relative insignificance in the Atuot relation to the world. The overall account would be deficient if the topic were ignored. Their relation to God through animal species is somewhat secondary, rather than direct, as demonstrated in the data on lightning and twins. The origin or "creation" of totemistic relationships occurs on a different level of experience than that of twins, for example; yet often to express the duality, and at the same time, unity twin birth is often cited as the cause of relationship.

Both Seligman (n. d.) and Westermann (1912a), among others, write that Shilluk totemism is largely thought to be "borrowed" from the Dinka. Evans-Pritchard (1956) indicates the same for the Nuer. Certainly the lengthy essay of Seligman (n. d.) and Lienhardt's (1961) exposition of Dinka totemism and totemistic relations give evidence of its difference from other Nilotic expressions and its manifest influence in social organization and religion among the Dinka. Simply stated, it is more prominent and essential in Dinka society, but this does not *necessarily* mean it is originally Dinka. Yet it is likely that the other forms or expressions of Nilotic totemism are derived from or patterned after the more embracing and complex system. This is another problem for further comparative study in Nilotic societies; here I only record what the ideas may mean for the Atuot (cf. Burton 1980e).

The text cited here is an open-ended conversation about *wet,* what is translated as "totems" for the time being. The sister of a former chief of the Luac Atuot, Iwer Deng, said:

> The fish called *cuur* is respected by me (cuur *thek e γen*) from the side of my husband and the uncles of my father. Someone named Dit was long ago seen on this fish and no sacrifice can be made to remove it *(thil ke puoke).* Dit had no father and no mother. He was brought and fed with cow's milk. Dit was also given *ring* by the fish. I can never eat it. If a girl is married she will never eat it in her husband's camp. It will never be eaten even when her children are buried.
>
> *Rou* (hippopotamus) is respected by my uncles. If a man eats it he dies. Sheep is respected by Jilek. Those who respect *againy* [Nile lizard], they are always Dinka or Aliab. If a man eats it he will die *(na cam e ke neu nuer).* Heart is the people of Kuek, and then it became ours. If we eat it now we would die.

I asked her if there were any people who "respected" snakes *(thol),* and her reply was instructive: "I suppose it could be *wet* if people respected it, but who would ever eat snake?"

> *Awai* [the small bitter fruit of the tree by the same name] is respected by Rorkec. *Ajep* [palm tree] is respected by the people of my paternal aunts *(ji wacde). Ajep* kept them alive because they sat under it one time and suffered from thirst when there were always fights. Later durra and water came from it. It also brought out the calf Ayan. *Dier* [hedgehog] is respected by some. Antelope, well, there is no reason to respect antelope except that it has a long neck and if it is eaten the children would have long necks.

The "spirit" or power of a totem is analogically similar to that of other powers, for in a general sense, if a man has the ability to call rain, the power of rain *(buom kwoth* or *kaai kwoth),* it is akin to the idea that if a man respects lions *(thek ayao)* he may be asked to call them away from an area where they are bothersome. The difference is that there are no shrines erected to propagate a species while there are what Atuot call *luak kwoth,* "cattle byres" for the power of rain where periodic sacrifices are performed by a *gwan kwoth,* possessor of the rain. Other texts collected reveal a "just-so" attitude toward the origin of totem relationships. Carnivores, such as hyenas, lions, jackels, foxes, monkeys, and scavaging birds, are "respected" in the sense that their flesh it not eaten, though this prohibition is not a part of the totemistic system. Animals that eat people cannot be eaten by people.

Crocodile *(nyang)* is respected by many people who were originally fishermen.

Crocodile, Lang and Ber were born together as twins *(acuio diang diak)*. Their descendents are now found in all of *cieng* Reel. The three brothers had one mother. When they later saw that crocodile was created in a different way *(ce cak murro)* with four legs and a different skin and a long tail they led him away from their home and made a sacrifice to God. Then they led him to a river bringing with them a ram and a goat. The animals were tied up by their feet and thrown into the river with the crocodile, and then the twins returned home. They put their brother crocodile in the river and they were left with its spirit *(ca jii nyang yier ke nong thin, ke jokde ce duoth e ke)*. After they did this, they took a woman to be the wife of the spirit of the crocodile in order that children would be raised in his name [from *cuong* "to raise up"]. The people who now respect crocodile are called *gaat nyang,* children of crocodile.

The relationship imbues the people with a measure of control over the habits of the crocodile, a satisfactory adaptation for the fishermen who frequent the rivers. Another text illustrates the manner in which they expect the animal to help them in some way, and the assumption of the relationship because of such aid:

Apar [a section of Apak, originally from Bor Dinka] were on a journey when they became very thirsty, and they were unable to find water. They came upon the Nile lizard *(againy)*. When the lizard knew he had been seen by people, he ran off in fright. Twin brothers then took off after him and saw him dive into the water. They bent down to drink and satisfied their great thirst. Then they showed the other people the water and they all drank. They wondered what they could do to show their gratification to the lizard. The older people said the lizard should always be left alone to produce its own generation, because it had saved their lives, and they were thankful to God.

Generally the flesh of the lizard, as with the snake, is despised. As indicated, there is the feeling that the meat is inedible, hence, there is little reason for it to be respected. People who are related to monkeys may be called when the animals try to damage a durra cultivation. In this situation a man who respects monkeys will walk through a garden looking for footprints of the animal. When he spies one, he spears it with a fishing spear (an act called *yeth,* different from the act of spearing with a fighting spear, *muot*). He then scoops up the earth and throws it in the direction of the monkeys in the forest. When I heard this I asked the narrator if this would not be similar to spearing his own brother as an act of fratricide. He answered, "This is done to show that I am your brother and this is my grain. If you are foolish enough to try to steal my grain, I will spear you for trespass." This suggests an ideal of balanced reciprocity between human and animal or plant species. A person should not overstep his bounds in relation to paternal kin, while there is always a degree of expectation of a gift from maternal relatives and affines. Since full brothers are born of one vagina *(ce dieth mur kel)* they share a common interest. Traditionally there could be no blood compensation, so ideally brothers should never harm one another, a situation paralleled in the totem/human paradigm.

When married each spouse must respect the *wet* of the other, especially if it can be eaten, which is implicit. One man stated, "When a child is made, the two of you mix your blood and the blood of the animal, if it was eaten, would come out in the child and poison its blood *(riemke jiek)*. So a man must *thek* his wife's *wet* in order to protect the child you will make." The idea of mixing blood in this way has some connotation to incest. If sheep are respected but eaten, the child will be seen to have qualities which liken it to a sheep. The belief that the evil consequences of action will be reflected upon those who have had nothing to do with the initial transgression is another common Nilotic theme. Failing to respect totemistic avoidance can cause the death of the child. The pollution of the blood will cause the child to become senseless or mad, and he will walk aimlessly eating human excrement.

If one eats the fish *cuur* (river perch) and should not, the skin will turn brownish in color and a person will begin to mumble. The same act in regard to sheep may result in blindness, and for hippopotamus, leprosy. The spirit or power *(jok)* of the non-human species are angered by the lack of respect shown toward them, and seek their vengeance, *cien*. We will later see how ghostly vengeance *(cien)* is seen in the same way. I have seen a man mistakenly eat a small bit of lamb, his totem, and he cut off a bit of fat and carried it wrapped in a leaf to the home of his mother-in-law. She dropped it into a fire and he inhaled the smoke, thereby removing the likelihood that there would be any physical or mental malady.

After a time, usually estimated to be three generations, the responsibility to respect the species inherited by maternal kinsmen lessens and after a time is ignored. The relationship of *wet* is thus traced patrilineally, "through blood." The severance of the respect can be achieved in a number of ways. The first is simply forgetting about it altogether, for example, if the relations between affines have deteriorated. A man may also pay direct compensation to the parents of his wife. If his wife respects the flesh of sheep, a cow may be given to cut apart or sever *(dhol;* the same word that describes cutting the throat of an animal in sacrifice) the relationship. A third mode is cited in a text:

> I inherited the respect of the *agep* ⌊palm nut⌋ from my father's sister, who was married by Luac from Akot. So the children had to respect heart because all of Luac respect heart, and also *dau agep* ⌊the seed or calf of *agep*⌋. My grandmother was the one who suggested this could be ended. One of the fruits was cut down and opened up, and placed over a fire in her home. The smoking and scorched inside was then passed around to me and all my brothers to inhale, and this ended the respect.

A person can then say, *ca ye liab,* "I have left it," a phrase derived from the verb *lieb,* to leave behind or leave alone. Members of the same age-set will all observe the same respect.

The social significance of totems for the Atuot is minimal, so I am inclined to agree with Levi-Strauss (1963) that they are good to think. To share a common totem does not necessarily imply a relationship of kinship and does not therefore affect marriage prohibitions. Atuot men and women never mentioned totemism as relevant to the arrangement of a marriage. The single exception to this statement is for twins, people who "respect" birds, and cannot marry twins, but this has already been shown to be unrelated to totemistic avoidance.

On the basis of this brief discussion I suggest that Atuot notions of totemism are a less important part of their wider and more embracing system of cosmology, which is importantly structured by beliefs about blood and life. Atuot expressions of totemic relations may have been adopted from the Dinka, particularly through intermarriage, and then interpreted through the Atuot idiom of powers. In a religious context a Dinka man may petition the totem (*yath;* in Lienhardt's usage, "clan divinity") of his forbears, while I have never heard a similar statement among the Atuot. The second most important consideration in deciding upon the marriage of a couple, following the primary assessment of the degree of relationship between parties, relates to age, not shared totems. The fact that all the people of Luac respect "heart" does not prohibit people of different clans within this section from marrying one another. The criteria of age are determinate, for the elder must marry first, or "walk ahead" as they would say. While insignificant in terms of marriage, totems are equally a minor aspect of religion or cosmology.

Their ideas of totemism may be seen in part as analogous to domestic roles, but not in a socially integrating manner. A totem was long ago a twin of a lineal relative and should thus be treated with the deference accorded to ancestors, and the respect which is ideally shared among people of one blood. The totem inherited through maternal kin is forgotten. The life or blood of a totem is respected in the way paternal kin should respect their common bond of blood relationship by not killing one another.

Even while they may be understood through an analogy with spiritual powers, the *jok* of a totem is qualitatively and figuratively different from the other powers. There is on the other hand a similarity in the nature of twin birth, *col wic* and totems, for each enters their life by a means other than their own. God reveals himself to man through twin birth, and twin birth is often seen as the origin of a totemistic relation. Like the power *col wic,* the totem is not an active agent. Neither can be manipulated to bring misfortune to others; rather, they both prevent misfortune from coming to people who have the power, as for *col wic,* or who respect the non-human species, like fishermen and crocodiles. An understanding of their religious beliefs is possible without necessarily making reference to totemism.

The reader may be inclined to think that since a single term, *jok,* can refer to totems as well as any other power, they are essentially similar. An analogous situation applies for the Nuer, where *kwoth* can mean God or a minor spirit. The Atuot *jok,* known as *ring,* is an all embracing power that guides their spiritual and physical livelihood, while even the power of a root used for medicine can be called *jok.* They do not confuse the divergent qualities of each, even though a single term designates both. In the course of interpreting a foreign ideology, homonym should not be mistaken for synonym.

This chapter explored the way in which cosmological order involves the central idiom of "powers" and has dealt with a number of situations where God is seen to relate directly to man, and we may call these manifestations as they involve people, "passive" experiences. The next chapter is concerned with the dominant powers through which Atuot in turn communicate with God, which can be labeled "active" agents. The terminology suggested corresponds with their experience.

CHAPTER IV

# The World of Powers

## 1. The Division of Powers

To the Atuot human fertility, illness, herd productivity as well as a sense of spiritual well-being are related to their perception of the presence or absence of a power (jok). This association is idiomatic of their religious and cosmological ideas. In the course of daily life, the most frequent reference to the word jok is its manifestation in the form of physical illness where peculiar symptoms indicate a particular power.

Brief reference should be made to the variety of translations of the Nilotic root jok as a background to the discussion which follows. A variety of referents in the Nuer language share in common a sense of things relating to the past. In Atuot as well, jok can mean simply "those things behind" or "in the past." For the Nuer the word also designates the southwesterly winds preceding the rainy season and also "ghost" (see Huffman 1929, 1931a, 1931b; Westermann 1912b; Howell 1953a, 1954; Crazzolara 1933, 1953; Jackson 1923). In Dinka jok connotes spirits associated with illness and to the sentiments of the ancestral dead (see Lienhardt 1951, 1961, 1970; Deng 1971, 1972, 1973; Johnson 1934; Seligman 1932). In the Shilluk-Luo languages the same term generally signifies a dominant and supreme being (see e. g., Kronenberg 1960; O'Bitek 1963; Ogot 1961; Southall 1956, 1971, 1972; Driberg 1923; Hayley 1947; Lienhardt 1954, 1970; Evans-Pritchard 1950b, 1953; Westermann 1912b; Hofmayr 1925). Throughout the Nilotic world, jok refers to some aspect of a supernatural power or being. Buxton (1973: 67) notes for the Mandari, formerly speakers of a Bari dialect, but of late increasingly influenced by their northern Nilotic neighbors, the word jok is now used to describe any illness thought to have spread from neighboring peoples, notably the Aliab Dinka and the Atuot.

The notion of a supreme being with ultimate powers over their lives is central to Atuot religion, while direct recourse to the powers they perceive is through the active agents of joks, and through these they communicate with God. Atuot are resigned to accept the death of a loved one as the work of God, but they also want to know particular jok actually caused the death. Two broad categories of such powers are imagined, those which came from God to man in creation and are associated with the sky, and lesser powers which dwell in the earth. The latter are said to have become more numerous in living memory, and will probably increase in the future. Included among them are such diseases as malaria and cerebral-spinal meningitis, which Atuot claim were brought to them during the British administration. Others are said to have been introduced into their cosmological world by Dinka, primarily the Agar. However, the more powerful spirits of the sky are in their eyes uniquely Atuot, and assume more of the quality of divinity. These include the powers called ring (flesh), nhial (a revelation of God) and the power of rain, usually referred to by its ox name, awumkuei. This color pattern is the most aesthetically pleasing for the Atuot; it signifies a boldly marked black and white animal, with a fully white head and red nose. All of the other powers are also known by their ox names, and many are said to have a number of wives. Each power has in addition its own songs which are recited in the course of sacrifices to propitiate them. The songs of the powers of the sky were taught to man by God long ago, while the lesser powers make known their songs to individual people who are possessed by them.

The powers are further distinguished by a peculiar mode of sacrifice for each. A man with wide knowledge of the powers can relate tales in detail about the origin of one or another *jok,* yet there is no myth that accounts for how people first began to make sacrifices. When asked about this directly, they say, "This is a thing of long ago that Decau gave to man with cows." The first cow, Ayan, was given to man by God, and with it he gave them spears to protect and fight for it. Because they are their most valued possessions, it might be argued they deduce implicitly that the sacrifice of a cow is called for by God (see Burton n. d. *a*).

As a general rule, the powers of the sky (*jao nhial*) are known to Atuot through psychic symptoms, while those of the earth are experienced as physical disabilities; correspondingly the powers of the sky or above are associated with creative powers of God while the lesser powers are minor revelations of divinity. The distinction is also made apparent in terms used to refer to the mediators of their religious experience. The *gwan riang* or *gwan nhial* (the terms are usually interchangeable, and most often refer to males) is a person who has *within* him and as a part of his being the power *ring* or *nhial*. They are not prophets, for Atuot do not recognize such a category of inspired persons. The *tiet* by contrast are persons who have bought a power, or who have been possessed by a power associated with an illness, and who later recover from the malady and thus gain power to control it. Further distinctions between religiously inspired specialists are discussed later. The adjective *gwan* (derived from *guar* "my father") refers to father or possessor, in a manner similar to that in which God can be said to be the father or possessor of life. *Gwan nhial* is a person who is said to have God within him. The *tiet* is a person with a controlling power over a certain *jok.* The two categories necessarily merge into one another, for as we have seen, *jok* refers to powers in a most general sense, and any sacrifice performed by either type of specialist is ultimately accepted by God.

I asked a man said to have "the power to call rain" within him to explain what happened between the power and God in the situation of sacrifice. The text also reveals some of the differences between *gwan nhial* and *tiet.*

> When a power comes, people will go and look for a *tiet* or a *gwan nhial* and he comes and finds the power and the power says it wants a sacrifice. It is given to the power, so the man will recover his health (*a be nien* "so he will sleep"). If the sacrifice is not made for the power, the man will have a great suffering and will die. If the sacrifice is made, you bring *yang* Nhial |a cow to be sacrificed to God|. The people will ask what is that God wants. I tell them that God wants the sacrifice of a sheep. God wants the sheep so that the man will recover with his life. When it is given, the power will pray to God and say, this is the sheep that is given by *acuok* |the ants of God|. I am such and such power, and I have been sent to bring it. I am the messenger |derived from *dol erap dal* "I have been sent"| and God will then say then let the person have sleep. God says to the power, if you are given a sheep like this then you take it and leave the man so he can sleep. God does not want goat. When it is *gwan nhial,* God speaks through the mouth of the man. When God speaks through him he will *cuer* |rock slowly and rhythmically back and forth|. If it is *tiet* who is making the songs of *jok* he shakes from the fire of the power in his body.

A number of comments on the text will be instructive. The first is a problem of simple translation. In the Atuot and other Nilotic languages, pronouns do not generally discriminate sex or animate from inanimate objects. In translating certain terms like "power" to a number of Atuot who also had a knowledge of English they agreed that *jok* should be called "he"rather than "it," because the power is "more knowledgeable than the human beings who are blind to their ways." The power *nhial* is sometimes referred to in song as being a big hairy man. In the text an implicit distinction is drawn between the hot and uncontrollable character of powers of the earth known to a *tiet,* for they come into him like a fire, and powers of the sky which are conceptually cool and slow. The powers *ring* and *nhial* are said to be "lame" and ancient, though their presence is permanent. Every power of the ground is known by distinct bodily physical symptoms and are thus "felt" by people. The powers of the sky are instead said to "speak" through the mouth of human agents, and as these partake more closely of the world of Creation, their experiential referent is likened to psychic phenomena.

While their religion is free of dogma and their rituals casually organized, there are a number of stories offered to explain the origin of powers, and these have the quality of true myth, for they explicate religious belief and ritual. The stories are known by most people and are not a body of secret knowledge such as one would find in a situation where magical oracles and formulas dominate ritual action. The first was recorded with a *gwan riang* and the second with a *tiet.* My question was how had the powers first come to human beings.

> Man was created long ago with cows. A spear was put on the back of the first cow Ayan by God. He told *nei me car* [the black people, a category that includes the Nuer, Dinka, Shilluk, Anuak, and Atuot] that this is their cow and they will always have to struggle with it. You *dingelese* [English-speaking people] were given guns to help and protect you. We were given the spear and the cow Ayan. We then met with powers *(jao).* We were in the camp and went to fish and we quarreled over the *toic.* When we went to fish we roped the fish of Abiel [a power of the ground], and Abiel cried and went up to God and said to him, the people you gave the spear to have now become very strong. They have roped our fish. God then said, I will close their eyes. He addressed Abiel, when you go back down later you put your fish into the fire to roast. People will smell the fish but when they look around they will not see you. Then you stab the fishing spear in one of them. They will rush off and will not know what is killing them.
>
> Abiel went to fish, and he killed them and put them in the fire to roast. People smelled it and said, where is this smell of fish coming from? Abiel then took up the spear and he speared a man in the left side, and the man fell and cried until blood came from the nose and mouth. People said among themselves, what is it that is killing this man?
>
> God then saw people suffering and he said, I will catch one man [the text reads here, *be dom e ɣen nuer me kel;* the verb *dom* is that used to describe a power catching or possessing a man] and he will become his power. It will not leave him. I will open the eyes of that man and when he goes, Abiel will remain with him to help save the lives of other people.
>
> When people came again to fish, the power speared one man, and this was the one whose eyes had been opened by Decau. He said to his people, quickly – you take me over to the other side of the river [symbolically the referent here is to the notion that a man taken by a power partakes of the experience of another world, an idea also represented in the footnote of this chapter]. I see Abiel over there. People ran and did as they were instructed. The man who saw Abiel called for a cow to be brought, and he sang
>
> I spear him with the fishing spear of powers
> And people dispersed
> Who are you? I am Abiel
> I speared the man in the ribs

And people dispersed
The ox of Abiel has a sour heart
Abiel killed a man in the *toic*

This is how the suffering of powers remained with people, and they took people, and then people learned their powers. They took men called *tiet* to be the servants of powers *(aluak jao)* to see them.

The second text begins also with reference to Creation.

People were created long ago by Decau. *Jok* was a different son, and all the people that are now in the world were different sons. They were all in one cattle camp, and each had their own side. Whenever the powers went fishing, Reel roped their fish and insulted them. One day the powers went to God and said, you have created us, but now whenever we go fishing they are stolen by Reel. God listened to their word and told them that later in the afternoon he would send a great wind filled with dust. He told the powers that this would blind the eyes of Reel and allow the powers to go on with their own things. He told the *joks* to hide in the ground.

A dog happened to be nearby and overheard the conversation between God and the powers. It ran off quickly and unnoticed to the side of the camp of Reel and told them what he had heard. He told people that when the dust came they should cover their eyes or else they would be made blind [the association between light and spiritual foresight is discussed by Lienhardt for the Dinka]. When Reel heard this he became angry with the dog and as he beat him he yelled at dog, you go off with your lies. When did you speak to God?

In the meanwhile the powers had gone to fish, and when they returned to the camp the dusty wind began and they hid themselves in the ground. The people in the camp sat around and expected nothing out of the ordinary to happen. The wind came, and dog buried its head in the ground. When the wind had passed, dog took his head out of the ground and he could see that people had been blinded.

Then the power called Abiel said, why is that people are not insulting and beating us? The other powers replied, perhaps it is because they are waiting to see if we have returned with fish. Abiel decided to test the people. It took up a fishing spear and stabbed a man in the ribs, and the man cried out in pain. Abiel went off unseen, and people said among themselves, what is it that is killing us that we cannot see? In the evening Abiel returned with more fish and put them in the fire to cook, and he realized that he had not been seen by people. They ate the fish, then all the powers dispersed, each one going to live with a different family. This is how the powers came to us, and why the dog who covered its eyes can still see the *joks* at night.

The themes of these two myths relate to the manner in which Atuot experience the powers. The pain of a power is occasionally compared to that of a spear piercing one's head and emerging from the base of the spine. They are things that are found in the ground, as are the roots or medicines said to be required by different powers. The setting of the stories is in the dry season cattle camp, the only type of settlement in which "people lived long ago." The man with the power over a *jok* is said to be able to "see" it. We see also that the power may be recognized individually, while it is God who figures as the ultimate mediator in deciding the life or death of a man. God made some men to be blind to them, and others the power to call them out.

Jok was created by Decau, like he created sleeping, water and all the things we people of Reel have. Sleeping through the night is God's will. Upon awakening in the morning the *jok* awaits with good health. In the night the *jok* has gone for a walk and left you alone. *Jok* and man were created as one *(jok kene nuer cak me kel)*.

Other versions of this story differ slightly by adding that in the afternoon when the other powers were returning, they were led by *ring,* the elder of the powers. When Abiel speared the man, *ring* ran to him and reprimanded this power. *Ring* said, "Abiel, why are you killing them. God has seen this," and then *ring* gathered all the *jao* together, and God said, "You *ring*, from now on you will be respected by these other *jao* and will be their elder." An elder woman of *ring* explained,

> The first powers were from the Creator, and later people bought the others from foreigners [*jaang*, i. e., Dinka]. The people with guns have their own powers. It is you *dingelese* and the others who brought malaria. Before this, we had only *ring, nhial* and *kulang,* these were the old powers of God. They were born with us and cows. You people do not take your teeth out like we do and this is one of the reasons why we have different powers than yours. It was God who put something in the eyes of human beings, so they could not see powers, and then he gave people *tiet* who can see them. The person of *jok* sees *jok,* but the person of *ring* does not see *ring.* He is given *ring* by God. When a person has big troubles, he goes to a man of *ring.* If he has a feud, the man of *ring* will make it work for him. A *tiet* sees the power and sucks it out of the body. The man of *ring* only says his words in a simple way. When there is a great suffering of many people, the songs of *ring* and *nhial* are sung.

This characterization of *ring* as the eldest power accords with the evaluation of age in Atuot society. Older people are not shown respect and deference simply because they are old, but because their longevity is evidence of their moral integrity, their "coolness of heart" and their spiritual prominence. They are conceptually closer to the world of the collective dead *(thuom)* and ancestors, who are the ultimate representation of morality. Likewise, the power *ring* is often said to be lame and "slow," and is compared with the sheep, while the power of the *joks* is likened to the goat. The same woman continued,

> *Ring* and sheep are *abuojek* [in this usage, "stupid"]. They do not move much and they take time. You just look with your eyes – you can see a goat is more active than a ram. This is the like the *joks* of the earth that run fast to people and stab them quickly. But *ring* and sheep go slowly.

Women are also compared to goats, for unlike men and their herds of cattle which are seen as permanent and perpetual groups, "women stray off into the forest alone like goats" to become members of different families, like the powers in the myth.

People are said to be "blind" to the powers. This has an experiential referent since powers are said to be active only at night, and during an evening where there is no moon, it is often difficult to see beyond the sparse illumination of a wood fire in a homestead. That there are powers moving about is made evident by the dogs who bark through the night, having themselves seen them. Those sacrifices in which God is directly petitioned are under normal circumstances always carried out in the earliest hours of the morning, often before the sun has appeared in the eastern sky. The newness of life associated with the rising sun represents the creative and life-giving attributes of God. Sacrifices for the lesser powers of the earth *always* take place during the night, the time of the day when the powers themselves are imagined to be most active. Evening is the time when people who suffer from a power are said to have "no sleep."

In their cosmological system, therefore, they see great powers in their lives as uniquely Atuot, given to them by God to guide their lives. This notion places them centrally in the world as a people whom God has favored. The lesser powers are typically said to have come from the Dinka, and less commonly, from the Nuer. A similar idea is recorded by Evans-Pritchard (1956) for the Nuer, who suggest God is the "true" Nuer phenomenon, and the variety of his refractions are Dinka in origin. From his account, one gains the impression that it is sacrifice to God which is basic to their Nuer beliefs. This was my impression of the ethnography, though I began to reason differently after my own experience among the Atuot. Evans-Pritchard based his writing about the Nuer on observations recorded in dry season cattle camps, and as far as we know, he never stayed in a wet season settlement. Atuot told me that it is only God *(Nhial)* who comes to them in the camp, while the powers are only in the villages *(te cieng apath)*. Among the Atuot the lesser powers figure in their lives on a day to day basis much more importantly, and more frequently, than the powers of the sky and God. There is a marked difference between Atuot social, economic, and religious activities in the wet season settlements, and the cattle camps. The lesser powers are foreign to the world of the cattle camp, but not to the cosmological order.

Nearly every homestead has a *jath jao,* forked branch shrine, on the western side of the hut. Here periodic sacrifices are made for the power that takes up residence within the shrine. When sitting one afternoon in a cattle camp I asked a friend where these shrines were to be found in the camp.

> There are no *jath jao* here in the camp like those in the village. The powers do not come to people in the camp, it is only God. A peg is made like all the other pegs for the cows and it is driven into the ground. There is the cow that God has chosen, and this peg is used to tether that cow. When we move the camp to the *toic* we carry that peg with us. When we arrive we put that peg in the ground for that cow. When the cow first gives milk they will make *ngat yang* [clarified butter] from the milk and take it to the village, and make the sacrifice of a sheep for God, and put the butter on the head of the sheep.

Population densities in the camp are far greater than those in the village settlements. The affirmation of a collective and cooperative sentiment makes social life in the camp possible, whereas each family leads its own domestic life in the village, separated from another hut by a considerable distance. Specific powers are owned by particular families, and sacrifices for them usually include only close kin. The camp is the world where the powers do not come, but where God minds the welfare of the people collected there with the cattle. Hence in a gross sense, we can outline a distinction between the religious experience of the village and that of the camp, where the former is individual in orientation, and that of the latter a collective affirmation of shared sentiments. The distinction has a rough equivalence of meaning to what Mauss (1972) saw as the essential difference between magical and religious ritual. The definition does not refer to the structure of the rites, but to "the circumstances in which these rites occur, which in turn determine the place they occupy in the totality of social customs" (Mauss 1972: 24). Magical acts are those by which individuals hope to affect the social world, whereas religion designates a degree of collective action. Magical acts can therefore be "anti-social." This is reflected by the belief that an individual frequently uses the power of his *jok* to bring illness to an enemy, typically a kinsman of some degree. A sacrifice to a power of the earth is made to affect some immediate situation, while sacrifice to God is a collective petition for him to consider the general plight. Powers come to people through sickness, while God is revealed to them in such things as twin birth or an abundance of sweet grasses for their cows to eat, which in turn produces thick rich milk. The story of the origin of powers tells how each power went off to live with a different family. In this way they became dispersed among the people. An elder woman once made this distinction between the power *ring* and the more numerous powers of the earth. We were sitting together in my hut at a table that was covered with a red and white checked tablecloth. As we spoke she pointed toward individual squares of color and said, "These are like the many powers, and they are scattered among all the people. This whole piece of cloth is like *ring,* for it is covering everything."

## 2. The Powers of the Sky: Ring, Nhial, and Kwoth

The powers of the sky are unlike those of the earth because they have no separate physical manifestations, nor are there any medicines associated with them. They do not come and possess a man like the lesser powers, but are inherited from ancestral kin. They cannot be bought, and in this sense, are beyond human control. A person with the power of *ring* is thought to have the ability to guide the lives of people and among his functions are a number of rituals which he leads to insure the well-being of people who imagine they are suffering without reason.

> *Gwan riang* speaks only the truth. When a man has a wife who is without a child, he will go to the *gwan riang* and explain his situation. He will bless the woman and smear her body with ashes *apuo* "the burnt cow dung" and when she delivers later she will call the child Apuo. When the child is weaned, the husband will give the *gwan riang* an ox to sacrifice in thanks to God.

Literally *ring* refers also to "flesh," as distinguished from the other elements which collectively form a human being. While he may thus be called a "master of the flesh" he has power over the lives of people. This is made evident in a number of the sacrifices only he can perform. His power of life is especially associated with breath and moving air, as these are active life principles. Traditionally it is said, a *gwan riang* was not allowed to die naturally, but was suffocated over the grave before burial. I have recorded a number of texts explaining the sacrifice performed for a woman who is without a child, called *buong,* and they shed further light on the association between the power of a man of *ring* and breath *(kwoth)* and life *(yei).*

> When there is a woman without a child, a *gwan riang* is called for and he will make *buong.* A sheep is brought, and it is suffocated, and they do not slaughter it with a knife. This is done this way, so that the running of the blood of the woman will not run like the blood when the throat is cut. You try to keep the blood inside the woman, like when they kill the sheep by sitting on it, instead of making the blood run. If they cut the throat of the ram, it would mean that the blood of the woman would still run more, and she would not have a child. The suffocation keeps the blood inside.

This form of sacrifice is specifically reserved for the power *ring,* and is also performed to ward off a famine that may be expected because of too little rain, or at the time of the first planting. to insure a bountiful crop. The "life" of the ram is not lost through the blood, but is transfered directly to the woman.

> *Buong* is a sacrifice that can be made by any man of *ring.* A very fat sheep is needed. It can begin in the evening, and the sheep is pegged in front of the doorway. The man and his wife are inside the house. Later the sheep is brought inside the hut, and its tail is held over the anus, and the mouth is held closed by the *gwan riang.* Then they sit on the ram, facing the door of the hut, and they stay like that until the breath is gone. Then the sheep is cut up and boiled. Very early in the morning the fat is smeared on the woman. The hide is put between her sleeping hide and the ground. The bones of the sheep are gathered together and then hung from a shrine for Nhial God outside the hut. Later, when the bones are taken down, another sheep is slaughtered, then the bones are put into a calabash with beer and water, and these

are things for God. The people making *buong* stay inside the hut for a number of days, and a pot is brought for them to urinate and defecate into. When the child is born and it is a boy, his name will be Ring, because it is the power *ring* that brought him life.

*Ring* is recognized in a person only after he or she has come of age *(ce kaai)* and cannot be said to "be inside" a younger person. In the past, when a *gwan riang* acted as a mediator in the settlement of a feud, Atuot say, if one failed to heed his words, the *gwan riang* would bring a curse *(auyio)* by mixing ashes from his *gol* fire with water and clarified butter, throwing it in the direction of the offenders. The recalcitrant man would soon die. He could also perform sacrifices before a raid in order to insure that none of his people would be felled by the spears and arrows of the enemy, though he never actually took part in the fighting.

The burial of a man with the power *ring* was performed in a manner different from that for a normal man or woman. The following text was recorded with a *gwan riang* who claimed to have witnessed the ceremony a number of times.

> When a man of *ring* is dead, a sheep is brought and sacrificed over the spot where the grave will be dug. When he is lowered into the grave, another sheep is killed. Every son comes with a sheep to kill on the grave. If he was a big man like Mabor Deng [the first person who was recognized as a chief by the British], fifteen bulls may be killed also. If it is just an ordinary man, he is simply buried *(kuoiny apath)*. Then a he-goat is speared, and this is eaten by people who are not related to him. First it is hung up on a forked shrine that is put in the ground next to the grave. When this is done all his children are gathered, and they sit by the grave with the woman's skirt *(ayat)* covering their heads. Then the eldest son stands over the grave and he sings

> I keep *ring* properly
> Do not leave the power of my father away
> I bribed it with Malao [an ox sacrificed for *ring*]
> I bribe the power of my father with Mabor [an ox]
> I tether the bull down with a rope
> The *ring* of my father will wash my back
> The power of my grandfathers
> I will wash your back

> The *gwan riang* stays, and when the sun comes he dies. He is taken into the hut and washed with oil. He became so old he did not know things anymore. When people have become too troubled with trying to feed him, they bring a long heavy log and press it against his neck, and he dies. Then *ring* has to look for someone, but *ring* goes slowly.

Two other texts offer additional detail.

> When the man of *ring* dies, *adhang* [the mudcovered platform used as shelters in the cattle camp] is made in the ground, and a sheep is slaughtered over the place where the grave will be dug. Every member of the family begins the grave by taking a handful of soil, to give them lives *(kene yei ken)*. When the hole is dug, a he-goat is taken by its hind legs and pounded to death over the grave, and then the goat is thrown into the forest. He is put in the grave, and a platform is made to cover him, so he will not touch the earth. Mabor Deng died with a bad heart, and that is why things have gone bad in this family. The *ring* of Mabor remains with his eldest son. The dance *ayumboi* is then made over the grave for eight days, and the songs of *ring* are sung. People say to him, now you have gone and you give life to the children and cows.

The last text I cite here was given by an elder chief of Kuek.

> Before the British came here, we had *gwan riang*. If you had difficulties, you came to him, and he would receive you in his *gol*. At night, you would tell him what was wrong,

if there was a fight, if you had murdered someone, or if there was no child in your wife. When he got so old that he could not walk or swallow, he was not allowed to die, but he was killed by suffocation like a sheep in *buong*. They bring a large heavy wood and lay him down on the ground, and put the wood across his neck, so there is no air going in. Sometimes he would just die from the dust of the dancing. They make a big dance, and his bull is killed and skinned, and the *gwan riang* is put inside the hide before he is buried. All the people are happy, and they sing the songs of fights and of *ring*. The grave should be about fifteen feet away from the door of his hut. They dig a shaft, and then on the right side of it they dig out more earth, so there is a cavity. Another hide is put down, and then a platform is made over it, so no dirt will touch him. The grave is filled, and then a small he-goat is brought and held by the hind legs and beaten over the grave until it dies. Then all the people take off their clothes and beads for mourning. Word is sent to his cattle camp not to milk the cows that evening. Early the next morning after he has been buried the eldest son brings a bull and tethers it next to the grave, and he cuts it in the face while it is still alive, and then it is speared in the heart. The sons of the *gwan riang* then put the woman's skirts over their heads. The he-goat is hung up from a shrine near the grave. People from all Atuot sections come and make sacrifices. They see the goat and they know there has been a sacrifice for *ring*. Before he died, the man of *ring* gave his walking stick to his son, and then would go into him. When the other Atuot sections came, they would approach with spears and bows and arrows as though they were going to make a fight, and the people of the *gwan riang* defend it and show that they are keeping the power there. Then the other people come and join the dance. The he-goat is for the ghost *(atiep)* of the man of *ring*. It is not cut so that the life will remain with the people. In the camp, the cows are led out a short distance, and a cow is sacrificed at the gate of the camp. It is just speared and the meat is for anyone who can grab it. Then the cows are brought back into the camp and they can be milked again.

The similarities of the mode of burial for the Atuot *gwan riang* and the Dinka master of the fishing spear are apparent. Among the Shilluk, "the grave of a *reth* and all *kwareth* ('people related to the *reth*') is a shaft dug in the ground with a cavity cut at the bottom of one side to form a vault" (Howell and Thompson 1946: 19). There is evident an association between the abilities of the *gwan riang* to provide life and satisfaction for people, and the suffocation of animals sacrificed for *ring*, as well as his own unnatural death. His power of flesh is likened to breath and life. The mode of burial seems a symbolic negation of death. Elsewhere (Burton 1976; Burton and Arens 1975) I discuss in detail similar notions which have been reported for the Nuer. The power *ring* thus appears as a manifestation of the life-creating powers of God which are embodied by people with the power of flesh. They combine divine with earthly powers, and Atuot recognize this implicitly in the sacrifices for *ring*. When I asked an elder *gwan riang* why this peculiar mode of burial was made for a dead man with that power, he suggested, "If he were buried the same way, then all the curses he made when he was alive would remain within the *gol* [i. e., the immediate family]. And if people took milk before the cow was killed in the camp, it would be like we were eating his blood."

There is little that distinguished a *gwan riang* from a *gwan nhial*, for Atuot say, the two powers walk as one *(ke jal kel)*, suggesting that both powers are known by the same characteristics. I describe here a sacrifice I witnessed called *nake yang Nhial*, killing a cow for God, in order to elucidate more fully what they have in mind when confronted with what Atuot consider to be a power of the sky. Atuot ideas relating to blood in the situation of sacrifice preface this discussion.

In the course of invocations before sacrifice, the animal to be slaughtered, whether goat, sheep, ox or a bull, is addressed as *yang* Decau, the cow of the Creator. Atuot explain that when they speak these words over the back of the animal, it is the Creator who hears the words, not the beast. "Decau is with the cow from creation. Decau hears the words." The life of the cow goes to Decau, where everything goes.

> When we make a sacrifice, the life and the blood go to God as one *(yei kene riem ke jal kel)*. The life of the cow comes with the dead person, or with the bad thing that has come, and the blood and the life join together to look for where the death came from to revenge it. Decau knows the blood is given, so he will listen to our words.

One may also hear Atuot speak thus,

> In sacrifice the blood is given to Decau and the meat *(ring)* is for the people. God takes the blood for the bad thing. When you are sick, and a sacrifice is made, you offer the blood in exchange for your own life. Because you are sick it means that God wants your blood, and you give him the blood of a cow so you can live.

When an animal is slaughtered, the blood normally runs off and soaks into the ground, so that it is impossible for God to take the blood. One man commented on this apparent paradox: "The blood has the life, so even when the blood goes into the ground, the life *(yei)* goes to God." The association between human life and blood, and these parts of sacrificial beasts, is not restricted to the symbolic act of sacrifice alone. A fight had once broken out between people who were arguing over the distribution of the flesh of a hippopotamus, and four people were carried to a local dressing station for treatment of their serious wounds. All had lost a great deal of blood, and would have lived if it had been possible to give them transfusions. Consequently, relatives of the deceased offered to bring cows from the camp in order to draw out their blood for the needy people.

With reference to the points I have discussed about sacrifices for the power *ring,* it is crucial to stress that no blood is shed. Under his guidance, life comes to man from God directly, for since no blood is shed, there is no exchange imagined.

A sacrifice for *ring* and *nhial* that I witnessed was performed in a cattle camp called Wunarok. I had asked the night before why about fifteen cows had been tethered together outside the perimeter of the camp, and was told that they were suffering from hoof and mouth disease. One cow of the color *ayan* stood some yards to the west of the other cattle and was separated from them by a small fire. The smoke was thick from the smouldering leaves called *gegoi,* which are thought to have medicinal qualities. The cows had become idle, people explained, and had not produced milk. As I walked toward the gathering in the early morning, a man was walking amidst the herd, sprinkling milk upon their backs using a small handful of the grass called *mayar.* A white ram was brought from the camp, and tethered near the fire. The gourd was then placed on the ground next to the stake.

I joined in the procession of younger and elder men who had gathered from the camp, as they circled counter-clockwise around the small herd of cattle three times. The man who was directing the sacrifice led the ram ahead of us, and he also sang a song of *Nhial,* while the larger group offered the chorus. The general theme of the invocation was repeated for me later. "God, you see your cows here and they are suffering. This is your sheep God, that we kill for you. Take the sheep and let the people of this camp have sleep." The song he sang included the lines,

The cow is *ayan,* the cow given by God long ago
The cow with the horns of the antelope
I keep the life of the cow
And the cow keeps my life

The procession ended next to the fire, and the sheep was then re-tethered next to the cow *ayan.* The same man who led the song then approached the ram with a handful of ash from his *gol* to begin an invocation. As he spoke, the words were repeated by the *gam long,* a person who "catches" the words of the invocation and then repeats them for the other people to hear. Each phrase was emphasized by a short stabbing motion with his spear in hand, acting as though he would spear the sheep. When the invocation was completed, the ram was again untethered, and lifted up into the air with its belly facing the sky. As it was held aloft, all gathered repeated the words "God, you see your cow and take away the badness that is killing our cows. The children are hungry for milk, and this badness is drinking it instead of them." The animal was then carried toward the cow *ayan,* and as the invocation was repeated again, the back of the sheep was pressed against the back of the cow and then raised into the air. This was done three times, I was told, to draw the sickness from the cattle into the body of the sheep. The sheep was then tethered again between the fire and the cow. A final short petition was made and the sheep was once again untethered, and held to the ground on its back. The man officiating the sacrifice then severed its throat, and then drew the spear through to the spine, ending the incision at the hip joint. A special effort was made to hold the mouth of the animal closed as it was slaughtered, so that the normal gurgling sound could not be heard. As this was taking place, an elder man drew me aside and told me the sheep would have been killed by suffocation, but there were no women present to sit on the carcass.

A small calabash was brought to collect the blood that flowed from the severed veins in the throat. That is, the blood was not shed, in a sense, nor allowed to soak into the ground. The heart was then cut out from the chest cavity and placed inside the calabash with the blood, and placed on the ground next to the peg. The man who had led the invocations then took the same bundle of *mayar* grass and aspersed the cattle with the sacrificial blood, ending with the cow *ayan.* The left half of the carcass was next fully severed from the right, and carried off into the forest, taking away the disease. The right half was later cooked and eaten by age-mates who had participated in the sacrifice. The heart was left in the calabash by the stake, where it would be seen by God.

By the Atuot mode of reasoning, this sacrifice was not performed to appease God, for the disease came of itself. Rather, God was asked to look upon their doings and grant them life. The blood of the animal which is the life was placed on the backs of the cattle, rather than being left to soak into the ground. This parallels the situation of infertility for women when sympathetic actions transfer the life from one being to another directly. Powers act as intermediaries or messengers between human beings and God. A man once referred to the powers of the earth as the "police of God." In the sacrifice just described, God is addressed directly. The sheep draws out the badness of the disease and its blood or life is taken directly for the well-being of the cattle.

The association of *ring* with life is also evident in the songs said to belong to this power. Here again, their character can be contrasted with songs for the lesser powers. The songs of *ring* might be more properly called hymns, for it is God who is addressed in them. The following illustrate these points.

The *ring* of my grandfathers said
I know my owner
The lame power of my fathers said
I know my owner
The power of Delang said I know my father
The *ring* of my father has shown me life
The *ring* of my father has shown me pity
The *ring* of my father has given me life
I had lain down in the forest to sleep
[i. e., he had abandoned all hopes of surviving]
But now I have known the *ring* of my father
The power of my father has shown me life

When they are carried out in a village, sacrifices for *ring* should ideally be performed under the tree called *awai*, a tree said to be "favored" by the Creator. This song recalls aspects of the mythical past in relation to the present dilemma faced by man.

The power of Makuec [an ancestor]
A man is crying under *awai*
You help him with his life
You, the *ring* of my father
Help the life of the man
You, the lame power of our fathers
You help the life of the man
It is *ring* that keeps the lives under the tree
You, the *ring* of my father
A man is crying under the tree
You help the life of the man

Because his powers are likened to those who are thought to provide for the lives of people, the *gwan kwoth*, possessor of rain, can also be described as *gwan nhial*, a person who owns or is possessed by a power of God. All of the powers of the sky, *ring, kwoth*, and *nhial*, can also be called *gaat Nhial*, "children of God," suggesting that they partake of a likeness of the Creator, the way children of a family resemble their parents. This designation further qualifies the powers of the sky as different from the less powerful and more numerous powers of the earth. The powers of the sky are seen to have more of the blessing and cursing power of God. Thus, the possessor of power over rain is not an individual who is respected because he is thought to have the ability to "call" rain, but because, like the *gwan riang*, he embodies a power which helps Atuot in their lives.

Among the neighboring Dinka, the divinity *deng* (rain) is most likened to their notion of God. Among the Nuer also rain *(deng)* is strongly associated with *Kwoth*, or God. As we have seen for the Atuot, the word for rain *(kwoth)* can refer to breath, an essential element of life, so it is easy to understand the association drawn in their minds between rain and a life-giving property. Evans-Pritchard (1940a) has noted for the Nuer, that while the material importance of rain is recognized for the needs of cattle and cultivation, persons with the ability to call rain are in no way privileged. This situation contrasts sharply with other Nilotic and Bari-speaking peoples in the Southern Sudan.

As a power of the sky and *gaat Nhial*, the power of rain cannot be bought, but is inherited through a lineage of ancestors who were known to have had this ability. One *gwan kwoth* explained how he has come to have the power within him. When his grandfather Anuer died, God called *awumkuei* (the ox name of rain) and *ring*, and he said they have to "see" someone. "Awumkuei was given to me, and God called Dhal (the speaker's paternal uncle), and the *ring* went to him." The common grandfather combined both powers within him, a situation which again points to the similarities between the powers of the sky, and to the fact a *gwan nhial* may have the power *ring, nhial,* or *kwoth.*

> When I speak to call rain *(be kwoth col),* maybe it has not rained for ten days. Awumkuei tells me he wants a sheep. People have come to me and said, if I start to cultivate now, the land will be burnt by the sun. They ask me what can be done. I tell them to bring a sheep to give to God to let the rain fall.

This expresses the idea that the "spiritual power" of rain remains passive until "directed" or acted upon by God. "I bring the sheep under the tree *abyei,* [literally, tree of life] and make the sacrifice." Typically, every person with a power over rain knows of a particular tree where it is said that God comes. In the course of rites performed to call rain, the *gwan kwoth* might sing,

> I worship God every year
> And the power of my father knows me
> I make sacrifices for Awumkuei every year
> The old powers of my fathers know me
> I prepare my body properly
> You bring *apuo* [dung ash] of my mother Dhiomgok
> So the animal will sleep to bring lives
> We collected our words with Aderwaak
> I went to bring Matuang [a generic name for bulls with large horns] from the son of Kiirbor
> My father asked me about the leaving from *cier*
> [i. e., the White Nile. The song recalls here the mythical story of the emergence of human
>     beings from a tree on the bank of the Nile]
> We will meet with misfortunes
> Awumkuei of my father
> Your gourd is filled with milk

The powers of flesh and revelations of God's powers have no material manifestation other than the human being of which they are a part. A shrine in a village homestead with the wild cucumber *(cucumis prophetarum),* called in Atuot *kuol,* planted at its base, indicates that the family resident there has the power of rain. Atuot explain,

> When you make a home for Awumkuei, you bring five things. Four are *kuol* and the fifth is a sheep. God wants the wild cucumber first, and then the sacrifice of a sheep. We know when a man has been possessed by *kwoth* he shakes and wants nothing to eat but the wild cucumber. Even if it is for ten days, he wants nothing else to eat. That is why God wants the sacrifice of wild cucumbers for rain.

Often in the cattle camp, people with the power of *ring* will also make sacrifices of *kuol* at the base of the cattle peg that serves as a shrine for God in the camp. In the villages, a string of the cucumbers is sometimes hung between the forked branches of the shrine. More elaborate "homes" or "shrines" for the power of rain are sometimes found near the homesteads of older men whose abilities are widely renowned. They are called *luak kwoth,* literally, "cattle byres of rain," and are of considerable ethnological interest. In his brief appendix to Lienhardt's (1961) study of Dinka religion, Howell *(ibid.:* 97–103) writes of what is called "Luak Deng, an exceptionally elaborate shrine of some significance among those Dinka tribes now living east of the Nile." This is in the general area the Atuot have in mind when they refer to Korlil or Akorthaar, near the junction of the Bahr-el-Jebel and Bahr-el-Zeraf. Howell records its name in Nuer as *luak kwoth,* and translates this to mean in their language "the cattle byre of God." Reference in the song just cited to "leaving from the White Nile" leads one to reason that Atuot perhaps know of the same shrine.

These texts were recorded from *gwan kwoth* about the shrines:

> When the *luak* is made four sheep, two cows and two goats are brought and killed. They are killed, and a dance is made. People sing *yaai* |war songs| and the songs of God. When the dance finishes, all the cows are killed, and God is brought into the hut. A calabash and a cow of the color *ayan* are taken into the hut. The pot for God is filled with *ngat yang* |"oil of the cow"; that is, clarified butter| and this is taken into the hut. The house is closed off with a mat, and the power is closed off in the hut. There is also a small gourd filled with water inside, and only the man of God can drink from this. God becomes his power. Last year when it was time to cultivate, there had been no rain. I went under the tree *abyei* and stayed and sang the songs of war, and a sheep was brought and killed under the tree. As soon as it was killed it rained until evening.

Another man explained,

> When my grandfather was created at Korlil he was given rain by God. When I call rain I go to the *luak kowth* and go inside alone. I fill the gourd with water and bring eight wild cucumbers, and I put these in with the water. I put some of the water over my feet and wash my hands in it. Then I wash my big fishing spear with the water and thrust it into the ground near the calabash. Then I pour the water over my head and go outside to sit in the sun, and when it is midday, the rain will come. If it does not rain I sacrifice a sheep early in the morning, when no one else is there, and then it will rain. Then I return to the hut and fill the calabash with the rain water, and make loops with the wood *aboic* |cordia *Abyssinica,* an extremely pliable woody vine| and put these inside the bowl.

The same procedure is reported for the Nuer as a means of calling rain (see Jackson 1923 : 136). One additional text was recorded with a *tiet,* a man with control over a number of powers of the earth, and the minor differences in detail are instructive in pointing out their different roles.

> A hut is made like the hut in the village. When it is completed, people of one section |clan| are called to come and make a dance there. They bring the wild cucumber, beer, tobacco, and a chicken. In the morning the cucumbers and chicken are sacrificed, and the power is brought into the hut. A small calabash bowl is brought, and inside it the wood *aboic* is coiled, and then water and clarified butter are put inside. The cucumber is cut and half is put in also. The power accepts this. When Decau created people he told them to go and make this *luak* for God to give the black people lives. When there is no rain, women come and make their dance and the dance for powers. God will hear this and he will let the rain come, so people can cultivate. They sing:

> > God let the water pour down
> > God my father poured down the rain
> > God let the moon come
> > And poured down the water

To bring rain, the possessor of the power pours water onto himself, as though he was its living incarnation. Symbolically rain has a strong association with the initial situation of creation, as seen in the song that recalls the tree at Korlil where people were created and some given powers of the sky. One text makes special reference to women coming and making their dance when the shrine is made for rain, and this also recalls the creative powers associated with feminity. In the initial situation water served as the husbands of women, and through the waves of the river, they bore children. The cucumber is one of the few species of plants to grow in Atuotland with a moist center.

The oozing liquid that seeps from an incision of the plant is compared with the moving of blood and life-giving powers of rain, and thus classify it as appropriate for sacrifice in these situations. The cucumber is addressed as "the cow of God," and sometimes is spoken of as the "poor man's cow."

> *Kuol* follows God. When killed it is cut in half and thrown up into the air. If it falls with one half up and one half down, this shows that God is angry. If both halves land facing up or down, then God has accepted the sacrifice.

With this outline of the more important powers of the sky (celestial powers?) completed, I next discuss the more numerous, and more active, powers associated with the earth.

### 3. The Earthly Powers[6]

There are numerous powers associated with the earth in Atuot cosmology, and many are known among the neighboring Jur and Dinka by either the same or slightly different names. I have some difficulty comparing the Atuot data on powers of the earth with the Nuer ethnography, for Evans-Pritchard calls similar notions "fetishes" and titles the practitioners of these powers "wizards." Both terms would be inappropriate for translating Atuot concepts. However, since Nuer also call them *kuth piny,* "spirits or powers of the ground," similar phenomena figure in Nuer religion. Generally, Evans-Pritchard attributes their recognition by Nuer as the result of Dinka infiltration, a situation recalling the varied expressions of totemism among Sudanese Nilotes referred to earlier. As already pointed out, Atuot view the celestial powers as "true" Atuot phenomena, and can relate detailed stories of how one or another of the earthly powers came from Dinka. Whatever their origin, these earthly powers figure importantly in their religious experience.

The most commonly recognized *jao piny,* powers of the earth, are *mathiang gook, thong alal, makao, mabier, agok, loi, arop, mangok, abiel,* and *koro.* I was able to record a list of the *joks* known among the Jur from Bernard Jenny, an anthropologist who was working among these people, and about half of these were recognized by Atuot, while the others were unknown or said to be originally from the Dinka. Many of the powers listed here are also known by ox names, and most are said to have a number of wives. I begin the discussion with a description of the power called *mathiang gook,* a power known also among the Dinka, the Nuer, the Mandari, and the Jur.

*Mathiang gook* is thought originally to have come from the Agar Dinka. Physically it is associated with a burning pain in the abdomen, and when a *tiet* is called to diagnose the malady, Atuot say he can see the power inside the stomach of the person. The power is said to have been brought by a poor Agar man from *mat,* a category of foreigners that includes such people as the Bongo and Azande. He returned from a

---

[6] I read one afternoon while living in Atuotland the following passage, which seems to reflect a similar idea associated with the earthly powers:

". . . there is no reason why a healthy man should see them, because a healthy man is, above all, a man of this earth, and he must therefore only live the life of this earth for the sake of order and completeness. But as soon as he falls ill, as soon as the normal earthly order of his organism is disturbed, the possibility of another world begins to come apparent, and the more ill he is, the more closely does he come into touch with the other world" (F. Dostoyevesky, *Crime and Punishment*).

journey into their country and brought *mathiang gook* into his hut and placed it on the roof. A *tiet* from Atuot went to see the man and found the power, and then brought a big ox to be sacrificed to it. The power returned to Atuotland with him, and he put down a shrine for it outside his hut, where *mathiang gook* then came to stay. This act is called *jok tete,* "putting the power in the ground." Like all the lesser powers of the ground, *mathiang* is owned by member of lineages, who can use the power to kill enemies or to destroy their crops. When a person has been taken by this power, the shrine is erected in the homestead by a *tiet,* and should he or she recover from the attack, the power will come to live in the shrine and protect the people of that family. Employing a metaphor that aptly suits the Atuot, Faron (1964: 63) describes a similar state among the Mapuche of South America. "Hawks of the sun are tethered to specific unilineal kingroups."

When a shrine is erected for this power, the *tiet* will go off into the forest to dig up the root thought to be its "home in the forest," and this is hung from the roof of the hut near the doorway. Ideally, since it is a powerful *jok,* a cow should be sacrificed when it first appears, and meat from the thighs of the sacrificial animal is hung from the forked branches as well as inside the hut by the piece of root. The wooden shrine should be placed in the ground some distance away from the hut, for while people want the power to stay with them to protect them, it is also a power that is feared for its strength and must be "respected." The flesh of the sacrificial animal is cut into thin strips and boiled, then consumed by the household members and any other close kin resident nearby. Periodically small offerings of meat should be placed on the shrine for the power to eat, and a goat or an ox should be dedicated *(puoc)* to *mathiang gook,* so he can see he is recognized and cared for by that family. When the power becomes angry, Atuot reason this because it has been neglected. The power will come to its owner in a dream and make its demands known. The person it has come to will rise quickly from his sleep and begin to sing one of the ox songs belonging to the power. The animal dedicated to *mathiang gook* will be led out of the hut and walked around the perimeter of the household, so the power will see it. Some of these songs follow next.

> A man who brought Tutbuong [an ox name of the power]
> He has given himself a fire
> I give *mathiang gook* what it calls for
> I dig the medicine *(wal)* of the power
> I do the work for the power until I am exhausted
> I make a sacrifice for *mathiang gook* every year
> *Mathiang* has told me everything
> I even know a power that is still far away
>> [suggesting that this power guides the singer's life, and is thus protected by yet unknown powers]

The next song also belongs to *mathiang gook,* and is sung by a *tiet* in the course of erecting its shrine in the homestead.

> Power of Ayi [the wife of *mathiang gook*]
> *Mathiang* has spoiled the things of a man
> and has no thought of our suffering
>> [this sentiment toward powers of the ground is markedly different than that they express in regard to the powers of the sky, which are generally benevolent]
> Atut *(mathiang gook)* always thinks good when it is bad
> *Mathiang* has spoiled a man's property
> I asked *mathiang* for peace

And the power does not agree
If it refuses me, I will spear his cows
I will pierce the man's anus
    |here *mathiang gook* is said to be singing|
I will spear the man and hold the shaft
    |i. e., be relentless in its revenge if ignored|
I will spear him until he has a tail like a cow
Angiel |a wife of *mathiang*| chases after things like dogs
*Makao* |a power said to walk with *mathiang*| is a messenger like a dog
I bought the power from Atim Akuei
And I slept away with it
    |this is a frequent line in the songs of the powers of the earth. The idea it refers to is that
    a man has travelled a great distance to purchase a power, and has learned of its ways
    when he slept with it in the forest, that is, away from his family and kin|
I bought the powers to help the lives of people
Makuei |an ox name of *mathiang gook*| makes the arms of the ants to bend in pain
Makuei spoils the whole village
My Makuei has become enraged
*Mathiang* has spoiled the land of Nuer
*Mathiang* has spoiled the land of *jaang* |Dinka|
*Mathiang* has spoiled the land of Atuot
*Mathiang* has hidden itself in the earth
The ants cannot see
The ants should hear the words
Let the people be cured
You *mathiang,* hear the sound of the rattle
The man has gone sour inside
He has no hope of life
*Mathiang* of my father
The power has filled the man
The strong power of Jur
It fills him with a strong smell

When a person is "caught" by this power, the pain increases until the *tiet* is able to draw it out from the body, an act called *puot,* literally, "sucking out the *jok.*" He will shake violently from the fire of the power and run to the edge of the forest to spit out the badness. That is, *mathiang gook,* like all powers of the earth, is imagined to have a physical property, not only in the manifestation of illness, but also as something that can be drawn out and discarded. In the observed sacrifices for the powers of the earth the *tiet* typically claims to draw out the bad blood from the human body, and more rarely he emits small pieces of black pebbles in the same manner. While they are said to be blind to the ways of the powers, Atuot do expect to see something brought out by the *tiet* in order for it to be considered a successful exorcism. There is an overriding association between the powers and the earth, indicated by such actions as digging its medicine from the ground, making its home with a product of the forest, and spitting out the badness in the direction of the woods in order to drive the power back to its abode and away from the homes of people. A number of these notions are illustrated in an ox song of *mathiang gook.*

The power breaks my father's spirit
The tree |shrine| of my father
The power breaks the tree
The bitter tree of my father

I have a hatred with you
The *mathiang* that always destroys
You Tutbuong, the bitter medicine
I am dangerous (*mathiang* singing)
You accompany me and make things ready
I am sent with poison for the hearts
If I come to speak [to the *tiet*] you put down *auyil*
   [the first of a series of payments made to the *tiet* for performing the exorcism. Unless
   the power "sees" that the payment has been made, it will refuse to cooperate with
   the *tiet*]
If it is a poison, you make the payment
It is something I do not know
The horns have broken six times
   [*mathiang* is sometimes said to have sharpened horns on its head. It has gored
   someone six times]
The bad things of the world are finding you
The shadow of life [*atiep* "ghost" or "soul"] is taken by the power
My power *mathiang*, the power with a hot heart
Bring the payment and throw it down
Bring the payment so the words will have meaning
The bitter medicine that kills a man
It does not give people sleep
The medicine that kills
Where did you find the medicine?
I wonder where the medicine was found
I can only wonder what is the source
It was found in a simple place
It is among the grass
What have I done for my father's *jok?*
I consider these things, power of my father
The medicine I bought from Rek [a section of Dinka]
It is overcoming me
This *mathiang* does not know my stomach
   [the *tiet* sings here; he says to *mathiang*, come out of the man so the people will
   see I have worked well and will make a payment to me of a goat or a cow]
The power that does not know the hunger of the *tiet*
I was so tired from travelling to buy *mathiang*
Why did I buy the power?
Because of the cry of people to come tomorrow
   [The power sings the remainder of the song through the *tiet*]
I have a bitter heart
It is hot like a fire
We meet over the lives
The troubles are behind me and in front of me
I fucked the people with my thumb

*Mabier* is another power said to have come to Atuot from the Agar Dinka. At the
present time, if *mabier* or any other "foreign" power catches a man, Atuot may say that
the power came on the back of a cow that was given in bridewealth in the course of a
marriage between Dinka and Atuot. In the days when inter-tribal hostilities were
greater, powers also entered their country through the blood that was shed by an
enemy. This remains in the ground for some time, until the power becomes active
again and seeks vengeance. Mandari have learned of these powers from the Atuot in a
similar way. Buxton (1973:66) writes:

> Certain punitive expeditions carried out against Aliab and Atuot are seen as directly
> instrumental in bringing powers into Mandari country . . . One of these armed forays
> was against a group of Atuot who were camping in open bush . . . a number of Atuot
> were killed and wounded. The Mandari constantly return to this incident declaring,
> "The blood of people with *jok* was spilt on our soil, so the angry *jok* belonging to the
> dead and dying Atuot were loosed in Mandari."

According to one of her informants, all the main powers of the Mandari were from the
Atuot. Atuot on their part suggest that the lesser powers are all originally Nuer or
Dinka, with the greatest proportion from the latter, for Atuot are rarely in prolonged
contact with the Nuer, and intermarriage is extremely rare.

*Mabier* is also called by its Dinka name, *thung mabrieu,* referring to the piercing pain
caused by the spear of this *jok.* When *mabier* possesses a man or woman, the pain is
described to be like a huge cat with long fangs digging into the chest. In the course of an
exorcism of this power, *mabier* may call out, "Move over, you are standing on my tail."
*Mabier* was found first by an Agar man who was travelling through Jurland. He carried
some food with him in a small sack as he travelled. As he was walking along he felt
hunger, but decided to travel on further before he ate. He grew tired and sat under a
tree. His sack of food fell to the ground and was scattered all about. He cursed his bad
luck, and *mabier,* who was sitting in the tree above him, asked who was making the
noise. The man answered that he was on a journey and had come to rest. Then *mabier*
said, why are you so angry? Is it simply because of the food you have lost? The man
replied that this was indeed the cause, and the *jok* then said, well I shall repay you for
this misfortune. After that, *mabier* stayed with the man.

Atuot explain that when *mabier* catches a person, it spears one in the head and
causes a pain as though the head had been split with an axe, and the thrust of the
wound travels down the arm and out the anus. "When the *tiet* comes to make *teet*
[perform a sacrifice] he will ask, 'How does it catch you?'" Once diagnosed as *mabier*
an ox should be killed in the early evening. The corpse is skinned and all of its flesh
is brought into the hut and kept there uncooked throughout the night. Early the next
morning a shrine is made for the power *(kua tete mabier),* and the meat is boiled and
distributed to the household members, a small portion and occasionally the horns
being reserved for the power, and placed at the foot of the shrine.

> It is made near the hut, not far away like the shrines for Nhial or *mathiang gook.* It
> should be close to the mortar where the women pound the durra. Everytime she cooks
> *simsim* (sesame), a small dab is put on one branch of the shrine. If this is not done,
> the power will always have hatred for the family. This is so because when the man
> dropped his food it was the doing of *mabier* who wanted to eat it. The same act should
> also be done for *mathiang.* Later on small children will come and eat it.

The songs of the powers of the earth cannot properly be called hymns, for in them
Atuot insult and bargain with the *joks.*

> *Acuok* [the ants of God] have put a fire in their lives
> The lives are with *mabier*
> This is the power that troubles
> But does not know anything
> The power of the ants that does not know anything
> A power of the forest
> You power, you fill my stomach
> You fill my stomach with beer

The power of powers [*kaai* "maturity," "wisdom"]
Is with me
You fill my stomach, so I can settle this case

I pray to you *kulang,* the red one
*Kulang* who keeps the lives
The power hates my words
I pray for the lives of people
I pray to you *kulang* for lives
I pray to *Tutbuong* for lives
*Mabier,* the power of the Jur, I pray for lives
The people ran away; things are bad
*Mabier* is blind to the trouble
*Kulang* show me what my eyes cannot see
I will go to the forest
Show me what I do not know
I will take away all the troubles
The *tiet* is making *teet*
I am appreciated by all the people
By all the people except one man
This *mabier,* a power of the forest
It has no use for us
*Mabier* only comes with a tongue
I will be a Jur in the forest
I will have some things to say
*Mabier* has become a *jok* of the forest
You *mabier,* you leave me to go walking
This is not a power of the front line
[reference is made here to a fighting formation; the bravest and most competent fighters are in the front]

Each power owns a number of songs. In the course of an exorcism, such as the one described in the next chapter, normally all the songs of the powers are sung. This is called "making a dance for the power," and Atuot say that it is more likely to leave the person afflicted if many songs are sung, and if the gathering of kin of the afflicted is large. There is a notion that the power can be "bribed" and even flirted with. The *tiet* leads the singing, and family and kin carry on the chorus. There is no fixed order for singing songs, and new songs are composed to accommodate the qualities of new powers. By contrast, the songs of the powers of the sky are always sung in order, and to the Atuot, they are unchanging and permanent, since they were given to human beings long ago in the situation of creation.

The power called *agok* (a term which can also refer to "monkey") is said to catch people in the stomach, causing diarrhea and severe stomach cramps. This is one of the more commonly recognized powers to enter their lives, and Atuot suggest it originated in their land. When *agok* catches a person, a *tiet* is called for to sacrifice a castrated goat by a shrine near the hut. In addition to this, in the course of a curing ceremony a string of pieces of wood and root is hung from the rafters inside the hut. This act is called *boce,* a verb that also describes the manner in which a mother carries her child slung from her shoulder in a hide made of goat skin. There is a tendency for women to be caught by this power more frequently than men, though Atuot offer no interpretation of why this should be so.

The power known by the term *kulang* is also said to be one of the older powers of the land and is therefore thought to be a true Atuot power. Some *tiet* told me, *kulang* is probably the oldest of all the powers. The symptoms of its presence are persistent vomiting of what is described as a white soapy liquid, and a deep and persistent cough. If this is the first occurrence of this power within a family, a goat must be sacrificed. The initial remedy is to cut off a portion of the goats's ear, and tie this with a string around the neck of the afflicted. The man of earthly powers then spits into the soil surrounding the hut, and collects bits of the saliva mixed with mud, then smears this across the nape of the neck, an area of the natural human body that is strongly associated with life, for beneath it lies the wind pipe. Following this the person should begin to recover immediately and cease coughing. If the illness persists, it is said that *kulang* is not satisfied with the sacrifice of a goat, but demands a cow instead. Another goat should be brought out of the hut during the course of this sacrifice, and after the cow is slaughtered, its ear will be cut in the manner of the first affliction, so that *kulang* will see that the goat belongs to it, and will cease harming the family. At a future time, this animal will be sacrificed to appease this power.

A number of other physical symptoms said to herald the presence of a power are discussed briefly. A person is said to be broken with pain in the lower back by the power called *grumbek.* Like the other earthly powers it requires the sacrifice of a goat. *Koro* causes a lesser form of diarrhea, and can be appeased by the sacrifice of a chicken. The wings are cut off and hung above the doorway of the hut on the inside. *Weltoic,* literally, "green medicine," also causes diarrhea and calls for the sacrifice of a goat. In the course of fieldwork another power called *jongbaai* (a Dinka term meaning literally, "power of the home") was becoming more mobile and increasingly recognized. This is a common occurrence, and Atuot learn of them from the men of powers in the course of curing ceremonies. He may say at such a time, "This is *mabier* who has come, and he has come with *jongbaai.*" The origin of *jongbaai* is explained in a short text.

> A man from the Palual clan of Apak named Awo Kuon went to look for honey in the tree. When he climbed to the top, he slipped and fell to the ground. He was travelling alone, and in the fall he broke both of his thighs, so he had no recourse other than to lie under the tree immobilized. He remained in this state for a month, by which time worms and maggots covered his legs. In his village, all his people had decided that he had been eaten by a lion. Then after a time a wind came, and it blew across his legs and healed them completely, and his body was filled with a power. He rose and returned to his home. When he arrived people thought that he had become mad for he stumbled often, and shook at night. The man told his people, "If you want me to live, then you had better sacrifice an ox." The ox was brought, and then the power came into him in a good way. The people asked him what it was, and he told them it was a power called *jongbaai,* "the unknown power." Then the power taught him this song:

> I am Awuo, the man with the unknown power
> This is a power that came to me alone
> I walk in the forest unharmed by the power
> I ask Deng,
> And it gathers the lives of cows and men
> *Jongbaai,* the unknown power came alone
> The power came to me alone

As indicated, the original encounter of a power is typically associated with the separation of a man from his kinsmen, and this necessarily implies travelling in unknown and dangerous territory, most commonly through Dinkaland. This is apparent in the song the man is said to have been taught, for *deng* is a powerful Dinka divinity, and is recognized only among those Atuot families who have for a long time exchanged women with the Dinka. By this sort of reasoning, and as a result of its social implications, all of the Dinka or Nuer spiritual powers could theoretically be grafted upon the Atuot system of thought. There is also an association between the manifestations of a power and the world of the forest, a feature of their ecological and ideational world that is fraught with unknowns and unpredictability, unlike the normally ordered and consistent experience of life in the cattle camp or the village.

A power is normally passive and only takes on an active role in protection of a family or in vengeance against another group of people, but it is also *potentially* active at all times. On one occasion while I was trying to take a photograph of an exceptionally elaborate shrine for the power called *makao*, I stood in a number of different locations around the forked branch in order to find a suitable pose. People, who sat watching as I walked around the shrine, paused and then moved to another angle, told me that this was the power pushing me away from the shrine, for it did not want its picture taken.

During the early years of the British administration there was a short period in which the number of powers increased rather suddenly. From one perspective this can be interpreted as the result of more peaceable relations between the Atuot and the Dinka. One such power was described by the assistant district commissioner in Yirol in 1944. Persons knowledgeable in the nature of powers agreed that they first learned of the power called *luoi* (literally, "to work" or "to make") about twenty years after the first punitive patrols led by the British against the Atuot. Mr. Crabb noted in a letter to his superior in the headquarters at Rumbek:

> I have told all concerned we frown upon it [*luoi*] and that the priesthood must be suppressed. This is in relation to what is now being called *luoi* practice and worship, which means as far as I can gather, "nothing to do with work." Under the leadership of Acok, demonstrations have been made and threats uttered against certain of our Christian congregation here. I have satisfied myself that these are real and saw myself the trampled ground near the Christian church [i. e., a mud hut meeting place] where the demonstration was held last Sunday. Blows have been struck, and when challenged by us, Acok made no denial of his possible intention to kill someone, probably the leading Christian.
>
> I know something of the history of the movement during the last year and reported it at once . . . They have frankly declared that mission [in Ceic country] and government are their sworn enemies . . . the leaders of their spiritual movement are strongest among the Ceic Dinka . . . to plant some of their sacred symbols in a Christian house.

The text highlights two points worthy of consideration: first, the power *luoi* "came from" the Dinka, and second, the way in which powers are manipulated with the intention of harming or even killing individuals who are despised. A comparable situation is evidenced among the Ngok Dinka, where for a period of time, the incarnate Mahdi was figured in Dinka cosmology as a divinity.

The powers of the earth partake more directly of the physical world, not only because they are associated with the ground, but also because they have a physical location in space. A man with the power *ring* can affect the lives of people who live quite far away, according to the Atuot, while a malignant power must be sent directly by an individual "at close range." In this, there is the invitation to categorize the notions surrounding *joks* as "magical," while the powers of the sky would then be considered as more religious in nature. Something must be actually done to bring illness to an enemy through a *jok*, while a person of *ring* has only to think of a means of achieving his ends.

The powers of the earth each require shrines of their own which are always erected on the western side of a hut in the homestead. This is done because "the *jok* comes from the east and it travels to the west where the sun sets. It should not face the direction from which it originates, but should be directed away from the hut. *Decau* long ago had the powers go to the black people. You do not face the power from the direction where the sun comes." Also, unlike the powers of the sky, *jao piny* are said collectively to have two "totems" or phenomena which they must respect. The first is they must face the west, the conceptual location of danger, death, and darkness. Powers of the earth are also said to "respect," that is, avoid, the bird called *guak* (stork) which frequents the marshes lining the permanent sources of water in their country. Atuot explain that this bird looks for the powers of the earth and tries to swallow them. Here again, the physical attributes imagined to characterize earthly powers are noted. A man with control over a power is said to be able to "see it with his eyes," as one man phrased it, "like you see yourself in the mirror." "The *jok* comes to claim its property. The *tiet* will know the reason because he can see it. If a man steals a cow, the *tiet* sees the *jok* keeping the cow. The power says this is mine. It says I am coming for this and that."

As the spiritual power of a man filled with *ring* merges toward the attributes of earthly powers, so too is there a slightly different evaluation of categories of persons who have control over the lesser powers. One may be a *tiet, me diet e mal,* a man with a great power over *joks,* or a *tiet me icuit,* an individual who has only bought a power to protect his interests, and who would never be called upon to officiate a ceremony in order to rid a person of an illness associated with an earthly power. Logically, the next lesser category of specialist includes persons with power to control the actions of natural species, such as in a totemistic relationship. Two texts are offered by *tiet* in explanation of how a man becomes a practitioner and is recognized for his curing abilities.

> *Tiet* begins with the effect of sickness. When the family has made many sacrifices for your recovery, and then you later recover your health, then you have shown that you have the power over the *jok.* It gives you the power to see it, like when it sits on the roof of a hut, and then they walk with people like shadows. Then you come to see and hear the powers, while all the other people are blind to them. When you first see *joks* they are like lizards, and they are not angry or wild yet. Later you see them like a hairy wolf with long fangs, like when you see *agok.* When you see them they are moving. All the *joks* are male, but every one also has a wife, and sometimes it is the wife of the power that brings the sickness because she wants something, like a goat. The powers of the earth are the messengers of God, and sometimes God comes directly to people. Then people know you have become a *tiet.*

Certainly not everyone who becomes temporarily possessed by an earthly power assumes the vocation. A casual observation about *tiet* in general is that they are usually rather more "hypersensitive" than others. Some overemphasize these qualities as a means of demonstrating their ability to communicate with spiritual powers invisible to most people, and such behavior is in fact expected of a successful man of powers, especially when he has been offered a goat or cow as payment for his services. There are women who may also become *tiet,* though I never saw one performing a sacrifice. The spittle of a woman who has borne many healthy children may be thought to be effective in assuring the fertility of a woman who has remained childless, or who has delivered a stillborn fetus. Older women are more commonly said to have the power *ring,* rather than some lesser manifestation of God. One man explained, "A woman will make *teet* like a man, but she will call for a man to make the songs of the powers [i. e., actually officiate the ceremony] because the *jok* does not recognize the voice of women." The man continued,

> There are two *tiet*. There are important *tiet* like myself who have *long* [a rattle], and the powers stay in the rattle. The power speaks through him to the people. When he looks for the power in the walls of a hut, the *jok* speaks to him through the rattle. The *tiet* makes *yor ghot* [rubbing the rattle against the wall of the hut] and the power enters the rattle and comes out of the person and into the *tiet*. There is also the small *tiet*. He only makes *teet* outside the hut, and the power does not speak to him. He can only diagnose the problem, but he has no real relationship with the *jok*.
>
> Only with the big *tiet* is the power in the body of the man. When the power comes into the man it makes him rock back and forth and shake, and the power he has tells him to suck out of the bad *jok* in the person. He pulls out the *jok* from inside that is making the sickness.
>
> A small *tiet* may sometimes want to become an important man of powers, and he can have the ceremony called *nguot long* [literally, "cutting the rattle"] performed. This is done in his hut. He goes to look for a *tiet* who is known to have control over many powers, and the man comes to his hut in the afternoon. A goat is cut in half through the abdomen, and the lower half remains outside the hut, and the upper part with the head is brought up into the *adwil*. It is a he-goat.
>
> The minor *tiet* holds the goat, while it is still alive, in a position as though he was to nurse it, and while he holds his rattle in his right hand, the powerful *tiet* cuts it in half. He then walks up to the steps into the *adwil* while other people and the major *tiet* follow behind him singing songs. Inside the hut the lesser *tiet* then sits on the lap of the man performing the ceremony. He puts his left arm around the man, and with his right hand he clasps the hand of the minor *tiet* and moves the rattle back and forth against the wall. Later, the upper part of the body of the goat is eaten by the new *tiet,* and the lower part, including the kidneys, is given to the man officiating. The new *tiet* must then remain inside his hut for six days, never going outside once. If he even sees the meat of the lower half, he would loose his power immediately. It is always a goat that is killed in this way, because all the earthly powers favor the meat of goat. And it always has to be a male goat, because it is hotter and more powerful than a female. Then the man must give the major *tiet* a goat and a spear for performing the rite. On the morning of the day when this is done, a goat is killed and placed in its entirety, unskinned, inside the hut of the *tiet* being initiated, and this is for the powers to eat during the night. The next morning a sheep is brought and killed, and then the corpse of the goat is brought down, skinned, and eaten with the sheep.
>
> These are the things that must be done before a man has the power to make *guor* [the power to look for and find a power. The word can also mean "to seek, to need, to want, to look for"]. This is how a man learns *tiet*.

The lesser powers are active agents manipulated for personal ends by human beings; the powers associated with and emanating from the sky are direct revelations of the powers of God. Persons filled with the power *ring* or *nhial* are therefore conceptually "closer" to God and are seen to have a similar type of creative and life-providing nature. The earthly powers are conversely bought and sold by people, and serve as media through which the deeds of the Creator are carried out only in an ultimate sense. As noted and as the texts illustrate, the lesser powers are thought to have an ability to act alone, without human beings necessarily directing them. Yet their actions are constrained by what might be called the overarching authority of God. Herein lies the moral rather than strictly religious quality of God the Creator: the ultimate and logical source of all life is God. In their daily lives, it is more commonly *tiet* who "help them have sleep." It is said to be only God who is responsible for the "giving and taking away of life." The moral source, represented by God in relation to the powers, makes human beings accountable to each other when they are related by "kinship." It would be of little benefit to seek to direct the malignant powers of one's *jok* against an unknown enemy, for there is no basis upon which a breach of morals can be measured. A man of *ring* on the other hand can curse his enemies and convince his own people, that their spears will not miss their mark. Like the image of God, *ring* and the other powers of the sky transcend the narrow confines of domestic relationships and have no defined territorial limitations. Infertility is most often ascribed to a condition which results from the power of God to bring life, while suffering from the *jok* called *agok*, for example, is more likely to be viewed as the consequences of neglecting to make good one's promise to transfer a certain number of cattle in bridewealth exchange. The resulting breach of moral commitments causes a physical illness, brought upon by the active agent of the angered *jok* of the party supposed to receive the cattle. The experience of the powers corresponds therefore in its general outlines to more tangible aspects to social organization and politics.

A community of kin is partially defined by moral commitments among its members, and these are the persons who would seek vengeance against one another, and eventually agree to compensation for imagined transgress of these bonds. Similarly, settlement of a long feud by means of blood compensation is only possible among a lineal or domestic group that recognizes their common economic and political interests. The moral and political world can be viewed in relation to the lesser spiritual powers of the earth.

From a Durkheimian perspective, the Atuot "experience" of powers of the earth might therefore appear paradoxically ill adjusted to the social setting. On any evening in an area of village homesteads one might hear the singing and rattling sound of a *tiet* who is beckoning a power to bring suffering to a not too distant neighbor. As Winter (1963) demonstrates for the Amba, however, it is precisely those persons who seek to harm each other who form the moral and kinship community. Seeking the aid of a power is a recognized and appropriate means of settling disagreements between persons who conceive of others as having some degree of kinship with them. Like witchcraft in central Africa, the Atuot experience of powers of the earth functions sociologically as a means of control. Winter (*ibid.*: 298–299) writes,

> When we treat the question of the influence of the social structure upon the set of ideas as a separate enquiry we find that the relationship is not a *functional* one in that the ideas exist in order to meet a need of the system of social interaction, but rather a *structural* one.

The Amba believe that witches attack only people who live in the same village and have the destructive power to harm them, and likewise for the Atuot, if in the course of his divination a *tiet* finds little wrong in the relations of the afflicted person with his kin, the source of his suffering will more likely be ascribed to the will of God, rather than the ill will of another human being.

The powers of the earth are, employing once again Faron's (1964) metaphor, "tethered" to specific unilineal descent groups, and are normally effective as a leveling mechanism or means of vengeance only within such a group. The powers of God transcend all categories of social life, and are more truely religious than moral in Atuot experience. Powers of the sky are psychic rather than physical manifestations of God. As such, the greater part of Atuot religion is "this-worldly" in orientation. God is knowledgeable of all things[7]. The spiritual powers that emanate from the sky are likewise "other-worldly," for they are more abstract and diffuse phenomena of God, affecting the lives of all people regardless of their agnatic or affinal relationships. These points will become more apparent following the description of a number of sacrifices.

---

[7] Faron (1964: 53) observes for the Mapuche of Chile a "structure" similar to that which characterizes this distinction in Atuot religion: "While it is to *nenechen* that final appeal is made, for only he is able to control the minor gods, the closest ties between men and the supernatural beings exist between the Mapuche and the regional gods and godesses." In the Atuot context, and more widely in Nilotic religions, one would replace the last phrase with "powers of the earth."

# CHAPTER V

# Sacrifice for God and the Powers

Earlier in this study it was suggested that sacrifice is the central act of Atuot religious experience and belief. This chapter attempts a further explanation of why this is so, and offers some comments about the intent of their sacrificial rites. In the situation of sacrifice, Atuot attempt to communicate with the creative being, hoping he will accept their offering in order that they may have life. Yet in addition to the performance in strictly religious contexts, sacrifices are made at wedding dances, during the course of mortuary ceremonies, following period of seclusion after the initiation of young men into adulthood, after the birth of twins, when the earth and their crops are scorched by drought, and at a variety of other times. Thus, while the act of sacrifice itself is *always* an expression of religious intent, there is no specifically associated "pious" attitude, since any sacrifice necessarily has its feastial as well as religious side. In spite of diversity of forms and occasions sacrifice *always* involves the substitution of the life of an animal in exchange for the life of human beings. This fact received its greatest recognition and emphasis by Hubert and Mauss (1964: 97) who wrote,

> ... fundamentally, beneath the diverse forms it takes, it always consists in one same procedure which may be used for the most widely differing purposes. This procedure consists in establishing a means of communication between the sacred and profane worlds through the mediation of a victim, that is, of a thing that in the course of the ceremony is destroyed.

The central role of sacrifice in both Nuer and Dinka religion has already received full examination (e. g., Lienhardt 1961; Evans-Pritchard 1956; Crazzolara 1953). For the present discussion, Lienhardt's (*ibid.:* 236) analysis is instructive:

> Therefore, to cut the throat of a sacrificial ox is merely the necessary physical conclusion of a sacrificial act of which the most important part has already been accomplished by speech. Without speech, or at least an intention which could be verbalized, there is no sacrifice . . . Like prophecies, the ceremony eventually represents as already accomplished what the community . . . intends. For the sacrifice is its own end. It has already created a moral reality, to which physical facts are hoped eventually to conform.

For the Atuot, if these comments were to be entirely representative of their sentiments in the situation of sacrifice, it would be necessary to ask why they bother to kill a beast at all, for according to one perspective a human being or a collectivity of persons are acted upon, rather than any sacrificial victim. The oral statement of intention is essential, while the slaughter of an animal is simply a secondary act, necessary for the conclusion of the rite.

Among the Atuot, sacrifices follow a fixed pattern, while the situation calling for sacrifice changes regularly and in accordance with the perceived needs of people and animals. The primary distinction occurs between sacrifices intended to ask for help for their lives from God *directly,* and the other types which are mediated by the presence of one or another of the earthly powers. Sacrifices for rain are, as we have seen, periodic occurrences, and those which are performed to appease the angered ghost of a dead man should also be made at intervals. I was present at a number of the latter type, and record here briefly what are their intentions in making a sacrifice in dedication to a dead man.

Ring Takpiny was the chief of the Luac section of Atuot and died suddenly in 1974. The burial itself was a rather elaborate affair, for he had been a prominent man, so that a great many individuals were called together to offer animals for sacrifice. In preparation for what is called in Atuot *yang neke yuic nuar,* "killing a cow on the head of the deceased," a dance is made nearby the site of the grave, and all those who attended the initial internment should ideally return at this time. It was said that the dead man would know that the sacrifice was being made in his name, for the ghost is still present around the place of burial and would communicate this to the late chief. As will be demonstrated in the next chapter, the ghost *(atiep)* is considered to be "alive" and represents to the surviving kin an image of the man, as when he was still alive. While his physical remains no longer have life, the ghost is imbued with the ability to seek vengeance *(cien)* against the living and cause them death or misfortune.

Thus in this situation, the elder son of the dead man was said to have been visited by the ghost of his father in a dream one night. As is the case with the powers which are thought to "walk the land" at night, a ghost too is most active in the darkness. In his dream the ghost told the son that Ring was calling for a bull to be sacrificed on his grave. An extremely large solid-black bull was eventually brought and sacrificed, and in the course of the invocations by senior kinsmen of his lineage the family *jok* named *makao* was also called for to help guide their lives and give them health. Soon after the son first had the dream, his half sister fell ill with her child, and a *tiet* was consulted, and told the collected relatives that this illness was brought on by the angered ghost of the deceased chief, and that a large black bull should be sacrificed over the grave. For the Atuot the concordance between these two separate events offered enough evidence that a sacrifice was demanded. Before the bull was brought from the cattle camp, a sheep was suffocated by the dead man's brothers and their wives, for this would make the ghost cease to be a harmful influence. The blood of the bull sacrificed over the grave would travel with the power *ring* to find out what was the initial cause of the death (see Burton 1978*a*).

I describe next a sacrifice that was performed in the household of a female relative of the same dead chief, which was intended to cure her state of temporary barrenness. Childlessness is attributed to God in an ultimate sense, but in order to offer a practical solution to the problem a *tiet* was consulted to seek out whatever *jok* was responsible for her condition. In their manner of thinking, it is most often a woman who is barren, rather than a husband who is impotent. A condition of barrenness is seen sometimes as both a moral and physical state, for it may also be that the ancestral dead are displeased with the way they see their living kinsmen going about their daily affairs. The curse of the dead is more effective and stronger than that of any living agnate, for the dead partake partially of the world of God and creation. Their physical remains vanish, while their moral superiority transcends the earthly boundaries of time and space. In this particular case, the woman, Akoi, worked part-time in a local dressing station as a midwife, so that she did have access to other forms of knowledge about the condition of childlessness. Instead, a spiritual agent was sought out as the cause of her misfortune.

As was the case with nearly all the sacrifices witnessed, only older members of the community of sacrificers were present. Four of her paternal relatives from the Luac and two maternal uncles from the Apak sections were gathered along with three wives of her brothers. Like most of the sacrifices which are intended to communicate with God, the rite took place early in the morning. A *tiet* from the Apak section had been consulted a number of days before, and since he had already done his work, his presence was not necessary. Further, there would be no exorcism. Akoi's elder brother had brought a white ram from the cattle camp, and when I arrived at her hut it stood tethered in front of the doorway. Sitting in a semicircle facing the doorway was Akoi in the middle, her paternal relatives to her right, and maternal to the left side of her. The spear to be used in killing the sheep was thrust into the ground next to the tethering peg. On the ground next to this was a small calabash filled with water, and another with durra flour. In the early morning sunlight, the ground around the hut and sheep seemed especially well swept. The elder brother untethered the sheep and led it around the hut three times in a counter-clockwise movement, while a paternal uncle began the prayer "to God" or invocation *(laang)* as he followed behind. It was not possible to record all of what was said, for as they passed in back of the hut their voices were inaudible. Part of the invocation included the phrase, "the father of Akoi has had only two daughters and no son. Akoi should be given a son for the family of Deng." This, as well as the other introductory statements, was directed toward the powers owned by the family. Throughout the period of invocation, the sheep was addressed as "the cow of God," and sentences were emphasized in a typical manner by thrusting a spear toward the animal as a punctuation of the oral statements. The circling of the hut is necessary so that the powers of the earth that are located *in* the walls of the hut can see the animal that is to be sacrificed, even while the life of the beast was not dedicated to them.

The elder maternal uncle then moved closer to the sheep and sitting on his haunches began to make an invocation over the back of the animal. After each sentence he would pick up a small pinch of the flour and rub it over the back of the sheep. His words were repeated by his younger brother for the others collected there to hear. Occasionally he would also toss some of the flour in the direction of the hut, and at one point he stood and sprinkled the floor with flour. He said as he did this,

> These are the things of God. You God, see this cow we have brought here for you. One time a girl came with water and put it up inside the *adwil*. In the morning she found it missing and when she later looked for it she found it where the pumpkins had been planted in the garden. You God, this is a thing you have done. After some time, a man in that family died, and we dedicated a sheep for you, and later you took this sheep and put it where the pot of water had been before. The man died in the same place. Then another time, you God took off the roof of the hut and put it in the middle of the garden by the pumpkins. These are your things God, and now you have called us to come and give you this cow, so that Akoi will have a child.

When he concluded he took some of the flour and once again rubbed across the back of the sheep, then walked to where Akoi was seated, and smeared the nape of her neck, her forehead, and her chest with the flour. Next, the younger maternal uncle took flour, and with both hands he rubbed it across her belly. Elder female kin of the woman also made short invocations. There is no fixed pattern, but generally elder people are required to speak first, for the power of their words are necessary for the sacrifice to be effective. Anyone collected for the sacrifice has the right, indeed, the obligation, to make at least a short invocation. The sheep was then untied and its rope was thrown onto the roof of Akoi's hut. When the sacrifice has been completed later, I asked Akoi's elder brother why so much of the sacrifice had been conducted by her maternal uncles, and was told that "the maternal uncle is often the cause of a bad thing, but it is the same person who also has special powers to cure."

The sheep was stretched out on the ground with its belly facing the sky, and its legs and mouth were held so that it was completely immobile. The elder maternal uncle said in a quiet voice, "God, it is your life and your cow." He then inserted the spear into the esophagus and drew an incision down to the middle of the chest. I was surprised to see how little blood had trickled from the incision. Once again, since the animal's mouth had been held closed, it died without making an audible sound. He then reached into the chest and severed the heart from the aorta, placing it in the calabash filled with water next to the tethering stake. The head of the ram was then washed with water, while the elder uncle carried the spear that had been used to make the incision to Akoi, who licked a small drop of blood from the tip. He then smeared a small bit of blood across the nape of her neck.

The carcass was then placed on its left side, facing the west, and was left there for about ten minutes. The heart was taken out in this manner, so that the powers of the family could come and sit on it *(bejao nyune thin)*. As I left the homestead, the flesh had been cut apart and was boiling to be eaten by Akoi and her family. The heart would later be eaten by the people from Apak, for none of Akoi's paternal relatives could eat this organ, because they were from the Luac section and respect *(thek)* heart.

Like the Nuer and Dinka, Atuot consider the heart to be the center of affective experience. A person who is generous and kind with his words can be said to have a very good heart *(teke loic me gau e mal),* while a wife who has refused to accept her domestic responsibilities will be said to have a heart that has gone bad *(loic ce jeo)*. The heart is not thought to be the center of intellectual experience, though someone who is "kind-hearted" is necessarily seen to be intelligent. To express anger in the Atuot language one would also say *loic ce jeo,* "my heart has gone bad" or is "heated," and the same phrase can connote jealousy, vexation, or mistrust. Joy, satisfaction or simple pleasure is expressed in the phrase, *ce loic de lim,* "my heart has become sweet." In the sacrifice just described, people also told me that "God likes the heart" and "the heart is given to God." This does not contradict the statement that it was placed in the bowl for the powers to sit upon it, for ultimately all sacrifices are accepted by God, and it is considered to be God who will grant the woman a child. In this context the Atuot express a sentiment that God too has the quality of affect and emotion, and the sacrifice is offered to please God in the sense that a human being can have a "sweet heart."

The blood which flowed from the sheep was allowed to sink into the ground, while that remaining on the surface was blackened by the heat of the sun, was dug up, and thrown into the bush on the perimeter of the yard. Akoi had in the meanwhile consumed a small portion of the sacrificial blood, "the life," of the animal. By partaking of some of its blood she too gained a part of the life that was exchanged to insure her fertility. In this sense, Akoi stands temporarily in a position of mediation between God and human beings, for not only did she take part of what was given to God in the sacrifice, but will also serve as the medium through which God will grant her a child. The heart also figures prominently in the sacrifice, for if there is something wrong with a person, it is necessary to first find out what has gone bad in his or her heart, that is, in her relations with her kinsmen. They offer the heart, the seat of affective life, to be wittnessed by God.

Moving air, animate breath, and the cooling breezes which follow a rain shower are associated with and symbolic of life. In the physical being blood represents life. Linguistically, both principles are combined, for the word for heart includes as its referent also the lungs, so that the internal organ that regulates both life and breath are one. This statement recalls a point made earlier, that what is buried in the ground at death is merely the physical remains of what was a human being, while blood and breath transcend the purely physical world. Hence, when Akoi licked the blood from the point of the spear, she was not only identified with the life of the animal sacrificed for her well-being, but the act also serves to emphasize the radical distinction between life and death. The life of the dead sheep became part of her own.

In the village setting durra flour is most often used when invoking a power of God, while in the cattle camp the same act is performed with the burnt ash of cow dung. The smearing an animal with ashes *(buk apuo)* is, as Evans-Pritchard and Lienhardt have demonstrated for the Nuer and the Dinka, an expression of the identification of human with non-human life forces. For the Atuot, in addition, the invocation with ashes of flour is also the first act in a series of transactions of a barter. The actions are calculated, which suggests that substitution itself has both a symbolic and material referent. In this case a ram is killed, so that a woman might produce a child, though this is not simply a pious plea toward God: the woman is *expected* to produce a life as a result of the sacrifice, and therefore she is ultimately acted upon. The ritual might be fruitfully contrasted to the earlier description of the suffocation of a sheep. The stated intention of suffocation is to keep the blood or life within it, with the idea that the woman too will cease shedding blood and become pregnant. In the ritual just described she seems to be temporarily barren and here she incorporates the blood from the sacrifice into her own body, so that she might "have blood" and give birth to a child.

A different form of sacrifice was performed in a village called Burtiit, also in the Luac area of Atuot. The family concerned most directly was in the process of erecting a shrine in the homestead for the earthly power called *thong alal,* "the power that speaks with a red tongue," while it had been delayed until the first durra had been harvested, so they would be able to make beer for the ceremony. They had not long ago bought a cow from the Ceic Dinka, who were unsatisfied with the price paid, and who, as a result, sent the power called *mangok* to cause sickness in the family. As already noted, the malignant power is here conceived of as having come on the back or in the blood of the foreign animal.

The power had come and caught a woman of about fifty years of age, causing suffering from stomach cramps so severe that she had become immobile during the preceding five days. A *tiet* was consulted, and he pointed out the source of the *jok* and told the family it was demanding to be given a sheep. When the *tiet* saw the power he knew it was *mangok,* because it had blood streaming down the side of its face. Preparation for the sacrifice had begun three days earlier, and my wife and I attended the singing for the powers on the preceding nights. Called in Atuot *bull jao,* "the dance and drumming for the powers," this sort of activity always precedes the actual sacrifice of an animal, for the power must be entertained, so it will become pleased and leave the afflicted person. On the fourth night, as we approached the homestead, the *tiet,* named Ijuong, told us that the goat would be killed that evening, so we walked a few miles in a different direction, where he found a small outcropping of stone and sharpened his spear. When we all arrived at the hut, the family and relatives who lived close by were sitting by the fire near the hut. We were seated and the *tiet* was given a pipe to smoke. After a short while he rose to his feet and slowly walked to the edge of the cleared yard and began to sing. As he did this, he began to circle the homestead, pouring out small libations of water at the edge of the yard, into the fire, across the doorway of the hut, and over the people seated around the fire. These were not songs belonging to powers, but others he himself had composed, including one ox song. Ijuong sang at the periphery of the yard so that his own power would come into his body, giving him the strength he would need to make the exorcism; these songs are translated here for their ethnographic interest as well as for the light they shed on the sacrifice which followed.

I   Awumkuei, my father, sent me away
    I am hated by the people of the camp
    I am sent away because of the good thing I did
    I am hated because of the cow I gave ⌊sacrificed⌋ to Myual
    The dance of the powers came from afar

II  The power fell to earth in Panther ⌈"The old home"⌉
    Iluong Deng, the power fell down
    And the lives were changed ⌊affected by the *jok*⌋
    I cross to the Nile, Abuk Ayual
    The land has been changed
    God, you make the land well
    The village has given itself to the owner
        ⌊i. e., people called the *tiet* and he recognized the power⌋

III In the camp of my people
    I was chased away in the fight
    I crossed to the other side of the river
    I released the white cow with the wide horns
    I released the cow of my father
    The camp Mager of the camp Atungyer
    The cow is so large like an elephant
    The chief of the camp crossed the river

IV  Awumkuei, you always burn the people
    You will turn my head down
    A man who is greedy
    And a man who overlooks me
    I will agree to the fight
    I cut the throat of the chief ⌊kills a cow for a power⌋
    So the people feared for their lives

V   It is the daughter of Majok Nhial
    This is my real father
    My father entered the grass by the light of day
    And the rains came
    My power has come to me
    I will see the way in the light of my power

VI  I went off into the grass
    I do not want the confusion of the words
    The words of the ants are confused
    The words are confused in the camp of Jel
    Oh, the confusion of my people
    The confusion in the camp of the powers of my mother

I wonder in the grass of the camp of Jel
⌊here, Ijuong begins to ready himself for his work. He has called his *jok* to him,
for it also recognizes his songs and voice. The confusion of the camp relates to
the temorary illness caused by the *jok* in the woman⌋

VII  If I leave you here to go and look for cows
The land will turn bad
A witch says I am invading the house
⌐A woman had deceived me
I am troubled for their lives
I find the shrine of rain
⌊the *tiet* begins to bargain with the people who have called for him to make the
sacrifice. He threatens them that if they do not give him the payment he deems
reasonable, he will abandon them and they will be left alone with their suffering,
hence he sings, "I am troubled for their lives." The reference to a witch recalls the
Dinka family who sent the badness into the family on the back of the cow⌋

Ijuong then returned to the central gathering of people, brought out his rattle for
calling his power to come into him, and then began to lead the songs of the powers. In a
short while about twenty people collected in addition to the members of the household
of the sick woman. She was carried out of the hut and placed on the ground with her
head resting in the lap of her sister. As he sang, Ijuong occasionally spit onto his rattle
and smeared the salivia across the nape of her neck and her chest. The songs increased
in volume and blended more rapidly from one into the next. The first song insults the
power.

I    The prostitute is causing the troubles
The mother of Acinbaai sits with her vagina open
Nyanken has a rotten vagina
The vagina has brought a case
A woman who is attracted to anything
The whore stumbles through the forest
Like a dog looking for a husband

II   God is walking above as though to kill people
I am confused with my life
There is good life in the air
The ox of Majong Damiit is tethered throughout the day
In the evening the air of life came
God came with life
I am helped in my life by God, my father

III  Acol is respected by my father
I pass with the cow Ayan near the camp
And the people were surprised
The people drooled when the cow was seen
Our camp went out and it frightened people
Our camp stated in the land of the ancestors

IV   Acol is the power of my father
The camp has gathered before me
Mayom said the shafts of spears have been broken
Mayen ⌊an ox⌋ do not break the shafts
  ⌊i. e., accept the role as the victim of sacrifice⌋
The spears we will use for the fight in the *toic*
So it will become ours forever
I am troubled for the lives of people
You, my father, the son of Nyong

> Help with the lives
> Abuk, my mother, bring the lives
> I am hated by all the people excepting one man
> I am hated by all the people

At this point in the ceremony Ijuong rose to his feet and began to dance with the beat of the singing, first across one side of the yard and then to the edge of the clearing, running back quickly to feign a spear thrust toward the hut or into the fire. Atuot explain that the more lively the dancing and singing, the more likely are the chances for a successful exorcism.

> V  Abuk, my mother, I am left like an orphan
> I carry the hatred of others
> I pray to you, I pray to you
> I am a man left out
> My head spins around from this life
> Majong's cattle have been tethered
> The rain that comes in the evening
> Abuk has come with life
> The head of a man is moving like the branches of trees
> Abuk, you come with the lives

As in the preceding songs, no power has been addressed directly, for at the beginning of all sacrifices the hymns of God are sung first. Abuk, sometimes said to be the first woman, figures in this song as the provider of life, and reference is made to her in the present context, for it is a woman who has been caught by a power. To suggest he is a man "left out" Ijuong compares the illness with a severence of social relations, for to stand alone implies that all things have been abandoned, including the will to live. When he sings "I carry the hatred of others," he makes reference to the evil associated with the power which he must draw away, for it has been sent as an act of hateful vengeance.

> VI  My grandfathers, you help the land
> A spirit has fallen in the evening
> Where has it gone to
> Where did the spirit fall
> It has fallen into these lives
> You children of Abuk, help yourselves
> We are going to argue [i. e., bargain with the power]
> It is said that a great man hopes for nothing
> These people are tiny ants compared to Creation
> It is *ring* that helps the land
> *Ring* comes with a strong wind and cracks the branches
> Do not spoil the edge of the spear
> I pass with Ayan in the middle of the camp
> Ayan is blessed by all the people
> Acuil, the spirit of my Creator
> People all collect together
> The spear has been thrown
> The people of long ago fought for this land
> And I am hated by all the people
> Take the life of this cow to give me life
> My stomach turns inside
> Go and bring life into the hut
> This is a cow for blood
> I pray to you my great father

VII Mayual breaks the tree with a wind
And carries off the troubles of the village
The *ring* of my grandfathers
The *ring* of my grandfathers helps the village
Break the tree with the wind
And take away the troubles of the village

VIII I pray to God like a monkey
I am praying to my father
I am troubled by the things of the ants
I do not want the annoyance of people
The bad things that come to the ants of God

Having sung this series of songs, Ijuong then shouted out *arum,* "everyone keep still!", the first sign that he has made contact with the malignant power. People converse quietly among themselves, and the *tiet* calls for a pipe to be lit, so he can smoke, all the while keeping his rattle moving. When the power enters the *tiet,* he no longer has complete control over his actions, and that the power comes into the rattle and makes it move by its own force. In fact, it seemed that as the seance continued over a longer period of time, the rattle became an extension of his arm, and it would jerk suddenly and unpredictably, a sign taken once again by Atuot to indicate that communication with the power has been established. Ijuong spent more time now sitting close to the woman and shaking the rattle in time with the singing and clapping, often pausing to massage her body with it, paying special attention to the nape of her neck and her lower back which seemed in retrospect preparation for a later stage in the sacrifice, when he sucked at the same places with his mouth to draw away the badness of the disease.

Followed by four other men, Ijuong led the goat around the perimeter of the hut three times. The goat was tethered close to the fire and about ten feet away from the woman. There was a pause in the singing, while each of the men made an invocation over the goat, repeated by the *gam long* and emphasized by the characteristic thrust of a spear. They were seated and the singing began once again.

IX I am praying for the lives of everyone
I pray for the lives of people
I am praying for the lives of Atuot
I am praying for the lives of Nuer
I am praying for the lives of Rek [a Dinka section]
I am praying for the lives of Agar
I am praying for the lives of *jaang*

X If there is no one here
The owner of the home is away
The words of the *tiet* are away
The words of a great man are absent
There is no need for lies, the words are absent
If the *tiet* is absent, who is to do the work
Who is to do it when I have not come
No one is to go ["bring life"] if I am absent
No man can go in my place
My father, my God, give me strength in my heart
To put away the hatreds
Make mine a strong heart for the work
My mother Abuk, wash my heart

> To take away these hatreds of people
> Any man here, you give me an ox for blood
> Give me a fat ox to exchange for life
> Give me the bull of Wunjur for the lives
> If the animal goes to someone else
> I will not accept

XI  Manyuong *juol,* the power of God
> Give me the cucumber to exchange for the lives
> You pray Abuk, for the lives
> The cucumber is the cow of a poor man
> God, you see the cow
> To exchange for life
> Someone is sleeping
> There is something hiding, something sleeping
> I am staying here for the lives
> You *anyijong* [hawk] and *apoltok* [kite]
> You come near me now
> You, the sons of the tiny black ants
> What I told you long ago,
> No man has yet opened up his ears to hear
> No one heard my word of long ago
>> [apparently this song draws reference to the situation of creation where the dog told man to hide his eyes or he would be forever blinded to the doing of the powers]

XII  Separate and untie the hatred of witches
> My father has brought lightning
> I am overcome by a great thing
> I hear the words of a great chief and I come
> Disperse these hatreds of witches
> My father *awumkuei,* make the thunder again
> Scatter the hatreds of witches
> I have found a man helpless in his life
> This is a man I have found struck down
> This is a man known to everyone

Atuot suggest that unless enough people gather to sing the songs of the powers, there can be no hope for helping the afflicted person gain his or her health. In this sense, at a sacrifice to rid a home of a malignant power, there is a collection of people who can be called the community of suffering. It is a basic social obligation to demonstrate one's concern for a kinsman's health, and failure to participate may lead others to suggest one is guilty of witchcraft *(apeth)* or simply longing for the things that belong to another person. The curing of a person is thus not entirely the work of the *tiet,* but is most importantly a collective enterprise. There is also a responsibility to become temporarily overcome by or possessed by the power of one's family, for this too will help draw out the malignant power. And as we have seen, the sacrificial community is typically co-terminous with a defined group of kin, for they share among themselves the same powers.

The *tiet* once again cried out *arum!* and began to shake violently all over his body. Possession would not be an entirely accurate description, for his own power is within him at all times. At this point it became an active agent within him, indeed, a part of his being. At this point he began to act as the "mouthpiece" of the *jok* that had possessed the woman, and since it was said to be a Dinka spirit, he began to speak this language.

There was a period of rapid speaking, making it impossible to understand the gist of his words, but when his own power began to speak from within him, he once again spoke Atuot and called for a chicken to be brought out of the hut. Ijuong stopped his shaking as suddenly as he had begun and stood above the woman, so that her outstretched legs lay on the ground underneath his. He grasped the chicken in his right hand, spit on it a number of times, blessing it with the power of his *jok,* and then began to circle it around the woman's head and body, and then dragged it across her breast and back. As he did this, he occasionally held it aloft and said, "You God, see the life given to you. Take it for the woman." He repeated the same acts on the bodies of the woman's two sisters, her husband, and a small child, and then it was released on the ground to walk about. What seemed peculiar about this was that normally a chicken will run away from the noise and confusion caused by so many people, but in this case it seemed content to stay in the midst of the crowd.

Soon after this, when the singing had begun again, a woman unrelated to the afflicted person in any immediate sense became possessed by the power of her own family, and I turned around quite startled expecting to find a dog growling and barking, when I saw instead the same woman bouncing up and down on the ground in double time to the beat of the rattle and singing, with every bump emitting a piercing growling sound. Ijuong had stood up by this time, and began running back and forth between the sick woman and the outside of the yard, carrying his rattle and spear in his right hand. When he re-entered the circle of people he approached the woman's face from a distance of only inches and sang at the top of his voice, only to turn around almost immediately and run back to the edge of the clearing, "throwing away" some of the badness of the power with thrusts of his spear. This continued for about fifteen minutes, at which point the other possessed woman stood on her feet and blurted out an unintelligible utterance. Then, as though she had been hit solidly in the back with a heavy club, she emitted a high pitched screech, and fell limp to the ground. The *tiet* began hopping and dancing on one foot nearly on top of the woman and back to the tethered goat. The violence of his movements in such close quarters made the presence of his *jok* appear all the more obvious. He told me later that it was his power *agok* that made him run back and forth in order to convince the power called *mangok* to leave the woman's body. Ijuong also later explained the reason why the other woman had become possessed was because his own power *agok* was speaking so quickly through him that it had to seek another person to speak through also, and added that when this occurred, he felt the presence of "so many powers rushing in."

He sat momentarily and regained his calm, then began slowly to remove his clothing. As he began to lead another song, he started crawling toward the sick woman on his hands and knees, the way an animal stalks its prey. Just as he was to touch her, he again started shaking violently and emitting gutteral barks and groans. He then lowered his head to bring his mouth against her stomach, while her kinsmen gathered close by to watch the proceedings intensely. Then he lunged at her chest and began to suck out the power, while the woman was held secure by her family. She appeared to be suffering great pain. Ijuong rose to his feet quickly and ran off to the edge of the yard, out of sight of any people collected for the sacrifice, and spat away the badness he had drawn off into the forest. He repeated the same acts, concentrating next on her lower back, her shoulder, and her neck. The other woman who had been possessed then demanded that the song continue, so the power would be courted out of the older woman. In the midst of her remonstration the *tiet* recoiled away from her body and shrieked, and his body jerked violently, while he became rigid, falling onto the sick woman. Two men then dragged him away from the homestead and returned to the woman's side without the *tiet*. Ijuong rejoined the gathering shortly. At this point it seemed easier for me to appreciate what he had told me before: he draws a power out of a person, which then enters him and burns like a fire.

When Ijuong was seated by the woman, apparently having regained his calm, he took up his rattle, spit on it, and massaged the places of her body where he had sucked out the *jok* with the spittle. The singing ceased for the first time in over two hours. He next placed his mouth softly against the nape of her neck and spat very gently there, an act caled *tiol,* which is necessary because "this is where the life is" *(ke yei te thin).* Ijuong then went to the goat and started to rub its back with his left hand. Next the goat was brought to where the woman lay prostrate, and its head was brought against hers, while the *tiet* drew his left hand across her head from back toward the temple and in a single continuous movement onto the head and back of the goat. This was explained to me as indicating that the *tiet* had now brought the earthly power out of the woman and was placing it into the body of the goat that would be sacrificed to appease it. He then turned to her kin and said *teet ce thu, tuiny ce wei,* "my work of exorcism is finished, the badness has gone."

The goat was then retethered, and short invocations were made over its back. The atmosphere had changed remarkably, for instead of the singing and rattling and grunting people sat calmly and relit their pipes. In soft whispers they began to discuss how much work it had been. As Ijuong sat down, he patted his chest vigorously, and now, he said, the power had stopped speaking in him. The goat was then held to the ground, its throat severed by Ijuong, and the blood collected in a calabash, while two other men held it aloft upside down so that the blood would flow out more quickly. The corpse was carried into the hut, where the small livestock are tethered during the night, and placed on the ground next to the calabash of blood, "so *mangok* can sit on the animal tonight and drink its blood." The act of slaughtering the animal appeared to me to be anti-climactic in relation to the rest of the ceremony. It was now about twelve-thirty in the morning, and the singing had first begun five hours earlier.

Early the following morning the goat was cut up, and a "hash" was made of the kidneys, liver and other internal organs which are considered by the Atuot to contain the "life" of the animal. Half of the mince was placed above the doorway of the woman's hut and the other placed in the ashes of the fire to cook and be eaten later. The food placed over the doorway was said to be for *mangok* to eat, and so that it would see at all times that the family was respecting it. When we emerged from the hut, a smaller number of people had gathered in preparation for the sacrifice of a chicken "for the wife of *mangok.*" A brief invocation was made over the fowl, and Ijuong dragged the chicken across the woman's body a number of times, then held it aloft saying "God, see your chicken and give the woman life." In what followed next the people saw what was taken to them to be further evidence of a successful exorcism. The chicken's head was cut off, and instead of running across the yard and scattering its blood about, the decapitated bird hobbled directly to the stake where the goat had been tethered the night before, and fell dead upon it. The *tiet* said in an almost inaudible voice, *lang e mal, lang e mal,* "very good, very good." The wings were cut off the chicken and hung inside the hut for the livestock, an act which was described as "giving a cloth for the wife of *mangok* to wear on her head." The blood that remained in the calabash was then poured into another container, to which was added the cooked mince of internal organs, and eaten by the woman, her husband, and her sister. For his work in making *teet,* the *tiet* was given two Sudanese pounds (approximate value at the time of this research, U. S. $ 2.87), the hide of the goat, one hip, and one leg. The remaining flesh of the animal, except for the heart and lungs, which were snatched by my dog but would have been eaten by the woman and her family, was prepared for people who happened to be around the household.

The next morning I brought some medication for amoebic dysentery, which is what I had thought was the cause of her illness. Her condition as compared to the night before was remarkably improved, for she was walking and even doing some light work. She took the medicine, but later in the afternoon she threw it up entirely. Ijuong told me that the *jok* did not want this medicine of the government or foreigners. They had seen evidence of the successful exorcism anyway, especially in the manner the chicken had died. It was said that "*mangok* is taken back with the goat. The chicken found where the power went. The *tiet* saw *mangok,* and it told him, this is what I want, and then I will go back."

As I noted at the beginning of this description, the family is also in the midst of preparations for erecting a shrine for the power *thong alal* or *mabier.* A sheep and a goat were to have been brought in November when the durra ripened. Then the same *tiet* will make *gor γot,* "bringing the *jok* into the hut with the blood of the animals," and it would remain in the walls. When the power is later consulted by a *tiet,* his rattle will draw the power out to speak.

In chapter IV, some of the formal aspects of Atuot ideas relating to "powers" were discussed. Having now described the praxis of some of their sacrificial rites, we can begin to consider the underlying notions of a religious nature revealed in sacrifice. This can be accomplished relatively briefly. It is somewhat apparent that their intent in sacrifices to God is different from that observable in sacrifices offered to lesser powers. The distinction is obvious enough to them, as the preceding texts have revealed. In the first instance, sacrifices addressed directly to God partake of a more religious quality, while those for powers are ultimately of a moral nature. Sacrifices for powers are necessary because of the affairs of people and their relationships with each other. Sacrifices for God are made in response to "the things of God." The presence of a malignant *jok* is the result of human action, for one person "sends" his power against another. At the same time, they will explain, if God does not consider it just, there will be no such spiteful vengeance. Dissatisfaction with a bridewealth payment is on the other hand adequate cause and ultimately of a moral nature, for in a sociological sense it relates to social control and the integration of values and norms. There is a corresponding difference in practitioners of the different categories of powers, for each reveals to Atuot powers of a different capacity. A *tiet* must know well the affairs of a family in their relationships with others in order to indicate the likely source of the problem. Each category of power is equally important in their religious thought, for they deal with different realms of experience, the relation of man to God, and of human beings between themselves. Hence, if a *tiet* is unable to define a problem in reference to a power, Atuot will be resigned and account for it as the will of God. There is no occasion for a successful sinner in their world view.

Lienhardt's (1961:64) observations for the Dinka apply more generally to Nilotic religions:

> . . . [medicines] are not to be regarded as of great *religious* importance, and the Dinka themselves are quick to point out the difference between the characters and abilities of such earthly medicines and their owners and those of priests and prophets . . .

There are no sacrifices performed to "take away God," for in the situation of twin birth, *col wic,* and other sacrifices it is to recognize God's presence that they take the life of an animal. They do on the other hand perform many sacrifices to separate (*dhol:* the act of cutting the throat of an animal) the influence of *joks* from their lives. It would offer little help toward our understanding, if we said that one or the other modes or conditions of sacrifice are "collective" or "individual" in orientation, as Evans-Pritchard seemed to think was so essential in explicating Nuer sacrifices. The stated intent of a sacrifice performed by a *gwan riang* or *gwan nhial* is to provide for the lives of people, and we have seen that in the course of an exorcism its success is measured in part by the number of people who participate. Instead it must be understood that there is a difference between sacrifice to God and those directed toward one of his agents. The observation may serve to draw into relief the active-passive contrast I have argued characterizes respectively their relations with powers of the ground and the revelations of God. Human action is necessary to "send" a *jok,* and consequently the situation requires a human response. Atuot react passively, by contrast, when they consider that their only recourse is to the benevolence of a fatherly God. In another sense, we could point out in line with Atuot usage, that powers of the earth are conceptually "hot" and those powers which emanate from the sky as "cool." Employing a similar analogy, the flesh of a goat, a conceptually "hot" animal, is deemed necessary for the appeasement of an earthly power, while a sheep is nearly always offered to a power of the sky, which by their nature are more like God. The slaughter of an animal for a *jok* is intended to remove the heat and suffering that ensues when a person is caught. Sacrifice to God is a petition for life, often associated in their songs with the coolness of the wind that brings health to people. Thus, the powers of the earth may be viewed as primarily "destructive" in nature, and those of the sky as "productive." This point is especially evident in considering sacrifices, which involve suffocation, as a means of insuring life. When Atuot say they are giving the life of an animal to God, we should understand this to imply they are making a petition *for* life from its conceptual source. The situation of sacrifice for a power is the attempt to remove the malignant force inhibiting this universal human desire for health and well-being.

Those acts which can be called religious in orientation therefore involve, for the Atuot, a relationship with God, while other sacrificial rituals are best understood in reference to social origins and are as a result, moral or "this-worldly" in orientation. To employ a classic distinction, one could view these forms of sacrifice as concerned respectively with categories of "sacred" and "profane," though there is not in their language any means of easily translating these two concepts. Nevertheless, they effectively highlight the real difference between types of sacrifice. There is of course also the feastial side of sacrifices, and this is especially apparent in the situation of a marriage settlement and following the initiation of young men into adulthood, once again, situations that are domestic in origin, where moral commitments are made explicit and reinforced. A man with *ring,* such as the *gwan kwoth,* may make a sacrifice entirely on his own that is intended to affect the lives of a multitude of people who may not share any degree of kinship or economic responsibility.

There is a further kind of power in Atuot cosmology which does not partake entirely of the same quality we have outlined for other powers. This is the experience of ghosts and spirits of the dead, which are not entirely of the world of God, nor of human beings, but rather transcend these larger categories. Since their notions pertaining to the dead cannot be entirely described under the title of religion, nor are they completely related in their mode of thought to spiritual powers, they are discussed in the next chapter. Ancestral ghosts represent moral precepts of Atuot society, for they bridge the world of the long deceased with that of living descendents. Yet, since they also are considered to be closer to God in some sense, so these notions are necessarily an aspect of Atuot religion.

CHAPTER VI

# Living with the Dead

When Atuot are confronted by the variety of spiritual powers they consider to be some manifestation of God, they view the encounters as ultimately attributable to external sources. In a situation of death, each individual reflects upon an experiential reality that is *internal* in origin, namely his or her relationship with and feelings toward the recently deceased. Notions of the afterlife form an important part of the study of Atuot religion, not so much for what they reveal about man's relation to God, but toward an understanding of their sense of individuality and personal identity. Physical death is not co-terminus with psychic non-existence, since among the Atuot the "spirit," "ghost," or "soul" of a dead person remains cognatively and even physically associated with living. This chapter outlines Atuot views of the metamorphosis of a human being at death, and then describes a mortuary ceremony. The conclusion introduces comparative data on similar themes from the Nuer and Dinka ethnography (see also Burton 1978*a*, 1978*b*, 1978*c*).

Human death is normally attributed either to the workings of a malignant power or as the result of direct action by God. Death *(lia)* is defined as the absence of life or breath, a state poetically phrased as "asleep" or "intoxicated" or "behind." Socially the situation of death involves women publically more than men in an immediate sense, for they are expected to gather and mourn in piercing high wails together for a period of days. Generally, the men discuss this situation involving the ancestral dead toward redefining their roles in relation to the physical properties (e. g., cattle) of a lineal group. This point helps shed some light upon the ideas presently under consideration, for while death creates a social vacuum, the sentiments of the deceased prior to dying are considered to be in some ways real and demanding of attention and consideration as though the person was still alive. In this, death parallels the demands for individuality every Atuot man or woman expects in life: here, one's "very own wishes" must be considered somberly.

> The first reaction to death of a relative is weeping and a great deal of mournful noise by the women. All the close relatives gather as well as other people who may live further away. After they have cried and older women must calm them, and collect them together to sit under the roof of the *adwil,* by the mud windscreen where the cooking is done. The body is taken up into the *adwil* of the man who has died, and the door is closed and no one enters. After this, cooking cannot be done in the hut, nor can any fires be lit. If it is a man who died, his elder relatives take care of this, and if it is a woman or a child, then women officiate the rite.
> A man is buried on the west side of the hut about ten feet away from the building. A woman should be buried underneath the *adwil,* where the food is prepared. If a man dies in the camp, he may have told his people that he wants to be buried under the *adhang,* so he can always stay with the cattle. The grave for a woman is dug on the right side of the windscreen. An older man begins the digging by making three piles of dirt, and four if it is the grave of a woman. No small children or unmarried people should

be present. The grave is dug to the depth of a man's shoulders. The dirt from the hole should not be mixed with the soil on the surface of the ground, because the soil from the grave belongs to the dead. The arms and legs of the corpse should be broken, so when he is put into the grave it will be like before he was born. The back faces the east, and the front of the body is made to face west. Before he is put in the hole, the inside should be packed smooth, so no dirt gets on the body. Then one half of the sleeping hide he had used is placed in the bottom of the hole for him to sit on. This is the hide for the burial *(akol kuiny).* When this is done, an older woman enters the hut with another agnatic relative and they shave the hair off the body, and wash it, and then smear some oil over it. The wife and immediate family do not do anything. They just sit under the *adwil* and watch from a distance. Then the corpse is brought down and placed in the grave, and another part of the sleeping hide is placed over the ears, so no dirt will enter. The eyes must be left open, so the dead man will always be able to see after their things. The people who dug the grave then squat down on their haunches with their backs toward the hole, and each pushes in some of the dirt from the piles with his elbows, three times, and then they turn around to fill in the remainder of the grave. A man will enter the hole to jump down on it, so it will be tightly packed, so no animal can dig it up. A small hump of earth remains after the burial, and then this is covered with dark hard mud. A small goat is then brought and it is pounded over the grave until it dies, and then the dead animal is thrown off into the forest. It cannot be eaten, because it takes away the badness of death and the burial. All the beads and bracelets of the dead man are then placed in a calabash, and the point of his axe is bent to show that he has died and does not do the work of living people any longer, and so that death will not come to that house again. The spoon and gourd he had used for eating are also placed on top of the grave. Sometimes, if it was an important man, beer is poured over the small mound, and a pot is left there for him to drink.

For the next four days no one cooks or sleeps inside the house. Relatives must bring food for the family of the deceased, and they sleep outside next to fires. After four days a goat is killed over the grave, and then his beads are aspersed with water and then taken back into the hut. The inside of the *adwil* is then swept for the first time since death. All the dirt that is collected is placed inside the calabash with the beads, and then carried off by an old woman into the forest and placed on the ground next to an anthill. This is how they take the dead away from the house. Sometimes a witch will go to that spot in the forest and steal the things. Then new mud is placed on the floor of the hut, and people can begin to sleep and cook inside again. Then the old people who carried out the burial will go to the hut of the deceased and demand from the people a goat, and this has to be given. It is carried into the bush close to the hut, and they get a vine that is growing down from a tree.

Then the goat and the vine are brought into the yard, and a fire is lit on the center of the vine. The people of the dead man sit on the side by the hut, and the goat is on the other side near the bush. Green leaves are brought to put on the fire and make a lot of smoke. Then the smoke of the fire is fanned over the living to wash away the badness of death from their bodies and carry it into the forest. Then they each cross the vine three times to leave the death on the side of the forest. The goat is then killed and eaten by all except the immediate family.

The physical remains of the deceased, the flesh *(ring)*, is buried in the ground, while the life and breath go "up to God." A woman may point out that her husband is dead, "here in the ground" *(te piny wene).* What remains behind, physically in association with the place of burial and conceptually in terms of the experience of the dead by the living, is the ghost or shade *(atiep).* Atuot say the shadow walks with a man through life and only leaves him when he is buried in the ground. The word *atiep* may be derived from the verb *tei,* which means "to stay" or "to have existence." At the same time Atuot say, the dead man (not his physical being or his life) "has gone to the cattle camp of the dead people who are below. He is now inside the fence of the dead people."

There are a number of complex issues raised by such statements, for while the notion of an eternal existence is an entirely foreign idea to almost all Atuot, excepting those very few who have "converted" to Christianity, the continued existence of the dead and their interest in the living is recognized in the course of their daily affairs. An understanding of their ideas concerning death necessarily involves at least brief reference to other features of their social life, particularly the institutions of ghost marriage (*cuong:* literally, "to stand on end," "to stand on one's head") and their mode of naming people.

Approximately ten days after the initial internment a cow is brought to the gravesite, and the same collectivity is expected to regather. In the invocations over the back of the animal an elder may utter the words, "These are the bad things that should not happen in this family again." Addressing the collectivity of the previously deceased he will say, "Your son has now come to you. Receive him with this cow that is sacrificed, so he may come and join you and leave the people in health." Without this sacrificial act the ancestral ghosts would not allow the man to enter their world, forcing the ghost to remain among the living for an indefinite period, a consequence that no Atuot likes to imagine, for this portends additional misfortunes in the future. Both Evans-Pritchard and Lienhardt record that they encountered a certain amount of resistence toward the discussion of the dead, but I did not have the same experience among the Atuot. In the proper context people were indeed quite willing to discuss these matters, especially if the person was a good friend or close relative of the deceased. What they do seem to wish avoiding in conversation and especially in their dreams, is an encounter with the ghost or shade of a person who died with an angry or "bad heart." To call him to mind for no good reason is to invite many mental images of lingering jealousy or shame. It is purposeless, like singing songs of *col wic* on a heavily overcast day. The ancestral dead are considered to have a beneficial effect on their well-being, for they share strong common interests in a herd with the living descendents. One cannot be sure what may have been lingering in the heart of a man who died recently, however, so it is better to avoid such discussions altogether. The recently deceased are in this way, still "close" to the living, for they are not yet ancestors, but no longer true human beings. In a categorical or structural sense, this factor of mediality accounts for their reserved attitude toward the recently deceased.

Recognizing old age and the possibility of a natural death, a man or woman may call brothers, sisters, and children together to address them from the deathbed. This is a most solemn moment to all concerned, for life and death, otherwise radically distinguished, have temporarily come so close together. An elder man related what his father had said:

> You stay with the cattle. If you do not do this well, I will see you even while I am in the ground. Do not let the things of our land go bad. Even if I am dying now before you, you keep the black people well. You keep the powers of the family well. When it is time for the marriages, you consult me for a word. When the rains come, sacrifice a cow. When the dry season comes, sacrifice a cow.

These are the things, Atuot say, that a father wills to his family *(ken a te cien yi guor)*.

When a man dies while the rightful possessor of the use and distribution of a herd of cattle, yet without a male heir, it is a fundamental responsibility of his surviving kin to marry a wife to his ghost (i. e., to his name) as soon after the death as possible. If this should be mentioned by him in his last words to the living, the responsibility is paramount. The worst consequences of neglect are known in the form of a curse *(acien)* uttered by the dead against the living in the attempt to cause barrenness among the wives of his family or even the destruction of the herds through disease. These notions seem closely related to Atuot ideas of individuality and the right of every adult (male) to have legal offspring and a name that will be remembered through the generations. The institutions of marriage, ghost marriage, and naming offer the only means whereby a man may gain this limited sense of immortality. They have few material possessions that outlast the lifetime of single individuals (obvious exceptions being bracelets, spears, and beads), while the collective rights of ownership of a herd of cattle and land in the *toic* or a village cultivation area are inherited and passed on collectively. Therefore the legal corporate group necessarily includes the living and the dead (cf. Deng 1966).

The encounter with the "living dead" occurs most often in dreams, when the darkness of night is the opposite of life and the brightness of day. Even in a physical sense a dark night obliviates all spacial categories. There is a conceptual merging of the two worlds. Atuot say, if a dead man comes "crying to you" in a dream, it can only mean the ghost will soon bring malise to the person for having ignored him in some way. The ghost may even clearly state the consequences, if the demand goes unanswered, and name those who may suffer as a result. In the morning a goat should be sacrificed above the ground where the man was buried. Some people speak of a life after death in quite realistic terms, suggesting that a dead man has gone to live with his friends who died before, where he will plant durra and take the cows seasonally to the *toic*. Even marriages and dances are sometimes said to be performed in the abode of the dead. The preceding chapter noted a sacrifice performed to honor the name and memory of a dead chief. In later years, it is likely that the same man will be recalled as the apex of a number of smaller lineages, and the people called after him "the people of Ring". So while it is an ideal that every man's name will be remembered, in fact (and this becomes apparent in recording their genealogies), only few people are ever figured in the position as having a section of people named after him.

The ghost is imagined in some ways to be a dynamic force which is "alive," not because it has breath and life, but because, like a power, it can affect the well-being of people. *Atiep nuer,* the ghost of a man, watches daily the activities of living kinsmen. The limiting factor of this behavior is human memory, a point that Atuot implicitly recognize. A small diagram helps to illustrate this:

    Dak Angoiny (died approx. 1880)
    Deng Dak (died approx. 1900)
    Takpiny Deng (died approx. 1919)
    Ring Takpiny (died at age 45)
    Marial Ring (18 yrs. old, 1977)

Atuot explain that the ancestor called Dak Angoiny still has an active ghost. There is a "sliding scale" of the powers of ghosts which is fixed in structural time in the memory of the deceased by the living. The world of ghosts, which are individually named, merges into that of the world of the ancestral dead, designated by the single word *thuom*. There is no singular form of this word, since it only refers to the collectivity of dead. This underscores Atuot conceptions of time in relation to the dead. After eight or ten generations, all people who are related patrilineally to Dak, and who have died, could be called *thuom* of the family of Dak, not ghosts of Dak.

The curse of the dead is not differentiated from that of any living relative. However, like the power of a *jok* it is only thought to be effective against a kinsman of some degree of affective relationship. The curse of a father is the worst sort. A man may say he was cursed by his father to live a long life, though all his children and his wives would die. Similarly a man may lay the blame for the death of a number of his cattle to the curse of his father, whether living or dead. There is here a "materialist" paradox, for one might expect a man would not curse the cattle of his son, since they are in fact also his.

These notions and sentiments draw into further relief the intense feelings of individuality which is so characteristic of Atuot ethics. The curse *(acien)* is one such means of self-assertion. The curse of a maternal uncle *(yueo nere)* is different, for in their daily lives the relation between a son and his mother's brother are characterized by the highest degree of respect and formality. A father may be an authoritarian figure, but the mother's brother is more often said to be a friend and a potential source of economic aid. His curse may cause a man to become senseless and unable to care for his concerns properly. However, it would be unlikely for an individual to be visited by the ghost of any maternal relative. That is, the ghostly curse is in one way an extension of the economic ideals which unite the family of one man. Another text illustrates this well.

> When a person is dead, he looks at us, as we are staying here, with you, Mayen. We are now relatives, because you stay here in our home, and we have come to know one another. If a man dies and he has children, you have the family and the household of your father. When the night comes, the ghost walks among his relatives and sees, where his children are, though you cannot see him. You come with Decau as one. The ones who died long ago walk as one group. If there is something that has gone wrong with the cattle, the dream will come and say, "You Mayen, you tell the people of my *gol* and slap them in their sleep, and tell them it is the dream talking." It is I, so and so. This has gone wrong, and then this must be done to correct it. The ghost comes exactly as a person, in the same shape. The ghost comes right in front of you and sits with the dream. It does not die. The life of a man does not die. The blood is like water that soaks into the ground and becomes mud.

To the best of my knowledge, when a man has died a natural death, rather than having died from a spear wound in which he bled to death, the blood is left within the body when it is buried. There is no written source making reference to this point for the Nilotic speaking peoples, for it is an obscure issue. When considered in relation to their ideas pertaining to the effects of the dead upon the living, it seems consistent with other notions in their cosmology. The blood is life, along with breath. Since the breath is said to return to God, it would follow necessarily that the blood, or another metaphor of life, remains in the corpse. If this were indeed the case, it would add further to our understanding of how a ghost can be said to be alive, for in itself it is nothing but an epiphenomenon. No one ever suggested, however, that the ghost of a man was alive because of his blood. It is a question I failed to ask, yet deductively it seems related to another practice that occurs in the context of the burial ceremony.

In by far the majority of sacrifices the victim is killed by severing the throat with a spear, thereby letting the blood flow into the earth to appease a power said to be located there. When a man of recognized social influence dies, his ox should be brought to the gravesite and sacrificed over it, an act called *rim thek,* "spearing the ox," which is different from *dhol amel,* for example, "cutting the throat of a sheep." When an ox is killed in this manner, it is speared in the heart, and the blood only slowly seeps from the carcass into the grave, perhaps symbolically conjoining the life of the dead man with his ox. Following this act Atuot say, the blood of the ox will travel day and night to seek out the cause of the man's death. In a like manner, the ghost "walks among the living" looking for things which may have gone wrong. The ox is said to fall in the direction from which the badness that caused death originated. If after being speared in the heart the animal collapses on the grave, this indicates that the deceased is angry with the living family of his own *gol*. The "heart" of the animal is singled out for spearing, just as it is said to be the heart of a person that determines relationships with people, both while living and when dead.

> When a man dies, cows are sacrificed for him. He goes down and becomes one of the people of the ground. People who stay up remain. When a cow is sacrificed on his head, it is not because we want him to come back. It is so we can have lives so I will be protected in my life by the *thuom* of my ancestors. The cows are sacrificed on his head to walk with *thuom*. The bones remain in the hole he was put in, and he lives down there. His ghost walks after the power that killed him. All of the dead are like people here. They see us living. If *thuom* send a *jok,* because they are angry, there is no way a man can live, even if sacrifices are made for his life. *Cuong* is made for the dead by the ones who have remained up, so they will hear his name tomorrow. The ghost can kill cows because his heart is bad. It kills the children of a person remaining up, and the *gol* is destroyed. The ghost says, "You have remained with my things and you have not married a wife for me." The ghost should have a wife who is alive to cook and give birth to children, and then *thuom* will be happy. It is stronger with the *gwan riang,* because he dies with his power. If he is angry when he dies, all the people will suffer, but if he dies with a good heart, all the things will come well to his children. *Ring* is the head. It kills people or makes life, and this is there, whether he is dead or alive.

Before continuing it is appropriate to consider the various meanings of words which have a non-material referent in the Atuot language. The human being is composed of flesh *(ring),* which at death is buried in the ground, and life, which is blown into a human being at birth and returns to God at death. What Atuot call *jok* cannot be seen by ordinary people, but can speak to and appear before a man who has power over it. Unlike the collective noun *thuom* the word for an individual ghost does have a plural form *(atip),* so that one can speak of the "ghosts of the dead," which come to people in dreams and confront the individual with an image of the formerly living person, as he appeared in life. Thus, ghosts can also be seen and have the ability to speak to people in the manner of powers. *Thuom* refers to a category of "forgotten memories," for there is never a confrontation with the collective dead in dreams. There is no physical representation of the collective dead and no immediate way in which they communicate directly with the living. By this reasoning an appropriate translation of each of these different non-material phenomena may be attempted. *Jok* is best translated as power, for it is considered to be an active agent. *Atiep* is satisfactorily translated as ghost, for it is in his confrontation with a ghost, that a man is haunted and reminded of his responsibilities to persons he no longer has a social relationship with. *Thuom* therefore implies the collectivity of dead beyond living memory, and I think the phrase "ancestral spirits" adequately describes Atuot ideas about the character and qualities of the long deceased. The category of ghostly images therefore transcends the other categories of experience, for it connotes neither a physical being entirely nor only a social personality. Ghosthood is rather a medial category, which bridges the gap between the memory of the recently deceased and the ancestral spirits, a nameless collectivity, that occupies the dusty archives of an agnatic group.

In order to fully appreciate these formal features of Atuot concepts relating to the dead, it will be worthwhile to consider the evidence of a burial ceremony *(kuoiny nuer)*. The events discussed here were recorded in the context of the interment of the wife of a prominent chief, and therefore cannot be seen as absolutely typical to this situation, though since neither Evans-Pritchard nor Lienhardt seem to have been present for a similar ceremony in Nuer or Dinkaland, what I record here briefly is of ethnographic value.

I learned of the death from a friend who had come from the homestead, where the grave was being dug. Since a woman had died, the soil brought to the surface was placed in four piles, two toward the western end and two toward the eastern ends of the pit. When the body had been lowered into the grave and the remaining earth beaten down as much as possible, an ox was brought and tethered near the side facing the west. After a short invocation, with one thrust of the spear, the dead woman's brother pierced the flesh of the animal and struck the heart. It fell dead immediately. This was the "cow" to take away the badness of death, and its flesh was prohibited from immediate kinsmen of the deceased and prepared as food for the many guests that had gathered. Before the carcass was butchered, however, it was left for nearly an hour lying on top of the grave. On the other side of the hut meanwhile two other cattle had been slaughtered for food, and women were preparing large quantities of beer. Temporary shelters were erected, and over the next four days the wailing cries of women became less frequent, and the general atmosphere turned into one of festivity.

On the morning of the fourth day after the interment a black chicken was taken to the graveside by a senior kinsman, and an invocation was made. The chicken was then beaten to death over the remaining mound of earth and thrown immediately into the bush. This was done in order to cleanse the living relatives of the badness associated with the death and to carry this away from the homestead and the family.

The woman had been married from a family of the Ceic Dinka, and members of the lineage had come to represent themselves among the greater collectivity of Atuot. The paternal relatives did not participate when the family from Ceic brought another cow, made invocations, and sacrificed the animal. Early the next morning, the fifth day after the burial, we went to the homestead of the wife's husband's brother. Dominating the center of the homestead was a large forked-branch shrine for the power owned by that family named *makao*. Nearby were the remains of the cement slab laid over the grave of Mabor Deng, the first chief recognized by the British when they entered Atuotland. A goat stood tethered by the shrine and had just been brought out of the hut before we arrived. It was a cool clear morning, and most of the family and relatives stood huddled around a small brush fire warming themselves. The senior living representative of the family, a man called Tuiny, sat close to the goat on his ambatch headrest, and by his feet sat a small calabash filled with pounded durra flour. The invocation began in the familiar manner, with Tuiny rubbing the flour on the back of the goat after every short phrase he spoke. Next, it was untethered and led around the hut three times and then retethered. When the invocation began again, the goat urinated, and some of this was collected by Tuiny and scattered over the heads of those sitting. When an animal urinates while an invocation is in progress, it is interpreted to indicate that God has heard the words well and will accept the sacrifice.

The goat was then held against the ground on its back, while its throat was cut. The spear that had been used to sever the throat was next passed around to all collected there, in order that they would lick some of the blood of the sacrifice. The corpse was left to lie at its tethering stake. A black chicken was next killed by cutting its head off, and its body laid down beside the goat carcass. After a short while, when people began to discuss things in whispers and relit their pipes, a white ram was led out of the same hut. It was led around the hut, invoked over, and cut at the throat near the shrine. While there were about thirty people collected, no one sat near the western edge of the shrine. A short dance began, and they began to sing a number of fight songs *(yaai)* of Luac Atuot, whose dominant themes praise their fighting abilities and name the many ancestors who had killed enemies of the Atuot. These songs recall for the living a sense of their own achievements of the past, an optimistic activity in such saddening circumstances. They are resigned to death, but happy with life.

When reseated, a calm stillness was evident, which seemed to me peculiar for sacrifices in general. People were quiet, I was told, so that the power *makao* could walk in secret to find what had caused the death. After a short while a calabash filled with water was brought out from the hut, and Tuiny went around to each of the older women, washing their faces and making them stop crying. Immediately following this he picked up small bits of mud, that had been soaked with the urine of the goat, and dabbed it across the foreheads of the senior family members. Washing was intended to cleanse them of the death. The symbolism of the act is less explicit, but I suggest smearing them with the mud identified them with the intent of the sacrifice, as was the case when they each licked the blade of the spear. Perhaps it also recalls in Atuot religion the notion, when a man dies, "he returns once again to mud." Rather than repeating the rite of washing the faces of all the other men who were present, it was agreed that if the face of the sheep was washed instead, it could represent their own cleansing. To summarize, the goat was killed as a petition to the family power *makao,* both to guide the lives of the living and seek out the cause of the death. The life of the sheep was said to have been given to *ring,* so there would be no more deaths in the family. The chicken was beaten over the ground to disassociate the living from the dead.

Therefore, while there is a conceptual distinction between "powers" in a general sense and the attributes of ghosthood, both are alike as non-material phenomena and in sharing the ability to affect the welfare of human beings. In addition, both are notions which pertain to a relatively well defined group of kinsmen. A power can only be manipulated to affect a relative, and ghostly visitation is only considered serious enough to take action, when it is experienced by a close relative of the deceased. Further, both also single out individuals, either through sickness, as in the case of powers, or in the form of a curse from the ghost of a dead man.

Further action is sought in relation to a power, which caused the death. The elder representative of the lineage, who officiated these series of rites, later told me,

> The wife had been married from the Ceic, and we of *cieng* Angoiny of Luac have taken
> their women as wives before. There is concern on the side of Luac about these marriages.
> We have always made good our cattle exchanges, but then this woman, like many
> before her, dies after she has given us only three or four children. Those of the Ceic
> say, this is not a problem of theirs. Instead they say, it is a hatred within Luac from
> long ago over the chiefship, when teh British first came.

These comments shed further light on the way in which Atuot conceive of both the progression of time and the relations between living and dead. Even though the dead woman was too young to have ever known the persons involved in an old feud over chiefship, the cause of death is seen to be related to the "bad things in people's hearts" from long ago. He continued,

> When the Ceic killed an ox at the site of the grave, they said to it, "You take this death away. You go down and tell *thuom* and the ghosts, I am killed and have taken away all the death of the people. If the cause of the death is with us, let it not happen again." Ceic have said to us, you are fighting among yourselves. So they also brought a ram to kill, to show their good intentions. The Ceic are trying to make their hearts clear. But we cannot continue to marry their women, if they die like this. At a time like this everyone should clear their hearts to the people, so people can stay without suspicion. They are saying that without my maternal grandmother the chiefship would not have remained with Luac, and there is truth to this. This is why our maternal uncles [the text reads *cieng nere* "the land or people related through the maternal uncle"] suspect the reasons for these deaths are among the Luac themselves.

The particular details of this disagreement are more properly addressed in a discussion of traditional Atuot politics, while mention had been made of the problem in order to illustrate what Atuot consider to be the concerns which are put into relief in the situation of death. In the act of licking the bloodied spear, people not only identify with the intent of the sacrifice, but also offer an oath, that none of those involved in the rite are in way responsible for the death.

Six days after the interment a final sacrifice was made by the paternal relatives of the deceased. The leading invocation, spoken by her elder paternal uncle over the back of the ox, included the following statements:

> Our family has been broken down. The death has now started with the younger people. It will break the family completely. If it is *Decau* who has taken her life, then this is a good thing, and the ghost will be pleased, and the people will live untroubled by an old hatred. If she is killed by another human being, you Mamer [the ox], you see to it properly. Let him die also with the wife of my brother's daughter . . . this bad thing . . . what has gone wrong. We have built new huts and sacrificed cows, and yet this death comes. Even if someone thinks, he will kill us all, still, our chiefship will never be taken away. You, Kulang [the husband of the deceased], do not give it up. God, you take this cow. Our heads spin around.

The ox then urinated and was slaughtered. The distribution of the flesh of the ox was made according to the degree of relationship to both the wife and the husband's affines and agnates. In addition to a number of representatives from different clans of Luac, men and women from the Jilek and Akot sections were present. In the initial sacrifices made after the burial the flesh of the slaughtered animals is prohibited to the immediate family of the deceased, and its distribution is haphazard. In this, the closing sacrifice of the rites, particular portions of the beast are reserved for the consumption by the same group of people who were previously excluded. Symbolically we can argue that this is done to represent the unity of the sacrificial community which must persist in spite of the death of one of its members. Significantly, the male idiom is used to represent those people who form an economic and kinship group through their common interests in a herd, for *genitals* of the ox were given to the eldest members of *cieng* Dak, the senior and dominant clan of the Luac. Dak is considered to be a son of the first wife of the culture hero Cuonga. The people of this section of Luac can explain that it was Dak who "bore them all with his penis."

While the situation of sacrifice at death is a context in which a lineal group is collected, and where their own unity is emphasized, the memory of the deceased must not be merged into the larger corporate group, and it is for this reason Atuot explain their practice of leviratic and ghost marriages. These are briefly mentioned for their comparative value to similar practices of the Nuer and the Dinka, which are addressed momentarily.

Ghost marriage *(cuong)* refers both to the act of marrying a woman to the name of a man who died without issue as well as to the form of marriage where an elder widow takes a younger woman to be her wife in her own name. It is a common form of marriage and was probably practiced with greater frequency in the past, when a proportionately larger number of people met death violently (see also Evans-Pritchard 1945). Presently a lower age of first marriage for males and the participation of Atuot in the cattle trade of the Southern Sudan also affect its decreasing frequency (see Burton 1978*b*).

In the ghost marriage the formalities which typify a normal marital union are carried out, including the exchange of bridewealth between the representatives of the deceased and the bride's kinsmen. The same prohibitions regarding incest and marriage are applied to the potential spouse of a ghost. The levirate (*wa γot,* literally, "going into the hut") does not involve the exchange of cattle, for a brother or some other paternal kin simply bears children with the wife of his dead brother, in the name of the deceased. Atuot speak of this form of child rearing as "comforting" or "washing away the sorrows" associated with the death. Another way in which they assure progeny for a dead or sterile man is the institution called *amuom* (literally, "the nameless or unborn son"). If performed for a man named Mayen, his wife will be known among his living kinsmen as *cek amuom* Mayen, "the wife of the unborn son of Mayen." This is similar to ghost marriage, for it too involves the exchange of bridewealth. If a man is sterile or becomes sterile at some point after he has married two wives, the elder son of the first wife may be instructed to sleep with his stepmother "to raise seed in his father's name," and becomes therefore the father of his own brother or sister, by entering the hut of the wife of the father *(wa γot cio guar).* The maternal uncle may ask the same of his nephew, as may the paternal uncle. An additional variation of the same practice is called *γot cio degualen,* "entering the hut of the son of the paternal uncle." None of the latter forms of cohabitation are considered incestuous, though I was told that, before a son was to sleep with his father's second wife, he may want to demand that a sheep be sacrificed in order to quell the emotional trepidation he may feel about performing the act. An infrequently enacted form of soratic marriage is also practiced, called *guel γot* ("replacing the hut"). Women profess to despise the practice. If a woman dies without having born a sufficient number of children, after the bridewealth has been exchanged, the paternal relatives of the husband may demand that the sister of the dead woman "comes into the hut" to replace her. The children she bears in the union will be known among her natal kin as the children of the first wife. Only the last child she bears will be known by her name, "to pay for her work." Other forms of cohabitation and marriage are to be noted for the Atuot, but their inclusion in this context would detract from the present concern with ghosthood and individual identity (see Burton 1980*d*).

The material recorded here for the Atuot may now be compared with similar data from the Nuer and the Dinka. The discussion will not only examine the way in which a man gains his place in the lineal archives, but will also point toward other parameters of the cultural and social similarities and differences between these three pastoral Nilotic societies. We may recall that Fortes (1959, 1965) has claimed, Tale social structure *demands* a form of ancestor veneration, and with a similar concern with the supposed functional attributes of religious ideology Gluckman (1937: 133) suggested that ancestor cults provide "a means of maintaining kinship groups." Yet among the three societies under consideration, which to a greater or lesser degree all conceive of social relations in terms of patrilineal descent groups, no such cult is practiced. One of the more fundamental differences between Atuot/Nuer and Dinka religion lies in the individual orientation of sin and sacrifice among the former peoples and the affirmation of collective sentiments which typifies much of Dinka religious ritual (see Douglas 1970: 126).

Evans-Pritchard (1956) suggests that there is no single Nuer word that can easily be translated as "soul" or "ghost." Nuer say that at death a person "disintegrates into his three component parts, *ring,* flesh, *yei,* life or breath, and *tie,* intellect or soul" (*ibid.:* 144). Like the Atuot, Nuer suggest that life is given to them at birth by God and returns to him at death (Evans-Pritchard 1949b: 57; 1956: 154). All death is ultimately accountable to the intention of God (Evans-Pritchard 1935: 74). The physical remains of the deceased ought to be buried to the left of a man's hut, and in eastern Nuerland the corpse should be placed in the ground facing west, the direction from which their ancestors originated. Dinka say that the body should be placed either under the floor of a cattle byre or somewhere nearby it outside (Lienhardt 1961: 263), though, as is the case among the Atuot and the Nuer, its head should be facing west in the grave (see also Stigand 1923: 18; Huffman 1931a: 9; Kiggen 1948: 52; Evans-Pritchard 1934: 33).

As a result of the polluting and potentially dangerous character of the corpse it should be buried as soon as possible after death. As indicated for the Atuot, the worlds of the dead and the living are conceptually conjoined at this time (cf. also Huffman 1931b: 52; Deng 1973: 56). The Nuer idea that if a man is left unburied his ghost will seek immediate vengeance against the living, is paralleled in Atuot and Dinka experience (see Lienhardt 1961: 290). Among all three groups there is a further association between the dead and the antisocial practices of witches and ghouls (see Lienhardt 1961; Fergusson 1921; Howell and Lewis 1947; Howell 1953a; Stubbs 1934). Nuer are said to conceive of the living as having a debt to the deceased, an idea made evident in the phrase used to describe the mortuary ceremony, which implies paying the debt through sacrifice, and as a result, severance of the relations between the temporarily conjoined worlds. Like the Atuot, Nuer consider that the recently deceased carry with them into the grave the same feelings toward their living kinsmen that they held in life. Normally a number of months elapse between the burial and the mortuary ceremony, and Nuer consider this to be the time in which the power of the recently deceased is especially prone to seek vengeance *(cien)* against the surviving kinsmen (see Evans-Pritchard 1945: 17). The cautious or guarded hostility of their feelings toward the recently deceased suggest for both Atuot and Nuer a sentiment of negative reciprocity between the ghosts and human beings. For the Nuer ghostly vengeance is imagined to be manifest in the form of sickness or some other misfortune that may ultimately result in death (Evans-Pritchard 1949b). The ghost *(jok)* of the recently deceased is imbued with the ability to fetch a living kinsman for his neglect and will come to the man saying *ban wa jok,* "let us go behing to the ghosts" (Evans-Pritchard 1956: 174).

The wronged ghost does not exact vengeance by his own action so much as by making his cause known to God. The same principle is evident in Atuot ideas about earthly powers. The potential to impart revenge is mitigated against by God, if sufficient cause is not apparent. This has a moral rather than strictly religious overtone. Among the Nuer a mortuary ceremony is not performed for a person who has "become" *col wic*. Evans-Pritchard (1949*a*; 1956: 56) writes,

> The difference between an ordinary mortuary ceremony and a ceremony to commemorate a *col wic* would appear to be that whereas in both, one purpose of sacrifice is to cleanse the living, another purpose in an ordinary mortuary ceremony, to send the soul of the dead to the ghosts, is lacking in the commemoration ceremony for *col wic* . . . this ceremony is performed not only to cleanse the living and to commemorate the dead but also to fix his soul firmly in the above so that there will be no return to the living, just as an ordinary mortuary ceremony fixes the soul in the underworld of ghosts.

Nebel (1954: 450) similarly notes for the Dinka, that mourning is not allowed for a person who is struck by lightning. Likewise in the case of twins, a woman is not married to the name of a dead twin, since at death a twin becomes a bird and could not therefore marry a human being (see also Evans-Pritchard 1936). In these somewhat anomalous situations, the deceased partake immediately of the spiritual world without passing first through the mediating status of ghosthood, which is the more common disposition.

A mortuary ceremony is performed by all three peoples from four to six months after the initial interment (see Evans-Pritchard 1951, 1956; Lienhardt 1961: 209; Deng 1973: 56), and at this time the ghost of the deceased is addressed and petitioned to leave the living in peace. While the sacrifices in each case are said to be for the honor of the dead person, they are necessarily directed toward God as well, who oversees these affairs. I have tried to indicate the way in which, for the Atuot, ghosts can be defined by negative qualities, for these are the features by which they are experienced. The ghost of a recently deceased person is associated only with vengeance, sickness, or death, and their demands on the living are strongest soon after death. Precisely during this period the social disorder, which accompanies the situation of death, is greatest. Further, both Atuot and Nuer associate vengeance *only* with the memory of ghost of the *recently* deceased, while ancestral spirits are rather more sources of moral values of a positive nature (cf. Evans-Pritchard 1940*a*: 236; 1951: 66, 68, 125; 1956: 175). I suggest then, that through the progression of what we can call historical time and what is for the Atuot and the Nuer perceived in a structural continuum (see Evans-Pritchard 1939), the memory of the recently deceased merges closer into association with the ancestral dead, and is thus also "closer" to the spiritual and divine nature of God (see also Seligman n. d.; Ogod 1961: 127–128). Buxton describes a similar notion for the Mandari (1973: 151, 155):

> Three generations after death, a deceased person is merged in the ancestral collectivity, and the dropping out of the long dead reflects the actual memory in relation to passing time . . . It is rare for |ghostly vengeance| to be the case after more than three generations have followed on from the death . . . ghostly visitation is not used in reference to long dead ancestors.

That these factors are related to other principles of social organization is clear, but they cannot be explained only by reference to such strictures. There is an additional psychological aspect that should be investigated. This would be at least in part related to the images of the world of the dead, for since they are occasionally said to live in the fashion of earthly human beings, so ghosts necessarily have human characteristics. This is not so in regard to "powers."

Evans-Pritchard explained Nuer notions of ghosts in reference to an outline of Old Testament theology. If a man's "soul" or "life" ascends to God at death, there does not seem to be in Nuer or Atuot cosmology any dogma which positively locates the dwelling place of ghosts. According to Evans-Pritchard the distinction he makes between "soul" and "ghost" "would seem to allow both for the idea of the dead leading some sort of existence in the Nuer sheol as shadowy replicas of the living and also at the same time for the idea that their souls are taken on high by God" (1956: 160). This directly contradicts a different statement, that "Nuer do not think of the ghosts as spectres" (1949a: 292). One of the obvious difficulties implicit here is that of translation. I know of no word in Atuot that could be translated as "sheol" or "spectre," and I am skeptical that the Nuer language would differ that markedly from Atuot in this regard. I think therefore that it can be said with some certainty, that neither Atuot nor Nuer cosmology embraces ideas about a life after death other than those which relate to the responsibilities to perform ghost marriages, and these in turn are restricted by social principles as well as human sentiments. The afterworld is thus the moral collectivity of long dead ancestors, while ghosts do not dwell permanently anywhere, but are merely the reflections of an experiencing self upon dead kin, with whom one had an economic relationship. Additional evidence for this assertion comes from that fact, that neither Atuot nor Nuer erect any long standing physical reminders of the dead. In the course of time, burial sites merge into the general landscape, but since their ancestors are buried in the land they live upon and cultivate, there is a more general and overarching moral association with particular cattle camps or village areas. A man gains social and moral immortality through the memory of his "very own name," and in this we can see that notions of the afterlife deal more directly with the experiential world of human beings living in society rather than with the religious associations of God. We could understand Atuot religion without making reference to their ecology or political organization, but we would learn rather little about their notions of ghosts, unless these ideas were seen in light of the social context in which they are expressed. Their herds of cattle, inherited from and raised by long dead ancestors may be seen as their wondering shrines of the dead. For both the Atuot and the Nuer one feature of ghosthood may be understood as a transitional and ambiguous medium, through which a dead person becomes an ancestor, while the institution of ghost marriage and other forms of cohabitation offer a means whereby the living recall the dead.

Though generally similar in outline, Dinka notions pertaining to death and the afterlife are subtly different from those of the Nuer and the Atuot. As Lienhardt (1970) indicates in his consideration of death among the Anuak, ecological, political, and historical divergences must be recognized at the outset, when comparing these with other Nilotic ideas (see also Lienhardt 1958; Evans-Pritchard 1940a: 275–276; Stubbs and Morrison 1938). The developed priestly-political office of the Dinka master-of-the-fishing-spear *(beny biith)* is qualitatively different from other statuses of authority among the Atuot and the Nuer. This point is immediately apparent in the religious sphere. Lienhardt (1961: 219) writes,

> It is rare to see a Dinka pray individually . . . much the greater part of their religious practice is collective and formal. I have heard Dinka remark upon their difference, in this respect, from the neighboring Nuer, whose frequent individual prayer seems to be consistent with their less developed priesthood.

The principles of agnation and residence offer a further contrast. While among the Atuot prominent "mouthpieces" for the people are called *tuot wuic*, "bulls of the camp" (among the Nuer, *twot wec*), among the Dinka a nuclear group of a tribe or sub-tribe may be referred to as *naar wut*, "maternal uncles of the camp" (Lienhardt *ibid.*). There is among the Dinka a correspondingly less rigid patrilineal bias.

> . . . the Dinka think in terms of the association of lineages, linked to each other in various ways, while for the Nuer a single agnatic principle is enough to explain all significant political identification of a lineage with a territorial segment . . . It is found moreover, in the way Dinka see the historical formation of their political groups, not as the grafting of strangers on to a single or original descent group, but as the division of their land between a number of equivalent groups which have spread out and displaced each other on the ground (Lienhardt 1958: 128).

Atuot generally know a great deal more of the historical traditions of individualized descent groups than of their wider migrations. Lienhardt (1961: 119) notes for the Dinka, "the pre-eminence of clans of spear-masters, and their hereditary priesthood, is established by the myths which the Dinka recount in some detail, and with much interest" (see also Deng 1972; 1973: 58–65).

While differing slightly in individual experience, the Dinka too conceive of the composition of a human being in terms of three principles. Life and breath are indicated by the term *wei.* At death, the ghost *(atiep)* is distinguished cognatively from the physical corpse that is buried. The term *atiep* can have as its referent both the ghost of a dead person and a power of divinity. For example, "A man whose source of possession is not known may equally be said to have an *atiep* in him, as to have Divinity of Creator in him" (Lienhardt 1961: 155). Lienhardt suggests that for the Dinka the *atiep* remains in the minds of the living when remembering the dead, an experience of the person that is identical to that of the person when alive. Seligman (1932: 17) noted, "While *atiep* are at their strongest immediately after death, and in a few generations may safely be forgotten, *jok* retain their strength."

The separation of the living from the dead emphasized in Atuot and Nuer mortuary rituals is equally apparent among the Dinka, though subtle differences are seen, for the severance of relations seems less pronounced. Ghostly visitations are in Lienhardt's words "encounters within the self," and while ghosts normally are omens of evil, "it is not dangerous for the living deliberately to call their dead to mind" (Seligman 1932: 153). Whereas peoples from all three societies erect minor shrines for domestically located powers or divinities, among the Dinka, shrines dedicated to "free divinities" (what I call for the Atuot "powers of the sky") and elaborate mud shrines found in the homesteads of masters-of-the-fishing-spear are unparalleled in either Nuer or Atuot religious experience (see Lienhardt 1961: 259–265). Spear-master clans legitimately represent political and religious influence, and are sometimes said to possess the only original divinities. The strongest similarities with the Dinka data for the Atuot appear in reference to the huts built as shrines for the power of rain, though there is no single myth, as there is for the Dinka, that unites all the people in possession of this power as descendents of an original possessor of rain, or of the power *ring.*

Ghost marriage (*koic,* Howell 1951: 283; Deng 1971: 140; Mayall 1924: 200) is practiced among the Dinka although it is entirely unclear if it accounts for as many marriages as among the Nuer or Atuot. Significantly, in a manner *most* unlike the Atuot and the Nuer, Dinka do not express an aversion to taking the name from one's deceased father, for his presence among the living is thus explicitly acknowledged (Lienhardt 1961: 149). This fact has a direct relevance to the query raised by Evans-Pritchard (1948: 167; 1956: 164) concerning the Nuer practice of naming. The over-emphasis on the necessity of taking a name different from one's father among the Atuot and the Nuer is consistent with the greater frequency of ghost marriage and the resulting or concordant beliefs pertaining to the individuality of the deceased. It may also be related to the absence of a more centralized political institution among the Atuot, who mock the Dinka for paying submission to chiefs-of-the-fishing-spear. In the same vein, it would therefore seem as though the Dinka custom would allow for a greater occurrence of the levirate, a point consistent once again with the continuity of naming (cf. also Buxton 1958; Howell 1953*b*: 104). Lienhardt (1961: 319) concludes his discussion of the mode of burial for a spear-master with the following lucid analysis:

> Notions of individual immortality mean little to non-Christian Dinka, but the assertion of collective immortality means much, and it is this which they make in funeral ceremonies of their religious leaders (see also Bedri 1939; Titherington 1925).

In his possession of the divinity flesh *(ring)* the Dinka spear-master is imbued with an overabundance of the life principle, so that the lives of ordinary Dinka are sustained by the spiritual transcendence of the physical and social world by these priestly-political figures. The Atuot *gwan riang* functions within a less developed or centralized role, and no one ever suggested to me that a sense of immortality was intended to be expressed for the collective well-being of people by the suffocation of them in the past. Symbolically the rite may have this component, but certainly not in the sense that Lienhardt observes for the Dinka. In a gross sense demographic features of Atuot and Nuer societies are inconsistent with such a priesthood, while the Dinka model is evidenced in an even more ritualized and centralized form among the more densely settled Shilluk, through the institution of the *reth* or "divine king."

Atuot ideas of collective immortality are expressed in the notion of *thuom* rather than an association with any political or priestly office. Individual immortality is in effect an ideal that can be realized only retrospectively by living kinsmen of the deceased in relation to the benevolence of God, who may have granted a human being "life" and the ability to satisfy what are considered to be the most sought after goals, namely, a large family and many healthy cattle. Since they do not imagine these goals await them already satisfied in some heavenly netherworld, Atuot religion does not evidence a notion of the redemption of souls. Immortality is temporally limited by the memory of living descendents. The chances of achieving either of the goals are in large measure predetermined by what is inherited in the situation of death from father and forefathers. Collective immortality is evidenced in physical form by the herds of a corporate group of kin who share collectively the rights of use in the cattle, and Atuot are quite conscious of this. As I sat underneath a shelter in a cattle camp, my friend Abielthok asked who would read what I was writing. I explained that anyone who wanted could read it, but the purpose of writing words down on paper was to make the information known to future generations who would live long after my own death. He told me then, that "this is the same with our ropes. Every cow has its own rope, and each rope is our writing. The writing of our ancestors are these cows in the camp."

While I have made no direct reference to such identification, for it has been made explicit elsewhere (e. g., Evans-Pritchard 1956), the strongest sense of a man's personal identity is in relation to his ox. Though a junior man has no immediate control over the cattle he herds, the ox from which he takes his name and his sense of personal identity is his *very* own.

Ancestors are most often recalled in song by their ox names *(rin theo),* and a most common feature of these songs is reference to paternal ancestors, who likewise composed similar songs, in which the experience of the singer and his ox are conjoined. A respectful means of keeping his memory alive is for a son to sing his father's along with his own ox song. In an obvious sense then, when a man composes an ox song *(ket tuar),* he is recording oral traditions. The social and cultural importance of song in Atuot society would be difficult to overemphasize, and every single man who stays with cattle has his very own songs. One is cited here for its relevance to the issues under discussion.

> The heart of our age-set is suffering
> But my eyes do not fear the arrows
> Abilduk [ox name of the singer's paternal grandfather] is walking with a fire in his heart
> The sons of Jiluoth [a section of Kuek] are roping the pasture in Panther
> I burn people with the fire, as though driving them like goats into a hut
> My Anguak [a bull] of the camp of Ithoiny
> My Maduol [a bull] of the camp of Gol
> I listened to the sound of my bull
> The animal I bought from Lieng
> I went and bought my bull from Akot
> [his sister was married into this section and the bull was received as part of the bridewealth]
> The camp where the people of words settled
> The people of a small section cannot speak big words
> We left the animal
> We left with Mabor [a bull] and the *ring* of my fathers
> Without the cows of his father
> A person will remain always unknown
> The cow of my grandfather Abilduk
> This is the cow that does not die
> [i. e., his grandfather and his progeny are recalled and praised. In saying that the cow does not die, he intends it to be understood that what is referred to is the family who herds the cattle]
> Ajuot, words are said that I do not understand
> Is it because of the cows that I am hated?
> Is it the curse of people?
> Or is it my way of doing things?
> Oh, the bull of my grandfathers
> I will not desert the camp

When a man dies and his ox is killed over his grave, the physical manifestations of his individual identity are destroyed, while his spiritual or moral identity will remain in the memory of the living. Thus it can be seen that an understanding of Atuot notions pertaining to death and the afterlife must be sought in the social context, for they are only peripherally revealed in Atuot cosmology.

In concluding this chapter it might be mentioned, that these ideas may be open to significant changes. In the contemporary Sudan the Atuot have the opportunity to increase herd sizes dramatically by participating in the cattle trade. The money earned is reinvested in what they consider to be high quality stock, and while a younger man still has no direct control over the cattle he may buy in this manner, he has a stronger voice in arranging his first marriage, probably at a younger age than would have been possible in the past. One can readily appreciate that, if a man had four sons long ago, the likelihood that the youngest son would marry while still alive is slim, unless the family was extremely wealthy in cattle. Modern influences of the cash economy may in time be reflected in Atuot social and cultural forms by a decreasing age of marriage with a corresponding decline in the frequency of ghost marriage.

# CHAPTER VII

# God's Ants: Religion and Social Values

This concluding chapter summarizes the central concerns and intentions of Atuot religion to the extent possible through the interpretation of ritual and oral statement. This is a far more difficult task than simple description, for the data are ideas, not observable facts. Enough has been said in the course of presentation about general notions to allow us here to discuss a more limited number of problems. Atuot are not prone to reflect on their religion, except perhaps as they are involved as individuals in the situation of sacrifice. They rather accept as a result of socialization, what has been passed on by ancestors as their own distinctive culture.

If one were to ask Atuot "what are the things of politics," they would first discuss *ruac reth ghok,* "the words of the spokesman of cattle." The topic of marriage introduces conversation about the exchange of the rights of ownership over cows, women, and children. Relationships of descent and affinity can often be phrased in relation to the responsibilities of individuals to contribute to or receive bridewealth. In both their language and mode of thought religion is defined as *ruac* Decau, "the words and deeds of the Creator." As we have seen in the discussion of sacrifice, cattle also figure in their lives in religious situations as intermediaries for establishing communication with the supreme being. In the ideational and experiential sense Atuot religion refers to the human response to the "things of God." Politics and marriage are relationships involving people, "things" that people do. For the Atuot, religious expressions are their response to that which God has done. In a most crude sense, powers relate to social and moral experience, while the passive acceptance of the ways of God is a religious expression.

Atuot assert people are blind and ignorant when compared with the knowledge and omnipotence of God. In the course of their daily life Atuot are demanding of others, self-assertive and calculating in pursuit of their perceived interests and desires. In their response to God, seen collectively in the situation of sacrifice, they are resigned to and passively accept realities for which they imagine there is no means of assertive action. They act instead in accord with what they think God demands of them, and ask in the course of sacrifice that people might remain with their lives, in exchange for the life of an animal. We do not have to ask if they *believe* in the efficacy of these acts, but understand their intention.

Atuot religion has no credenda nor liturgy, and I believe this is related in part to a similar absence of priestly or other types of specialists. Practitioners are just as often participants. This in turn accords well with Atuot ethics, for in their society every person has some means of attaining individuality and a sense of dignity. A blind person may be said to be better able to see the "light," a notion associated with moral and religious correctness. Even while he is said to be the living incorporation of a power of God, *gwan riang* may be inept as a pastoralist. Atuot society is structurally undifferentiated, since its "component parts" are multifunctional (see also Deng 1971). Their sense of individuality and identity, characterized not so much by equality as aloofness, is consistent with a conception of God, who is similarly impartial to any one man and relatively removed from all members of society, indeed, from the world of creation.

A great deal of thought in social anthropology has been directed toward explaining such sentiments in terms of supposed "function," to the exclusion of their understanding. Gluckman's (1962:24f.) comments are typical of others which are both tautological and misleading.

> . . . 'ritualization' . . . [refers to] . . . a stylized ceremonial in which persons related in various ways to the central actors, as well as these themselves, perform prescribed actions according to their secular roles; and that it is believed by the participants that these prescribed actions express and amend social relationships so as to secure general blessing, purification, protection, and prosperity for the persons involved in some mystical manner which is out of sensory control.

The notion that there could ever be a "demand" of the social structure appears to be equally "mystical." For the Atuot we should understand that cosmological notions are precisely those which are amenable to sensory control. Their intent is to ask God for help. Lienhardt comments in a most thoughtful way on the same point for the Dinka. He writes (1961:251), "For the sacrifice is its own end. It has already created a moral reality, to which physical facts are hoped eventually to conform." Concurrently, for the Atuot, the prayers of an individual offered in seclusion could have the same efficacy in a moral and religious sense as collective petitions in sacrificial contexts: what is fundamental is personal intent.

Following the pioneering study of Nuer religion by Evans-Pritchard (1956), social anthropologists increasingly saw their task as concerned with "meaning" rather than social function, and this interpretative effort is also frought with its own problems which have psychological and linguistic parameters. Further, categorical classifications have little explicit meaning (cf. Rigby 1967). Structuralism offers one means of interpreting ideational experience, but does not reveal the manner in which people consciously experience the ideas discussed. As argued, even in the situation of collective sacrifice, a person "faces" God individually and necessarily has his or her own psychological attitude toward him. We cannot understand this as an observable reality, but only as a peculiar confrontation with an idea and associated imagery. The alien observer has access to these phenomena only through observation of externalized practical action and in the consideration of individual oral statements. We are here confronting "inner states."

One can translate the Atuot petition, "God, my father, help me," by reference to the sentiments that figure in the relation of father and son, as Lienhardt does for the Dinka.

> The ideas of "creator" and "father" are fused with each other when Divinity is thought of as the active source of live for his "children," men (1961:40).

While the Atuot notion of divinity is imbued with paternal interests in human beings, this is not the central cognitive meaning of God in their lives. A man might just as easily, and with perhaps greater success, address his own pater for help. I cannot say for certain what is really intended, but it is my impression based on the experience of living among them, speaking their language, and occasionally participating in their sacrifices as an adopted son, that a distinct level of affective reality is at the basis of their understanding of God (cf. Lienhardt 1961:42–44).

When religion is considered in relation to the individual, then one should make some attempt to realize what is the Atuot notion of the "experiencing self." Unfortunately this seems impossible, but having already discussed the encounter with powers and ghosts, some things can be understood about the internal self and the external world. Atuot do not make the distinction between the intellectual self and physical factors which westerners do, as for example, in the idea of conscious and unconscious experience. For the Atuot, when a person is seized by a power, the individual state is diagnosed by its physical characteristics, while exorcism can only follow the examination of potential psychic and "sociological" causes. The appearance of a power within an individual is seen as the projection of the passions of one man against his fellow. Likewise, the power is not external to the practicing *tiet,* but is fused within his physical and intellectual self. The source is always, and to their thinking necessarily, defined as another human "self" projecting an affective state of hate or jealousy experienced by the afflicted person as a physical malady. Ghosts figure in Atuot cosmology in a similar way, for ghostly visitation is an encounter within the "self" of the memory of a dead person, which has an active agent. From our analytical perspective a power or ghost can be viewed as the moral manifestation of an active psychic agent. Therefore, the external world of active agents and the inward experience of "being" are combined in the diagnosis of sickness, in which case sacrifice is performed to initiate the healing process. Conversely, when the heart of a human being is "cool," he is emotionally and physically at rest, at peace.

These comments might help to illuminate a thesis I have referred to throughout this study as passivity, typical of Atuot in their relationship with God. Assertive action is demanded in gaining one's livelihood through such means as raiding cattle or seeking to gain back one's stolen cow with the aid of a power. The earthly powers are associated consciously and symbolically with the world of the village, and the homestead is the proper location for the forked-branch shrine of a power. People live in relative isolation from their neighbors in the village, and every family desires to have a homestead situated in the midst of their cultivation. Individual and collective assertiveness through the manipulation of powers is evident at its strongest in the village, a world conceptually associated with women. Social norms are "reinforced" by vengeance through the active agents of powers. By their own reasoning, God would not allow for its realization unless just cause was apparent. The moral and religious qualities of identity merge in Atuot thinking at this junction, since like the Nuer, to be in the "right" with God, a human being must also be in the right with his fellows. The spoken word has the equivalent of purposeful action.

The submission of self-assertiveness, which promotes collective well-being, typifies the moral norms of the cattle camp, a point again, of which Atuot are fully aware. The world of the camp constrains people to maximize values of cooperation in the interest of their herds tethered together in a single camp. For our present concern, it would be difficult to overemphasize the significance of the Atuot statement, "Powers seize people in the village. It is only God who comes to us in the camp." While in either situation it is obviously the same individuals involved, seasonal variation in their modes or production and related economic pursuits are correlated with a difference in their moral and religious experience. It would be suspect to explain these variations by reference to the intrinsically "this-worldly" economic behavior. The human adaptation to physical environment is reflected in moral and religious notions which are expressed differently in accordance with seasonal changes.

This discussion soon calls to mind a similar state investigated by Mauss (1905) for the Eskimo, namely, that when social aggregates increase in density, they "generate kinds of behavior different from those found among the same individuals, when they are isolated and dispersed" (Lienhardt 1964:36). For the Atuot, either seasonal variation in living is no more moral than the other, as Mauss seems to imply for the Eskimo, but merely reflects the divergent social and individual experience of the cattle camp and the village. Mauss' general principle is illuminating, but there are more complicating realities than population and moral densities. In one way, moral density is at its highest in the cattle camp, an aggregate which in the past united in warfare against similar "units." God watches over their lives in the camp. Conversely, by far the greater number of sacrifices occur in the village after the harvest of durra, when sufficient food and beer can be prepared. However, effectively the community of sacrificers in this context is smaller, since a moral community can only exist in the exclusion of others. Hence, the intent of sacrifice is to provide for the well-being of the sacrificial group at the expense of others, by calling for an earthly power to express moral indignation and revenge against another group of people or individual.

In its most embracing meaning the religious community includes all Atuot who collectively assert that their existence is dependent ultimately upon the Creator God. The moral community is an exceedingly less inclusive group, since it is the one within which insult must be redressed and bloodshed revenged. These groups are regionally dispersed, according to Atuot social theory, in conformity with principles of descent and post-marital residence, yet to the alien observer, there is no necessary or consistently notable correspondence between these ideas and reality. Kith can usually be recognized as sharing some degree of kinship relation. The moral community is co-terminous with the economic units of production.

When one man has speared and killed another in warfare or as the result of an insult uttered at a dance, and if it is expected that compensation and reconciliation will eventually be realized, sacrifice must be performed to expiate the murderer of this sin. Atuot explain that failure to comply with the act would cause the guilty man to die as soon as he drank water, for it would be as though he had drunk the blood of the deceased. Thus, while ideas of morality and the breach of these norms, which are classified as "sinful," are intrinsically related, religious experience and morality are not meaningfully co-terminous. Moral values unite people among themselves, and since these necessarily overlap with economic interests, the moral community reaches its highest "density" (paradoxically, realized among the smallest social unit) in the world of the village.

Their relationship with God is viewed as permanent, and more or less a part of the immediate lives. Through the birth of twins his revelation is direct. When Atuot say that a man's heart has gone bad *(loic ce jeo)*, they imply that he has severed his relations with an individual or group of persons in a selfish and spiteful manner. This points to a feature of Atuot morality and even political theory evidenced also among the larger group of Nilotic speaking peoples. If people are to live together, in a cattle camp for example, they must submerge their individual interests to those of the community. God unites them all in a spiritual and ideational sense. The opposite of incorporation is the absolute severance of relationships, accompanied by the strongest sense of wanting to "get one's very own back" (see Lienhardt 1975). Social life is the constant interplay between individual values and the demands of social groups which are collective in orientation. Since they fear incorporation as equivalent to non-existence, the moral world is continually in a state of flux, as fluid as the changing social composition of villages and cattle camps. Moral values are as a result continually redefined in relation to particular and peculiar circumstances. Earthly powers are likewise individualized and owned by groups of people with their own self-interests.

By this reasoning, the notion of a distant yet ubiquitous God seems an important part of individual identity. Even while he is imagined to be removed from the daily concerns of people, God is said also to have a continual interest in each experiencing individual. In their system of thought this occurs at a distinctive level of psychic experience. At a time of sudden physical or mental distress a person should be left to himself for a short time before a *tiet* is consulted, since it may "only be God that has come to him." Though a man may be successful in concealing socially disapproved behavior from his world of kin, in the way we have understood this to be his experience of a moral community, Atuot say that God will see his actions and deeds regardless of the ignorance of others.

At the lowest end of their spectrum of "powers" is a quality of certain individuals which suggests they are witches *(apeth)* or sorcerers *(roadh)*. Witchcraft shares a quality typical of powers, since it also implies an assertive and active agent, but is really seen to be more of a psychological characteristic. Witchcraft is associated in their thought with the least enviable and most socially disapproved qualities of human beings, theoretically latent in all of "God's ants," but more or less apparent in any one individual. Their notions of witchcraft might be interpreted as the projection onto others of the worst qualities every individual notes about himself. Collectively the ideas are "the standardized nightmare" (Wilson 1951:313) of people; yet they have no great imaginative or moral importance among the Atuot, a point noted also by Lienhardt·(1951) for the Dinka (cf. also Baxter 1972). Atuot notions of witchcraft seem to be a logical extension of the analogical mode of classification combining individual identity and intent with non-human powers. A witch cannot be seen, but only sensed or detected intuitively. In the Atuot idiom, a witch has a kind of "power," but its origin is social rather than spiritual.

The individual and collective experience of powers in the lives of human beings relate persons to persons and reflect moral expectations in relation to experienced realities. And what of the relation between God and man? "God the father" is never said or imagined to exist in any physical form, nor sharing the needs of human beings. Indeed, either attribute would be inconsistent with Atuot ideas of divinity.

Since God is perceived as a permanent reality, a constant being identified with primordial creativity, transcending the world, he partakes of a quality that Tillich (1951:218) has called "ultimacy." Atuot religion projects images of a very great number of powers, which are in turn differentiated among themselves, but it is evident that their "beliefs" are monotheistically oriented. Employing the terminology of Otto (1923; see also Schmidt 1931), Evans-Pritchard (1956:316) perceived the same feature of Nuer religious thought, where the "refractions" of God are but "different ways of thinking of the 'numinous' at different levels of experience." Lienhardt (1961) and Deng (1972, 1973) both describe the formal characteristic of the Dinka supreme being as a unity in multiplicity. For the Atuot as well, the power speaking through a *tiet* in the course of exorcism is a different manifestation of "power" that gives a man the ability to call rain, or bring about the death of a man simply by wishing it to happen. They are conceptually distinguished in terms of experience while seen as a single type of phenomenon cosmologically.

Even if successful in defining and illustrating these general features, we still confront a problem intrinsically related to translation and interpretation. Only by employing their idiom of *jok* is it possible to describe Atuot ideas about witches, totems, ghosts, and powers of the earth by the same analogous principle that relates in turn *ring, nhial,* and *kwoth* to God. The symbolic statements imply metaphors which are peculiar to them. If their meaning cannot be explained, nothing is lost, for to understand them is the initial and primary task. Needham's (1973: xxxix) reminder of a philosophical principle is especially enlightening, for not only does it offer a partial answer to the problem raised, but also relates to the confusion, which has resulted in the interpretation of alien ideologies by anthropologists who are ignorant of the fact:

> . . . analogy does not mean an imperfect similarity of relations between two things, but a perfect similarity of relations between two quite dissimilar things.

All the "powers" of the world are alike in that they involve individual psychic and physical experience, and are manifestations of Divinity. The notion of *jok* is idiomatic in their religious thought, since it connotes the overriding similarity in the varied manifestations of Divinity.

In their social context, different qualities of powers relate to distinct moral, domestic, political, and economic groupings. The study might end at this point, satisfied with having "uncovered" these correlations and symbolic associations, and conclude that religion is socially constrained, but ultimately an interior state (see e. g., Evans-Pritchard 1956: 322). Ideally it would be preferable to understand why there are *differences* in religious expressions, for the more general similarities of this aspect of social life are all too obvious. Mental attitudes also vary. For the Atuot, economic constraints of transhumant pastoralism are revealed in moral values, but these strictures cannot explicate why people say twins are birds, or that *joks* favor the flesh of goats in sacrifices dedicated to them.

Atuot make the present exercise in interpretation and understanding all the more easy by comparing themselves metaphorically to tiny black ants. Possibly this in itself is an adequate summation of the religious side of their life. Atuot are skillfully in control of the means to provide for their immediate well-being as pastoralists, fishers, and cultivators, while in their view of the world, it is God the creator who makes the ends more or less an experiential reality in their lives.

# References

BARNES, R. H.
 1974   *Kédang: A Study of the Collective Thought of an Eastern Indonesian People.*
      Oxford: Clarendon Press.

BAXTER, P.
 1972   Absence Makes the Heart Grow Fonder: Some Suggestions why Witchcraft
      Accusations Are Rare among East African Pastoralists. In: M. Gluckman
      (ed.), *The Allocation of Responsibility.* Manchester: Manchester University
      Press.

BEDRI, I.
 1939   Notes on Dinka Religious Beliefs in Their Chiefs. *Sudan Notes and Records*
      27: 15–20.

BRYAN, M. A. and A. N. TUCKER
 1948   *Distributions of the Nilotic and Nilo-Hamitic Languages.* London: Oxford
      University Press.

BURTON, J. W.
 n. d. *a*  Sacrifice: A Polythetic Class of Atuot Social Thought. (Unpublished
      manuscript.)
 n. d. *b*  Life and the Left Hand: Lateral Symbolism in Atuot Cosmology. (Un-
      published manuscript.)
 n. d. *c*  Nilotic Studies: A Bibliographic Essay.
 1974   Some Nuer Notions of Purity and Danger. *Anthropos* 69: 517–536.
 1976   On the Interpretation of a Nuer Ritual. *Man* (N. S.) 11. 388–391.
 1977*a*  Nuer Prophets: Ethnological and Demographic Considerations of the
      Central Nuer. *Sudan Notes and Records.*
 1977*b*  The Peoples Called Atuot. *Sudan Now* 12: 42–44.
 1978*a*  Living with the Dead: Aspects of the Afterlife in Nuer and Dinka Cosmology
      (Sudan). *Anthropos* 73: 141–160.
 1978*b*  Ghost Marriage and the Cattle Trade among the Atuot of the Southern
      Sudan. *Africa* 48: 398–405.
 1980*a*  The Village and the Cattle Camp: Aspects of Atuot Religion. In: I. Karp
      (ed.), *Explorations in African Systems of Thought.* Bloomington: Indiana
      University Press.
 1980*b*  The Proverb: An Aspect of Atuot Collective Thought. *Folklore* 80:
 1980*c*  Women and Men in Marriage: Some Atuot Texts. *Anthropos* 75:
 1980*d*  Atuot Age Categories and Marriage. *Africa* 50:
 1980*e*  Atuot Totemism. *Journal of Religion in Africa* 10: 5–17.
 1980*f*  The Wave Is My Mothers's Husband: A Piscatorial Theme in Pastoral
      Nilotic Ethnology. *Cahiers d'Etudes Africaines.*
 1980*g*  Benign Neglect: British Colonial Administration and Local Response
      among the Pastoral Nilotes of the Southern Sudan. *Anthropology* 4:

– – and W. ARENS
 1975   Death by Suffocation. *Man* (N. S.) 10: 313–315.

BUXTON, J.
1958    The Significance of Bridewealth and the Levirate among the Nilotic and Nilo-Hamitic Peoples of the Southern Sudan. *The Antislavery Reporter* 6 (3): 66–75.
1963    *Chiefs and Strangers: Political Incorporation among the Mandari.* Oxford: Clarendon Press.
1973    *Religion and Healing in Mandari.* Oxford: Clarendon Press.
1975    Initiation and Bead Sets among the Mandari. In: J. Beattie and R. G. Lienhardt [ed.], *Studies in Social Anthropology.* Oxford: Clarendon Press.

CRAZZOLARA, J. P.
1933    *Outlines of a Nuer Grammar.* (Linguistische Anthropos-Bibliothek, 13.) Wien.
1953    *Zur Gesellschaft und Religion der Nuer.* (Studia Instituti Anthropos, 5.) Wien.
1950–1954    *The Lwoo* (Parts I, II, III). Vienna: Missioni Africane.

DENG, F. M.
1966    Property and Value Inter-play among the Nilotes of the Southern Sudan. *Iowa Law Review* 51 (3): 541–560.
1971    *Tradition and Modernizaton: A Challenge for Law among the Dinka of the Sudan.* New Haven: Yale University Press.
1972    *The Dinka of the Sudan.* New York: Holt, Rinehart and Winston.
1973    *The Dinka and Their Songs.* Oxford: Clarendon Press.

DOUGLAS, M.
1970    *Natural Symbols: Explanations in Cosmology.* London: Barrie and Jenkins.

DRIBERG, J. H.
1923    *The Lango: A Nilotic Tribe of Uganda.* London: T. Fisher Unwin.

EVANS-PRITCHARD, E. E.
1934    The Nuer: Tribe and Clan. *Sudan Notes and Records* 17: 1–57.
1935    The Nuer: Tribe and Clan. *Sudan Notes and Records* 18: 37–88.
1936    Customs and Beliefs Relating to Twins among the Nilotic Nuer. *Uganda Journal* 3: 230–238.
1939    Nuer Time Reckoning. *Africa* 12: 189–216.
1940*a*    *The Nuer: A Description of the Modes of Livelihood and Political Institutions of a Nilotic People.* Oxford: Clarendon Press.
1940*b*    *The Political System of the Anuak of the Anglo-Egyptian Sudan.* (Monographs in Social Anthropology, 4.) London: Percy Lund, Humphries and Co. Ltd.
1945    *Some Aspects of Marriage and the Family among the Nuer.* (Rhodes Livingston Institute Papers, 11.) Lusaka: Rhodes Livingston Institute.
1948    Nuer Modes of Address. *Uganda Journal* 12: 166–171.
1949*a*    The Nuer *Col Wic. Man* 49: 7–9.
1949*b*    Burial and Mortuary Rites of the Nuer. *African Affairs* 48: 56–62.
1950*a*    Nilotic Studies. *Journal of the Royal Anthropological Institute* 80: 1–6.
1950*b*    Ghostly Vengeance among the Luo of Kenya. *Man* 50: 86–87.
1951    *Kinship and Marriage among the Nuer.* Oxford: Clarendon Press.
1953    A Note on Ghostly Vengeance among the Anuak of the Sudan. *Man* 53: 6–7.
1956    *Nuer Religion.* Oxford: Clarendon Press.
1960*a*    *The Sudan: An Ethnographic Survey.* In: S. Diamond [ed.], *Culture in History.* New York: Columbia University Press.
1960*b*    Introduction to: R. Hertz. *Death and the Right Hand.* London: Cohen and West.

FARON, L. C.
1964          *Hawks of the Sun: Mapuche Morality and Its Ritual Attributes.* Pittsburgh:
              University of Pittsburgh Press.

FERGUSSON, V. H.
1921          The Nuong Nuer. *Sudan Notes and Records* 4: 146–155.

FEIERMAN, ST.
1974          The Shambaa Kingdom. A History. Madison: University of Wisconsin
              Press.

FORTES, M.
1959          *Oedipus and Job in West African Religion.* Cambridge: Cambridge University
              Press.
1965          Some Reflections on Ancestor Worship in Africa. In: M. Fortes and
              G. Dieterlen [ed.], *African Systems of Thought.* London: Oxford University
              Press.

GESSI, R.
1892          *Seven Years in the Soudan.* London: Sampson Low, Marston and Company.

GLICKMAN, M.
1972          The Nuer and the Dinka. *Man* (N. S.) 7: 586–594.

GLUCKMAN, M.
1937          Mortuary Customs and the Belief in the Survival after Death among the
              South Eastern Bantu. *Bantu Studies* 9: 117–136.
1962          Les Rites de Passage. In: M. Gluckman [ed.], *The Ritual of Social
              Relations.* Manchester University Press.

GOUGH, K.
1971          Nuer Kinship: A Re-examination. In: T. O. Beidelman [ed.], *The
              Translation of Culture.* London: Tavistock Publications.

GRAY, R.
1961          *A History of the Southern Sudan.* London: Oxford University Press.

HARRISON, M. H.
1955          *Report on a Grazing Survey of the Sudan.* Khartoum: Sudan Government.

HAYLEY, T. S.
1947          *The Anatomy of Lango Religion and Groups.* Cambridge: Cambridge
              University Press.

HERTZ, R.
1960          *Death and the Right Hand.* London: Cohen and West.

HOFMAYR, W.
1925          *Die Schilluk: Geschichte, Religion und Leben eines Niloten Stammes.*
              (Ethnologische Anthropos-Bibliothek, II/5.) Wien.

HOWELL, P. P.
1951          Notes on the Ngok Dinka of the Western Kordofan. *Sudan Notes and
              Records* 32: 239–293.
1953a         Some Observations on Earthly Spirits among the Nuer. *Man* 53: 85–88.
1953b         Observations on the Shilluk of the Upper Nile. Customary Law: Marriage
              and the Violation of Rights in Women. *Africa* 23: 94–109.
1954          *A Manual of Nuer Law.* London: Oxford University Press.
– – [ed.]
1954          *The Equatorial Nile Project and Its Effect in the Anglo-Egyptian Sudan*
              (5 Vols.). Khartoum: Sudan Government.

— — and B. A. LEWIS
1947        Nuer Ghouls: A Form of Witchcraft. *Sudan Notes and Records* 18: 157–168.

— — and W. P. G. THOMPSON
1946        The Death of a *Reth* and the Installation of His Successor. *Sudan Notes and Records* 27: 5–85.

HICKS, D.
1976        *Tetum Ghosts and Kin.* Palo Alto: Mayfield Publishing Company.

HUBERT, H. and M. MAUSS
1964        *Sacrifice: Its Nature and Function.* Chicago: University of Chicago Press.

HUFFMAN, R.
1929        *Nuer-English Dictionary.* Berlin: Dietrich Reimer.
1931a       *English-Nuer Dictionary.* London: Oxford University Press.
1931b       *Nuer Customs and Folklore.* London: Oxford University Press.

JACKSON, H. C.
1923        The Nuer of Upper Nile Province. *Sudan Notes and Records* 6: 59–107; 123–189.

JAMES, W.
1979        *'Kwanim Pa: The Making of the Uduk. An Ethnographic Study of Survivial in the Sudan-Ethiopian Borderlands.* Oxford: Clarendon Press.

JOHNSON, R. T.
1934        Religious and Spiritual Beliefs of the Bor Dinka. *Sudan Notes and Records* 17: 124–128.

JOSHI, N. R. *et al.*
1957        *Types and Breeds of African Cattle.* Rome: United Nations.

KIGGEN, J.
1948        *Nuer-English Dictionary.* London: St. Joseph's Society for Foreign Missions.

KRONENBERG, A.
1960        Jo Luo Tales. *Kush* 8: 237–251.

LEVI-STRAUSS, C.
1963        Totemism. [Transl. by R. Needham.] Chicago: University of Chicago Press.

LIENHARDT, R. G.
1951        Some Notions of Witchcraft among the Dinka, *Africa* 21: 303–318.
1954        The Shilluk of the Upper Nile. In: D. Forde [ed.], *African Worlds.* London: Oxford University Press.
1958        The Western Dinka. In: J. Middlefern and D. Tait [ed.], *Tribes Without Rulers.* New York: Humanities Press.
1961        *Divinity and Experience: The Religion of the Dinka.* Oxford: Clarendon Press.
1964        *Social Anthropology.* London: Oxford University Press.
1970        The Situation of Death: An Aspect of Anuak Philosophy. In: M. Douglas [ed.], *Witchcraft Confessions and Accusations.* London: Tavistock Publications.
1975        Getting Your Own Back: Themes in Nilotic Myth. In. J. Beattie and R. G. Lienhardt [ed.], *Studies in Social Anthropology.* Oxford: Clarendon Press.

MALINOWSKI, B.
1954        Myth in Primitive Society. In: Magic, Science, and Religion. New York: Ancor Books.

MAUSS, M.
1904–1905    Essai sur les variations saisonnières des sociétés Eskimos: Etude de morphologie sociale. *Année sociologique* 9.
1972    A General Theory of Magic. London: Routledge and Kegan Paul.

MAYALL, E. C.
1924    Memorandum on the Tribe of the Northern Dinka in the Upper Nile Province. *Bulletin de la Societe Royale de Geographie d'Egypte* 12: 187–203.

MCLAUGHLIN, J.
1967    Tentative Time Depths for Nuer, Dinka and Anuak. *Journal of Ethiopian Studies* 5: 13–27.

MIDDLETON, J.
1960    *Lugbara Religion*. London: Oxford University Press.

NEBEL, A.
1954    *Dinka Dictionary*. Wien: Verona Fathers.

NEEDHAM, R.
1963    Introduction to: *Primitive Classification*. Chicago: University of Chicago Press.
1972    *Belief, Language and Experience*. Chicago: University of Chicago Press.
1973    Introduction to R. Needham [ed.], Right and Left. Chicago: University of Chicago Press.

NEWCOMER, P.
1972    The Nuer and Dinka: An Essay on Origins and Environmental Determinism. *Man* (N. S.) 7: 5–11.

O'BITEK, O.
1963    The Concept of the *Jok* among the Acholi and Lango. *Uganda Journal* 27: 15–30.

OCHOLLA-AYAYO, A. B.
1976    *Traditional Ideology and Ethics among the Southern Luo*. Uppsala: Scandinavian Institute of African Studies.

OGOT, B. A.
1961    The Concept of *Jok* among the Nilotes. *African Studies* 20: 123–130.

OTTO, R.
1923    *The Idea of the Holy*. London: Oxford University Press.

OYLER, D. S.
1918    Nyikwang and the Shilluk Migration. *Sudan Notes and Records* 1: 107–115.

PETHERICK, J.
1869    *Travels in Central Africa and Exploration of the White Nile Tributaries* (2 Vols.). London: Tinsley Brothers.

RIAD, R.
1959    The Divine Kingship of the Shilluk and Its Origin. *Archiv für Völkerkunde* 14: 141–284.

RIGBY, P.
1967    The Structural Context of Girl's Puberty Rites. *Man* (N. S.) 2: 435–444.

SAHLINS, M.
1961    The Segmentary Lineage: An Organization of Predatory Expansion. *American Anthropologist* 66: 322–344.

SANTANDREA, S.
1968        *The Luo of Bahr el Ghazal.* Bologna: Missionari Comboniani.

SCHMIDT, W.
1931        *The Origin and Growth of Religion.* London: Methuen and Company, Ltd.

SELIGMAN[N], C. G.
n. d.        *Report on Totemism and Religion of the Dinka.* Khartoum: El Sudan Press.

1911        *The Cult of Nyikang and the Divine Kingship of the Shilluk.* (Fourth Report of the Welcome Tropical Institute.) London.

− − and B. Z. SELIGMAN
1932        *Pagan Tribes of the Nilotic Sudan.* London: Routledge and Kegan Paul.

SOUTHALL, A.
1956        *Alur Society.* Cambridge: Heffer and Sons.
1971        Cross-Cultural Meaning and Multilingualism. In: W. H. Whiteley [ed.], *Language Use and Social Change.* London: Oxford University Press.
1972        Twinship and Symbolic Structure. In: J. S. Lafontaine [ed.], *The Interpretation of Ritual.* London: Tavistock Publications.
1976        Nuer and Dinka Are People: Ecology, Ethnicity and Logical Possibility. *Man* (N.S.) 11: 463–491.

STIGAND, C. H.
1923        *A Nuer-English Dictionary.* Cambridge: Cambridge University Press.

STUBBS, J. N.
1934        Notes on the Beliefs and Customs of the Malwal Dinka. *Sudan Notes and Records* 17: 243–254.

− − and C. MORRISON
1938        The Western Dinka: Their Land and Agriculture. *Sudan Notes and Records* 21: 251–265.

TILLICH, P.
1951        *Systematic Theology.* Chicago: University of Chicago Press.

TITHERINGTON, G. W.
1925        Burial Alive among the Dinka of Bahr-el-Ghazal Province. *Sudan Notes and Records* 8: 196–197.

TUCKER, A. N.
1935        A Survey of Language Groups in the Southern Sudan. *Bulletin of Oriental and African Studies* 7: 861–896.

WESTERMANN, D.
1912a        *The Shilluk: Their Language and Folklore.* Philadelphia: United Presbyterian Church.
1912b        The Nuer Language. *Mitteilungen des Seminars für Orientalische Sprachen zu Berlin* 15: 84–141.

WILSON, M.
1951        Witch Beliefs and Social Structure. *American Journal of Sociology* 56: 307–313.

WINTER, E. H.
1963        The Enemy Within: Witchcraft and Sociological Theory. In: J. Middleton and E. H. Winter [ed.], *Witchcraft and Sorcery in East Africa.* London: Routledge and Kegan Paul.

# Glossary of Some Terms Mentioned in the Text

*aboic*  to fear; cf. *ce gai,* to be suddenly surprised or frightened

*abor*  seasonal flood, as in *aborpiny,* the earth has been covered with water

*abuojek*  a senseless individual, moron, a lame person

*abuoi*  a net used by women when fishing

*abuol*  late maturing groundnuts from the previous year's crop. These are harvested before the new crop matures, adding an important addition to the diet when it is most needed

*abyei*  literally, "tree of life" under which sacrifices to call rain are performed

*aceke*  the term for government as well as all persons and materials associated with administration. The term is derived from the verb *cak,* "to create" and was initially employed with reference to the British, who were in a sense likened to a great spiritual power due to their superior military technology

*Acinpuo*  a personal name meaning "without a heart"

*acot*  literally, "hornless" when referring to cattle. The word also refers to a group or individual male who has recently been initiated

*acuek Decau*  the ants of God, a phrase which Atuot employ in hymns and ritual for self-reference, underscoring their perception of God as an omnipotent being

*acuok*  human twins

*adep*  rope used for tethering cattle; also an adjective for a clever person and one who possesses aesthetic dexterity

*adhang*  the shelter erected over dung fires in wet season cattle camps. A variety of ropes, gourds and spears can normally be found hanging from the rathers and thatch of the roof

*adwil*  the traditional hut erected by Atuot, which encloses a space on the ground level for cooking, keeping utensils and an upper approximately ten feet above the ground for sleeping

*adjuaic*  a noun referring to all the vegetal species consumed by people

*againy*  the Nile lizzard, a common totem or clan divinity of fishermen

*ajuong*  indigenous iron smelters, who formerly made all the metal implements used by Atuot in cultivation, hunting and fishing

*akol*  sleeping hide

*akor*  from *akorlil,* the tree in the place of creation

*alet*  a story or folktale, as *alet lai dial,* the story of the origin of animals. The word is derived from the noun *lat* or word, as *alet ne mei,* ancient traditions. One can also ask, *teke lat,* do you have a word? or what is the news?

*aliab*  lies, confusion, chaos

*alier*  "the wind of life" which blows from the south in the early rainy season, cooling the land and heralding the return of life to the land with the ensueing rains. As distinguished from *jiom,* wind, *alier* has important religious connotations

*amel*  a sheep, the common victim for sacrifices to the power *ring*

*apeth*  a witch as well as the character and behavior of such individuals

*apuo*  the fine greyish ash produced from burning cow dung. It is often smeared on the body for personal adornment but also has immediate moral and religious referents

*arop*  a power of the earth thought to have originated in Nuerland

*arum*  in the course of excorcism when the diviner becomes possessed by a power he will call out *arum,* to signal that the power is about to speak through him

| | |
|---|---|
| *ater* | blood feud |
| *athin* | is present, is in existence, as in the phrase *Decau era thin,* God exists |
| *athoiny* | circumcized, a term of abuse applied to Arabs. Atuot profess disgust of the practice |
| *atuc* | the durra bird |
| *awec* | a sinful act, such as adultery or incest; cf. *dwer,* a human error committed by mistake, unintentionally |
| *awuot* | a fully matured man |
| *ayat* | the traditional clothing of a married woman, made from two triangular shaped hides of goat or sheep. They are often adorned with beads or bells, and are a source of great pride among women |
| *ayumboi* | the dance made over the grave of a person possessed by *ring* |
| *baar* | a salt lick, where cattle are driven seasonally |
| *biith* | a primary religious symbol to mark the status of a man of *ring* |
| *buk aₜuo* | the practice of smearing *apuo* across the back of an animal victim in the course of sacrifice, identifying the sacrificing group with the intent of the act. Also, when a man acquires an ox, bull or cow, he will bring it to his cattle camp and cover the entire animal with *apuo* to identify it as an animal of his herd |
| *bull jao* | making a dance for an earthly power to entice it out of a individual in the course of exorcism. Many songs are sung, accompanied by clapping to the rhythm of the diviner's rattle. The more active the "dance" the more likely the exorcism will prove to be successful |
| *buol* | a gift, as Atuot speak of life as a gift of the Creator, *buol Decau* |
| *buong* | an act of "sacrifice" in which the victim is killed by suffocation. This act often accompanies rituals performed to treat and cure barren women (see Burton 1976; Burton and Arens 1975) |
| *buoth* | hunger or starvation. A man or woman may also fancifully state *nake buoth tap,* "I am being killed by my need for tobacco" |
| *bur* | temporary fishing camps of the dry season. Cattle are left behind and tended by a few individuals so the rest can be free to fish |
| *cak* | as a noun, milk. As a verb *cak* means "to create from nothing something which did not exist before," as the Creator created *(ce cak)* people |
| *cam* | a verb describing the act of eating animal flesh, in contrast to the verb *mieth,* as in *mieth kuen,* eat this food |
| *cang* | the sun |
| *ce cek* | to have ripened, to have come to maturity |
| *cek* | a married woman, wife |
| *ce paar* | it is said when twins die, *ce paar,* they have flown away rather than the usual "he has died" |
| *cien* | ghostly vengeance |
| *cieng* | 1) a homestead; 2) a named territory; 3) in the broadest sense, Atuotland, *cieng* Reel |
| *cier* | the river Nile |
| *ciil* | the rhino |
| *cuer* | a thief; morally, a wrongful act |
| *cuong* | ghost marriage |
| *dainy* | as a generic term, women's dances |
| *Decau* | the Atuot image of the Creator God. It is only *Decau* that is embued with the puissance of creation |
| *de ker* | literally, when the year separates, that is, when the season of rain commences. The dry hot world is separated from the coming season of cultivation and plenty |
| *der cang* | the middle of the day, when the sun appears to be directly above |
| *dieng* | the beginning of the season of harvest |
| *dom* | a verb meaning to catch, as in the usage, *abiel ce yi dom e,* the earthly power *abiel* has caught you |

| | |
|---|---|
| *dor* | "social section." The Atuot people are divided into six *dor,* the Luac, Jilek, Apak, Akot, Rorkec, and Kuek. The term also refers to the ceremony performed at the settlement of a feud, when people *dor,* or come together |
| *gam long* | when a diviner has been possessed by a power, the words he speaks are repeated to all gathered nearby by the *gam long* |
| *gok* | a term referring to a type of forest with sandy soils |
| *guak* | the stork |
| *gwan kwoth* | an individual possessed by the spirit associated with the natural element rain, *kwoth.* As a possessor of the power he is also thought to be a genator of the life it brings |
| *gwan riang* | a person possessed by the power *ring,* one who brings life to human beings. The form of *ring* in the pronounciation *riang* is cognate with the verb *riang,* "satisfaction." One ought to say after a meal, *ca riang,* I have been satisfied by this food |
| *jaang* | the term used by Nuer and Atuot to refer to the Dinka |
| *jok piny* | an earthly power |
| *jok* | spiritual power |
| *juei* | fever, malaria |
| *kak* | garden |
| *karath* | the term for maize, which Atuot have adopted from the Mandari |
| *kot* | fighting shield, commonly made from the hide of a rhino or hippo |
| *kuen* | food |
| *kulang* | an important power of the above |
| *kuoiny nuer* | the burial of an individual |
| *kuol* | the wild cucumber, a plant that is "sacrificed" in ceremonies to call rain. Also the term referring to the season in which the first rains are expected to commence |
| *kwoth* | the spirit associated with rain |
| *laang* | literally, to pray, to raise one's hands to God |
| *lia* | death; as in *nuer ce lieu,* the man died |
| *luak kwoth* | a shrine (occasionally an enclosed hut) erected by a person possessed by the power *kwoth.* At such sites, the same individuals will perform sacrifices to call rain |
| *luoi* | the verb to make, as a potter makes a pot from clay; cf. the verb *cak,* to create |
| *muk* | the buffalo |
| *muon me car* | heavily black clay which is used in plastering the walls of huts |
| *mut* | the fighting spear |
| *nei cieng Reel* | the Atuot, people who are descended from the original ancestor who led a migration into Atuot country |
| *ngac* | to know; to have realized, as in *ca ngac thok Reel,* I have learned the Atuot language |
| *nhial* | literally, what is above; also a proper noun referring to God |
| *paai tieth* | the first phase of the moon; cf. *muoth,* a moonless night |
| *panther* | literally a Dinka word meaning "the old home." In their oral traditions Atuot frequently make mention of *panther* as the first place in which they settled |
| *pel ngac* | literally, "to leave milking behind," the rite of male initiation |
| *piny ce jaal* | the land has travelled, a phrase employed to connote that people have observed an historical progression of time, or a significant change in the social environment |
| *piny wer* | literally, the land has gone, night has come |
| *reth* | a noun derived from the verb "to speak." *Reth* is a spokesman |
| *reth wuic* | the spokesman of a cattle camp |
| *ric* | literally, "marriage class" |
| *ring* | perhaps the most important heavenly power, which in Atuot collective representations refers to the power of life itself, of corporeal existence |
| *roadh* | a sorcerer |
| *rol* | impotency |

| | |
|---|---|
| *rual* | incest |
| *ruon* | the ecological year, said to begin in mid-January |
| *tak* | an idea |
| *tau* | to think, ideate |
| *thaang cam* | the "left side" of the physical world |
| *thaang cuic* | the "right side" of the physical world |
| *thuom* | ancestors, the long deceased |
| *tie* | existence |
| *tiep* | ghost |
| *tiet* | diviner |
| *tiiar* | pounded millet flour. This is used often in place of *apuo* in the course of sacrifices performed in the village setting |
| *toic* | permanent inland pastures |
| *tonye* | the customary practice in which men will "fatten" themselves by drinking and eating large quantities of milk and beef |
| *tuar* | generically, a man's song, as in *tuar theo* (ox song) and *tuar tuot* (bull song) |
| *wel* | literally, medicine. The term most often refers to the *wel* of a *jok,* in the form of leaves or roots which are dug up in the forest |
| *wet* | totem, or clan divinity. The majority of Atuot tales which account for the origin of a totemistic relation suggest that the plant or animal was born long ago as a twin of a clan founder |
| *wuic* | a cattle camp (pl. *wei*) |
| *yei* | life |

# STUDIA INSTITUTI ANTHROPOS

1. PAUL ARNDT: Religion auf Ostflores, Adonare und Solor. XII–248 pp. 1951. DM 41,25.
2. FRANZ GIET: Zur Tonität nordchinesischer Mundarten. XX–184 pp., ill. 1950. DM 68,80.
3. LOUIS J. LUZBETAK: Marriage and the Family in Caucasia. XVI–272 pp., ill. 1951. DM 68,80.
4. J. A. VERHEIJEN: Het Hoogste Wezen bij de Manggaraiers. XV–240 pp. 1951. DM 68,80.
5. J. P. CRAZZOLARA: Zur Gesellschaft und Religion der Nueer. XVI–221 pp. 1953. DM 99,-.
6. PAUL SCHEBESTA: Die Negrito Asiens. Bd. 1: Geschichte, Geographie, Umwelt, Demographie und Anthropologie. XVI–496 pp., ill. Mit 21 pp. Anhang. 1952 (out of print).
7. M. VANOVERBERGH: Songs in Lepanto-Igorot as it is Spoken at Bauko. 141 pp. 1954. DM 27,50.
8. PAUL ARNDT: Gesellschaftliche Verhältnisse der Ngadha. XII–546 pp. 1954. DM 68,80.
9. JOSEPH F. ROCK: The Zhi mä Funeral Ceremony of the Na-khi of Southwest China. Described and transl. from Na-khi manuscripts. XV–230 pp., ill. 1955. DM 41,25.
10. WILHELM SCHMIDT: Das Mutterrecht. 186 pp. 1955. DM 64,-.
11. P. DRABBE: Spraakkunst van het Marind. 190 pp. 1955. DM 41,25.
12. PAUL SCHEBESTA: Die Negrito Asiens. Bd. 2: Ehtnographie der Negrito. 1. Halbband: Wirtschaft und Soziologie, XIV–340 pp., ill. 1954. DM 55,-.
13. PAUL SCHEBESTA: Die Negrito Asiens. Bd. 2: Ethnographie der Negrito. 2. Halbband: Religion und Mythologie. XIV–336 pp., ill. 1957. DM 42,-.
14. LUDWIG GOLOMB: Die Bodenkultur in Ost-Turkestan. Oasenwirtschaft und Nomadentum. XII–160 pp., ill. 1959. DM 41,-.
15. PAUL ARNDT: Wörterbuch der Ngadhasprache. 646 pp. 1961. DM 57,-.
16. HUGO HUBER: The Krobo. Traditional, Social and Religious Life of a West African People. 306 pp., ill. 1963. DM 55,-.
17. ALOYS KASPRUŚ: The Tribes of the Middle Ramu and the Upper Keram Rivers (North East New Guinea). X–193 pp., ill. 1973. DM 42,-.
18. Festschrift Paul Schebesta zum 75. Geburtstag. XV–568 pp. 1963. DM 77,-.
19. ALOIS PACHE: Die religiösen Vorstellungen in den Mythen der formosanischen Bergstämme. XV–272 pp. 1964. DM 77,-.
20. WILHELM SCHMIDT †: Wege der Kulturen. Gesammelte Aufsätze. XXXI–340 pp. 1964. DM 43,-.
21. *Anthropica.* Gedenkschrift zum 100. Geburtstag von P. Wilhelm Schmidt. Gesammelte Aufsätze. XII–452 pp. 1968. DM 63,-.
22. JOSEF FRANZ THIEL und ALBERT DOUTRELOUX [edit.]: Heil und Macht – Approches du sacré. 215 pp. 1975. DM 42,-.
23. INGE HOFMANN: Wege und Möglichkeiten eines indischen Einflusses auf die meroitische Kultur. 188 pp., ill. 1975. DM 54,50.
24. ALFRED HAUENSTEIN: Fables et contes angolais. 294 pp. 1976. DM 56,50.
25. HERMANN TRIMBORN et al.: Investigaciones arqueológicas en los valles del Caplina y Sama (Dep. Tacna, Perú). 129 pp., ill. 1975. DM 36,-.
26. JOSEF FRANZ THIEL: Ahnen – Geister – Höchste Wesen. Religionsethnologische Untersuchungen im Zaïre-Kasai-Gebiet. 200 pp. 1977. DM 39,-.
27. HENRY MAURIER: Philosphie de l'Afrique noire. 279 pp. 1976. DM 58,50.
28. *Al-Bahit:* Festschrift Joseph Henninger zum 70. Geburtstag. 324 pp., ill. 1976. DM 76,50.
29. GEORG HÖLTKER: Menschen und Kulturen in Nordost-Neuguinea. Gesammelte Aufsätze. 414 pp., ill. 1975. DM 59,50.
30. DAVID HICKS: Structural Analysis in Anthropology. Case Studies from Indonesia and Brazil. 133 pp. 1978. DM 32,-.
31. INGE HOFMANN: Beiträge zur meroitischen Chronologie. 248 pp., ill. 1978. DM 63,-.
34. ANTON VORBICHLER: Die Oralliteratur der Balese-Efe in Ituri-Wald (Nordost-Zaire). Musikwissenschaftlicher Anhang von RUDOLF MARIA BRANDL. XV–349 pp. 1979. DM 132,-.
35. JOSEF GLINKA: Gestalt und Herkunft. Beitrag zur anthropologischen Gliederung Indonesiens. 176 pp. 1978. DM 66,-.
36. JOHANNES MARINGER: Das Kreuz als Zeichen und Symbol in der vorchristlichen Welt. 149 pp., ill. 1980. DM 45,-.
38. ANICETUS B. SINAGA: The Toba-Batak High God. 264 pp. 1981.